ENGLISH DRAM

Series Editor:
Bruce King

ENGLISH DRAMATISTS
Series Editor: Bruce King

Published titles

Susan Bassnett, *Shakespeare: The Elizabethan Plays*
Richard Allen Cave, *Ben Jonson*
Phillip C. McGuire, *Shakespeare: The Jacobean Plays*
Kate McLuskie, *Dekker and Heywood*
Christine Richardson and Jackie Johnston, *Medieval Drama*
Roger Sales, *Christopher Marlowe*
David Thomas, *William Congreve*
Martin White, *Middleton and Tourneur*
Katharine Worth, *Sheridan and Goldsmith*

Forthcoming titles

John Bull, *Vanbrugh and Farquhar*
Barbara Kachur, *Etherege and Wycherley*
Maximillian Novak, *Fielding and Gay*
Rowland Wymer, *Webster and Ford*

ENGLISH DRAMATISTS

SHAKESPEARE: THE JACOBEAN PLAYS

Philip C. McGuire

Department of English
Michigan State University

MACMILLAN

First published 1994 by
THE MACMILLAN PRESS LTD
Houndmills, Basingstoke, Hampshire RG21 2XS
and London
Companies and representatives
throughout the world

ISBN 0-333-44257-1 hardcover
ISBN 0-333-44258-X paperback

A catalogue record for this book is available
from the British Library.

Typeset by Pure Tech Corporation, Pondicherry, India

Printed in Hong Kong

For Penelope –
'Your acts are queens'

It is a trew old saying, That a King is as one set
on a stage, whose smallest actions and gestures all
the people gazingly do behold. . .
　　　　—James I, *Basilikon Doron*, Book III (1603)

　　　　On the Life of Man
What is our life? a play of passion,
Our mirth the music of division,
Our mothers' wombs the tyring houses be,
Where we are dressed for this short Comedy,
Heaven the Judicious sharp spectator is,
That sits and marks still who doth act amisse,
Our graves that hide us from the searching Sun,
Are like drawn curtains when the play is done,
Thus march we playing to our latest rest,
Only we die in earnest, that's no jest.
　　　　　　　　　　—Sir Walter Raleigh (1612)

Contents

Editor's Preface

Each generation needs to be introduced to the culture and great works of the past and to reinterpret them in its own ways. This series re-examines the important English dramatists of earlier centuries in the light of new information, new interests and new attitudes. The books are written for students, theatre-goers and general readers who want an up-to-date view of the plays and dramatists, with emphasis on drama as theatre and on stage, social and political history. Attention is given to what is known about performance, acting styles, changing interpretations, the stages and theatres of the time and theatre economics. The books will be relevant to those interested in or studying literature, theatre and cultural history.

BRUCE KING

Acknowledgements

Over the inordinately long time I needed to write this book I acquired many obligations. Some are acknowledged in my notes, but others merit a different form of acknowledgement. Bruce King, general editor of the 'English Dramatists' series, was extremely patient as he waited for a very slow process to reach completion, as were the editors at the publishers with whom I was privileged to work: Beverley Tarquini, Caroline Egar, Alison Kelly, and Cathryn Tanner. Michigan State University provided an All-University Research Grant without which the demands on their patience would have been even more severe. I also had the benefit in this – as in all of my work (and much else) – of the friendship and knowledge of Randal Robinson and Douglas Peterson, valued colleagues at Michigan State.

All errors and shortcomings in this book are my responsibility, but they are fewer than they would otherwise be because Michael Friedman and Craig Bernthal kindly read parts of it in draft, and because Hillary Nunn assisted with the copy-editing, proof-reading and indexing. Barbara Hodgdon, who read and in some cases re-read virtually every word in this book as it was being written, provided generous help that was not only invaluable but also essential.

My daughter Lucy Mercedes Bassnett-McGuire, who also read parts of this book, repeatedly provided encouragement – sometimes in person, more frequently (alas) via trans-Atlantic phone calls – for which I am deeply grateful. My wife Penelope Victor, whom I met when this book was first taking shape, bore us a son well before it was finished. While Emmet is the greatest of the many gifts she has

ix

given to and shared with me, the truth is that without her insight, tact, humour, assistance, and full love, I could not have completed this book.

Note Regarding Shakespearean Quotations

For the following Shakespearean plays I have quoted from the most recent Arden Edition of each: *Antony and Cleopatra, Coriolanus, King Lear, Macbeth, Measure for Measure, Othello, The Tempest,* and *The Winter's Tale.* The bibliography provides details of publication for each of those editions. Quotations from all other Shakespearean plays are from *The Complete Works of Shakespeare* (1992, fourth edition), edited by David Bevington and published by Harper Collins (New York).

When quoting from Quarto or Folio versions of Shakespearean plays, I have used *Shakespeare's Plays in Quarto: A Facsimile Edition of Copies Primarily form the Henry E. Huntington Library* (1981), edited by Michael J. B. Allen and Kenneth Muir (Berkeley, Calif.: University of California Press) and *The Norton Facsimile: The First Folio of Shakespeare* (1968), edited by Charlton Hinman (New York: Norton; London: Paul Hamlyn). In those quotations, the Renaissance long 's' has been changed to modern 's' and u/v and i/j have been normalised in accord with modern practices.

Introduction

What is not known about William Shakespeare's career as a play-wright is considerable. There is no certainty about when it began – probably towards the end of the 1580s. There is also no certainty about when it ended – probably no later than 1613, three years before his death. No one can fix precisely when any one of his plays was written or even first performed. It is clear, however, that his career spanned something more than the last decade of the reign of Queen Elizabeth I and most of the first decade of the reign of King James I, who succeeded her as sovereign of England at her death on 24 March 1603. It is also clear that from 1594 onwards, Shakespeare was an 'attached' or house playwright, providing plays exclusively for performance by an all-male acting company called the Lord Chamberlain's Men during Elizabeth's reign and the King's Men during James's.

This book concentrates on Shakespeare's 'Jacobean' plays – those we are reasonably confident were written and first performed after James became king of England. Those prior to that are the subject of a companion volume by Susan Bassnett, *Shakespeare: The Elizabethan Plays*. Twelve of the thirty-seven plays now generally accepted as Shakespeare's are Jacobean, and the first of them is *Measure for Measure* (1604), a comedy. Among the twelve are six tragedies: three of his four 'major' tragedies – *Othello*, *King Lear*, and *Macbeth* (*Hamlet* being the fourth) – as well as *Timon of Athens*, *Antony and Cleopatra*, and *Coriolanus*. Shakespeare's Jacobean plays also include all four of those often called the 'late' plays or the 'last' plays and sometimes classified

1

as 'romances' or 'tragi-comedies': *Pericles, Cymbeline, The Winter's Tale,*
and *The Tempest.* The twelfth of his Jacobean plays is *Henry VIII*, a
history play, now widely accepted as having been written in collabora-
tion with John Fletcher, his eventual successor as the King's Men
attached playwright.

Of the eight chapters in this book, the first is more general, the
remaining seven more specific. Chapter 1 looks at the factors that
make Shakespeare's Jacobean plays different from his Elizabethan
plays, attending particularly to changes in the circumstances within which they came into being. The major advantage of using the
categories 'Elizabethan' and 'Jacobean' is that they make it less
difficult to consider how individual Shakespearean plays, the relationships among them, and indeed Shakespeare's playwri(gh)ting
career in its phases and as a whole took their shape from and reflect
a complex, shifting interplay between the extraordinary creative
powers that were uniquely his and the changing circumstances –
broadly cultural as well as specifically theatrical – within which he
and the acting company for which and with which he worked
functioned.

Each of the remaining chapters takes up individually, in what is
currently the generally accepted order of their composition, one of
those seven among Shakespeare's twelve Jacobean plays that have
been most often performed and most often written about and taught:
*Measure for Measure, Othello, King Lear, Macbeth, Coriolanus, The Winter's
Tale,* and *The Tempest.* Common to all seven chapters is a shaping
emphasis upon the dramaturgy of Shakespeare's Jacobean plays –
the ways in which they call attention to, and exploit their theatrical
character as works meant for public performance by a group of
actors in the presence of individuals who, paying money, assemble
in a specific place to form a collective entity called an audience. This
book focuses on Shakespeare as playwright rather than poet – and
as a professional playwright, responsive to commercial considerations
as well as artistic concerns, who worked in specific theatrical and
cultural circumstances that were changing then and have continued
to change, in ways that vitally affect how his plays are performed,
understood, and valued.

One area of change has been in conceptions of plays in general and
of Shakespeare's plays in particular. Today, his plays possess a status,
a cultural place and value, they did not have in the Elizabethan–
Jacobean era and did not begin to acquire until more than a century

after his death. When in about 1598 Sir Thomas Bodley began establishing what has since become the world-famous Bodleian library at Oxford, he specifically prohibited the inclusion of 'play-books' because he feared 'the harm that the scandal will bring unto the library, when it shall be given out that we stuff it full of baggage books'.[1] Shakespeare's 'playbooks' have since become, and remain, objects that library directors compete to obtain, and his plays are venerated cultural icons. As Maurice Charney puts it, they are 'after the Bible . . . our primary canonized text' (1988, p. 9).

Charney's use of the term 'text' points to another major change. Originally conceived and first presented to the public as works performed by a group of actors, the plays have since been transformed into works of literature, into 'texts' best understood and most deeply appreciated when read by an individual in private. The words of a Shakespearean play are crucial and essential. They deserve – and reward – close, sustained scrutiny, but it should be scrutiny that respects the difference between how words function in a play and in a literary work. A poem, a novel, or a short story consists exclusively of words meant to be read, and literary semiosis – the process by which meaning is generated and conveyed – is verbal, a function of its words, their interrelationships, and what an individual reader brings to, derives from, and makes of them. While words and their interrelationships are the essential component of a literary work, they are but one essential component of a play. A play consists not of words read but of actions performed, one of which – in Western theatre perhaps the most important of which – is the action of speaking words.

Theatrical semiosis involves not only words and their interrelationships but also – and essentially – the interplay between those verbal elements and all that the audience see and all that they hear, including the actors' physiques, facial expressions and body language, their gestures and costumes, the spatial relationships among them established by blocking (movement and grouping), stage business, stage properties, lighting, scenery, and set, as well as sound effects and music. Plays are polysemic; everything on the stage, including words spoken, functions as a sign, as a vehicle of meaning. In *Antony and Cleopatra*, for example, on the eve of the second and final battle, a stage direction specifies that '*music of the hautboys is under the stage*' (IV.iii.11) as soldiers in Antony's army discuss what the next day will bring. The dialogue that follows makes clear the significance of that

music, which no reader ever hears: ' 'Tis the god Hercules, whom
Antony lov'd, / Now leaves him' (IV.iii.15–16). The music is an
essential part of theatrical moments portraying a development that
cannot be presented effectively by the usual combination of actions
seen and words heard. Hercules's abandonment of Antony would
have less impact in the theatre if there were no music and the
soldiers merely talked about it. On the other hand, if there were no
discussion of 'What should this mean' (IV.iv.14), audiences would
not know what the music they hear signifies. The god's departure
is not – and perhaps cannot be – enacted physically, but the play
gives the audience a visual equivalent by taking advantage of the
need to clear the stage for the next scene. As the musicians out of
sight under the stage withdraw still playing hautboys, audiences see
the soldiers follow the departing music and make their exit. Whatever meanings the scene conveys arise not simply through words, not
simply through actions, and not simply through music. Its meanings
flow from the interplay of all three.

The emphasis on Shakespeare's plays as literature rests upon and
encourages a specific conception of artistic creativity shaped during
the Romantic era. That conception sees creation as an autonomous
act undertaken by an extraordinary individual whose solitary efforts
bring into being a work that is wholly original in the sense of being
essentially different from anything that has previously existed. That
work is specifically and uniquely that individual's because it is
understood to have its source in his or her creative imagination,
artistic talents, and moral intelligence – in insights, experiences,
responses, and skills – that are his or hers alone. Such a conception
of authorial singularity and sovereignty is at odds with what is known
of the circumstances and conditions within which Shakespeare
worked and within which what we continue to call 'his' plays came
into being.

From 1594 on, in his capacity as 'attached' playwright for the Lord
Chamberlain's–King's Men, Shakespeare was obligated to provide a
number of new plays each year for the company to perform. To do
that, Shakespeare drew upon not only his own powers of invention
but also the work of others – playwrights, historians, story-tellers,
travellers, essayists, translators – for incidents, plot lines, characters,
and even speeches. Among his most famous speeches is Enobarbus's
description of Cleopatra coming by barge to her first meeting with
Antony:

The barge she sat in, like a burnish'd throne
Burn'd on the water: the poop was beaten gold;
Purple the sails, and so perfumed that
The winds were love-sick with them; the oars were silver,
Which to the tune of flutes kept stroke, and made
The water which they beat to follow faster,
As amorous of their strokes. For her own person,
It beggar'd all description: she did lie
In her pavilion – cloth of gold, of tissue –
O'er-picturing that Venus where we see
The fancy outwork nature. On each side her,
Stood pretty dimpled boys, like smiling Cupids,
With divers-colour'd fans, whose wind did seem
To glow the delicate cheeks which they did cool,
And what they undid did.

(II.ii.191–205)

The speech is a re-working of a passage found in the principal source on which Shakespeare drew, Thomas North's translation (1579), via a French translation by Jacques Amyot, of Plutarch's 'Life of Marcus Antonius':

> she disdained to set forward [to meet Antony] otherwise but to take her barge in the river of Cydnus, the poope whereof was of gold, the sailes of purple, and the owers [oars] of silver, which kept stroke in rowing after the sounde of the musicke of flutes, howboyes, citherns, violls, and such other instruments as they played upon in the barge. And now for the person of herselfe: she was layed under a pavillion of cloth of gold of tissue, apparrelled and attired like the goddesse Venus, commonly drawen in picture: and hard by her, on either hand of her, pretie faire boyes apparelled as painters doe set forth god Cupide, with little fannes in their hands, with the which they fanned wind upon her. (Ridley, 1954, p. 246)

The issue is not whether the words Shakespeare set down for the actor playing Enobarbus to speak are 'better' than those found in North, but whether it is helpful or even historically accurate to speak of them as exclusively 'Shakespeare's' – as the product solely of his artistic imagination, of an autonomous creative effort that brings into being something utterly original. While it is true that Enobarbus's lines would not exist had Shakespeare not written them, it is equally true that they would not exist without North's efforts and Amyot's and Plutarch's. Neither exclusively Shakespeare's nor exclusively theirs, those lines are the product of a collaborative creative process in which Shakespeare participated, bringing to bear talents uniquely his that transformed what others had done.

What is true of Enobarbus's lines is equally true of the play of which they are part. There would be no *Antony and Cleopatra* for us to call (not entirely accurately) 'Shakespeare's', had Plutarch not written, and had North and Amyot not translated, his 'Life of Marcus Antonius'. And what is true of *Antony and Cleopatra* is true of other Shakespearean plays. They use what others have done as essential sources, dependent upon what is found there even as they proceed to change and build upon it. Given their reliance upon such sources, most Shakespearean plays plays are not 'his' alone, not the product of insights, experiences, and responses solely and uniquely his. They take their being from and through a creative process that is not wholly individualistic but collective and transformative.

As commonly used today, the phrase 'Shakespeare's plays' fosters misconceptions that are misleading in another sense. Ownership of and control over the plays Shakespeare provided for the Lord Chamberlain's–King's Men rested with the company, not with Shakespeare himself. Artistic, as well as financial and managerial, authority within the acting company was not exercised by a single owner, a board of governors, a star actor, a dominant director, or even an immensely gifted playwright. It rested with a core group within the company, the sharers.[2] As one of them, Shakespeare was in a position to participate in deciding what changes, if any, would be made in a script he wrote, how and when it would be performed, whether it would be published and, if so, by whom and in what form. There is no evidence, however, that such decisions were his alone to make simply because he was the playwright. It would have been inconceivable for a playwright in the Elizabethan–Jacobean era to do what Samuel Beckett did in 1984 when he threatened legal action to prevent performances of the American Repertory Theatre's production of *Endgame*, directed by JoAnne Akalaitis, at Lincoln Center (New York) because it did not conform closely enough to what he had written. A more historically accurate way of referring to the plays we reflexively call 'Shakespeare's' is to call them plays in the making

of which Shakespeare participated as playwright; the majority of them
– those written from 1594 on – are plays of the Lord Chamberlain's–
King's Men written by William Shakespeare.

The emphasis on Shakespeare's plays as literary works he created
autonomously fosters the assumption that the creative process that
brought each of them into being ended when Shakespeare put down
his quill after penning the last word of the play. That may be an
appropriate way of thinking about a poem or a novel – about a work
of literature written to be read in private by solitary readers – but it
distorts the nature of a Shakespearean play, a dramatic work intended for performance in public. Clearly, a Shakespearean playtext
has features in common with a poem; the language is often extra-
ordinarily rich and most of it is in poetic forms, usually blank verse.
Just as clearly, a Shakespearean playtext has features in common
with a work of narrative fiction – a short story or a novel; it has a
narrative line, it presents a sequence of events.

A Shakespearean playtext is also fundamentally different from poetry
and narrative fiction because it is, as they are not, a script, a code for
performance meant 'to lead a company of actors – and eventually
an audience – to matters that are not visible on the page' (Hardison,
1983, p. 137). Shakespeare's act of writing was a crucial, indispensable first phase in a collective creative process that reached completion not when he stopped writing but when the play he scripted came
to life on the stage through the bodies and voices of his fellow actors.
That completion is momentary and remains to be achieved anew
with each performance of the play, down to the present day.

Performing a Shakespearean play is not simply a matter of acting
out meanings embedded in the words of a playtext. Performing is
also, and primarily, a matter of *making* meanings, principally through
what theatre theorists, appropriating a term from linguistics, call
deixis. Just as such words as 'here', 'now', 'I', and 'you' take on
precise meanings only in relation to the particular context in which
they are used, so the meanings generated by the words of a playtext
become specific and precise only within the particular theatrical
context established by a host of non-verbal features. Because, in Jiri
Veltrusky's formulation, 'All that is on stage is a sign',[3] the words of
the playtext – and any authorial intentions immanent in them –
cannot control fully and precisely the semiosis of performance.

King Lear's command 'Give me the map there' (I.i.36) is an
especially clear example of theatrical deixis: of how much of a given

theatrical moment Shakespeare's words leave imprecise and unspecific, and of how much they rely on the talents of others to complete the creative process of which they are an essential, but not the only, component. The five words are simple enough in themselves – 'Give me the map there' – but what do they mean and to what action(s) do they refer? Is Lear ordering that a specific map, the one over 'there', be brought to him? Or is he ordering that the map be placed in a particular spot – 'there'? Each alternative is equally consistent with the words and their syntax. How does the actor playing Lear speak the words? Does Lear shout the command tyrannically, proclaim it majestically, or utter it with quiet but firm authority? Where is 'there'? On a desk, a table, the floor, a wall? And who moves in response to Lear's command, whatever it means? One or more attendants? The Duke of Albany, the Duke of Cornwall, or both? One of Lear's daughters (which?), two of them, all three? Do Goneril and Regan vie to be the one to carry out Lear's command, thus foreshadowing the sibling rivalry that Lear will soon unleash by asking each to declare how much she loves him and that later mutates into a deadly competition for Edmund's sexual favours? Shakespeare's words give no distinct sense of 'the map' and what is done with it. Is it parchment, a piece of hide, a sheet of paper, or possibly a tapestry or even a rug? Is it small enough to rest on a table or for Lear to hold in his hand? Is it so large that it must be displayed – hung on a wall, perhaps, or held up by several attendants – or even spread across the floor?

'Give me the map there' is a signal to do something with the map, but exactly what is for those performing the play to determine – be they the King's Men of Shakespeare's time or the Royal Shakespeare Company of today. It may be that Shakespeare did not write out fuller directions regarding what was to take place because he was in a position to tell his fellow actors what he had in mind, or because over their years together they worked out ways of dealing with such moments that made explicit stage directions unnecessary, or even because someone else in the company had responsibility for such decisions. It may be that Shakespeare did provide directions that were somehow omitted when the play was published, or it may be that he intended the moment to be one that could be played in different ways on different occasions. In any event, the fact remains that 'Give me the map there' summons all those involved in performing the play (primarily actors but also directors, set and costume designers, lighting and sound technicians) to complete the creative process of which those words are an essential part.

The tendency to prize Shakespeare's plays as works of literature remains deeply embedded to this day. It manifests itself in efforts to apply to them the techniques and assumptions of various species of *literary* theory and *literary* analysis. The editions of Shakespeare's plays currently most widely available offer a second and particularly telling example of the power that the idea of Shakespeare's works as literature continues to exert. In the overwhelming majority of them, the numbering of lines ignores the stage directions, even the ones present in the earliest surviving versions of Shakespearean plays: those published singly in quarto format, many during Shakespeare's lifetime, or those published as a collection in the First Folio of 1623, seven years after his death.[4] By not counting stage directions, which are the most direct guides to the actors' movements and gestures during a performance, editors say, in effect, that they are not part of the play.

The basis for both performance and criticism of Shakespeare's plays is the editions in which they are published. A feature that sets this book apart from others of its kind is the attention given to the impact of editorial practice, particularly its capacity to present as established fact what is, on closer examination, one among a range of options. The presentation in the Arden edition of *Othello* of what Othello says and does after stabbing himself provides an example of the constriction that can occur:

> OTH.: I kiss'd thee ere I kill'd thee, no way but this,
>   Killing myself, to die upon a kiss.
> > *[Falls on the bed, and dies]*.
> > (V.ii.359–60)

The same stage direction, with 'He' added at the beginning, is found in the New Cambridge edition of *Othello* as well as in editions of the play included in two collections of Shakespeare's complete works widely used in the USA: the Riverside and the Pelican. The New Oxford edition of the complete works has '*He kisses Desdemona and dies*'.

However, each of the two versions of the play closest in time to when *Othello* was first conceived and performed provides a stage direction notably less full and precise. The Quarto edition, published in 1622, six years after Shakespeare's death, has simply '*He dies*', and the Folio edition of 1623 has, even more simply, '*Dyes*'. The imprecision of those stage directions leaves open the very questions that editors today typically answer: does Othello die upon the bed where Desdemona's corpse lies, and does he manage, after mortally wounding himself, to carry out his desire to give her corpse a final kiss?

What cannot be emphasised too strongly is that the current editions of Shakespeare's plays – and those of previous eras – are not simply updated copies of those plays as they were first published, replications of them that reach us intact except for some helpful annotating and modernising. The editions that determine what the vast majority of students as well as teachers, performers as well as theatre critics and scholars, readers as well as theatregoers know of and do with Shakespeare's plays are *constructions* of that earliest material. One needs to remain aware that they may – as in the case of the stage direction typically given for Othello's dying – narrow the spectrum of possibilities offered. They may also, as subsequent discussion of *Othello* and *King Lear* will show, present as 'Shakespeare's' a play different at specific points and as a whole from anything that existed during or shortly after his lifetime.

Over the centuries since Shakespeare's plays were first conceived and performed, they have come to be – and continue to be – esteemed as timeless, transcendent, universal, immutable works that rise above the particularities and flux of history, that are, as Ben Jonson declared of the man who wrote them, 'not of an age, but for all time'. In fact, however, Shakespeare's plays are and have been deeply immersed in change, implicated in history. During the era when they came into being, they were an especially critical element in the process of cultural formation, the network of activities by which, in Clifford Geertz's words, 'this people, or that, this period or that, makes sense of itself, to itself' (1980, p. 167). In Shakespeare's day, the presentation of plays by professional actors performing in buildings erected exclusively for that purpose and before people who paid to be members of the audience was a novel and highly controversial cultural practice. In fact, as Stephen Orgel has pointed out, before James Burbage constructed a permanent theatre a little north of London's walls in 1576,

the concept of 'theater' had included no sense of *place*. A theater was not a building, it was a group of actors and an audience; the theater was any place where they chose to perform. When the play was over, the hall or courtyard or banqueting room ceased to be a theater' (1975, p. 2)

The name Burbage gave to his structure testifies to its uniqueness and priority; he called it simply 'The Theatre'. Other structures like it were built over the ensuing decades – The Curtain, The Fortune, The Red Bull, The Rose, The Hope, The Swan. The proliferation of public theatres is evidence of the space – physical, economic, and cultural – that they and the novel practices they housed came to occupy in early modern London. Stageplays became a distinct (but controversial) cultural form, an activity that happened regularly, almost daily, in fixed locations dedicated to that purpose, and playing itself became a distinct (and controversial) social calling, a way of earning one's living, a profession. The locations of the Elizabethan–Jacobean public theatres points to the marginality of what occurred within their confines. All were situated in areas outside the jurisdiction of the authorities of the City of London proper.

When towards the end of 1598, the Lord Chamberlain's Men found it necessary to dismantle The Theatre, which had been their home since their founding in 1594, they used its timbers to construct a new home, on the south bank of the Thames. The name they gave to the new structure reflected the domain that a form of theatrical practice less than twenty-five years old now claimed. They named it The Globe – as if assured that all human actions on this earth were within the scope, the jurisdiction, of professional players performing as often as six days a week, ten months of the year on stages in permanent theatres open to anyone willing to pay the price of admission.

The emergence of that practice was one of a complex of vast, interrelated changes associated with England's passage from the middle ages to what historians call the early modern era, from late feudalism to early capitalism, from a ceremonial and ritualistic conception of human life to an historical and psychological one, from a sense that identity is fixed and a function of personal and social relationships to a sense that identity is fluid and autonomous, the extension and expression of each person's distinct individuality. The Elizabethan–Jacobean commercial theatre – both the public play-houses and the private playhouses – was simultaneously a product of the massive change sweeping over England, an agent and promoter of that change, and a means by which it could be accommodated. That theatre was, in short, a site of cultural transformation. There

were embodied, rehearsed, and articulated that era's deepest values,
beliefs, metaphors, and assumptions – the ideological constructs that
shape the terms in which individuals conceive and experience, before
they consciously ponder, themselves and their places in a specific
social formation. There those constructs were also examined, tested,
judged, and even challenged.

Among the most fundamental of those constructs was the doctrine of a divinely ordained, unchanging, hierachical order in nature
and human society. A response to the impact of profound change
sweeping through all facets of a traditional and rigid society, that
doctrine was promulgated in the official sermons that Elizabeth and
James ordered to be read throughout the realm at the Sunday
services the English were legally bound to attend. One, the Homily
on Obedience, explained that

> Almightie God hath created and appoynted all things, in
> /heaven, earth, and waters, in a mooste excellente and perfecte
> order. . . . Everye degre of people in theyr vocation, callying,
> and office hath appointed to them, theyr duety and ordre. Some
> are in hyghe degree, some in lowe, some kynges and prynces,
> some inferiors and subjects, priestes and layemenne, Maysters
> and Servauntes, Fathers and chyldren, husbandes and wives,
> riche and poore, and everyone have nede of other: So that in
> all thynges is to be lauded and praysed the goodly order of god,
> wythoute the whiche, no house, no citie, no commonwealth can
> continue and indure or laste. (Bond, 1975, p. 161)

The capacity of Elizabethan–Jacobean theatre to promote change
by challenging that dominant ideological construct was not primarily a matter of what was said or done on the stage.[5] It arose
most profoundly from the very process of theatrical representation
itself, from the very act of playing. Playing blurred the fundamental
categories – nobleman and commoner, king and subject, male and
female – that were the basis for the distinctions and stratifications
upon which rested the Elizabethan–Jacobean conception of a society
organised as a divinely ordained hierarchy that was inevitable and
unchanging. On the stages of the public theatres, boys played
women, and commoners played nobleman and kings.

Hamlet says that 'the purpose of playing' is 'to hold, as 'twere, the
mirror up to nature' (III.ii.19, 20–1). In the very process of playing,

however, the Lord Chamberlain's–King's Men and their principal playwright not only held 'the mirror up to nature', they also participated, willy-nilly, in changing what that nature was. Knowingly or in ignorance, they acted out an alternative to the official doctrine of a rigid hierarchal order, presenting their audiences with what Louis Adrian Montrose calls 'a dramatistic world picture' (1980, p. 55) in which identity is not fixed and ordained but developed, acquired, learned, fashioned in the very process of adjusting to and coping with the changes living brings.

The power to show what nature is carries with it the power to influence what nature is seen and understood to be, and over the centuries since Shakespeare's plays came into being, they have been used to confirm or, less often, to challenge whatever the dominant ideology of a given moment presents as universal, timeless, natural. They have played an important role in the ongoing process of cultural formation, both reflecting and forming the perceptions and conceptions – the ideology – that enable individuals and groups at a given moment in history to discern in 'the very age and body of the time' what Hamlet calls its 'form and pressure' (III.ii.22–3). Shakespeare's plays are 'for all time' not because they transcend 'the age' in which they originated but because, charged with what Stephen Greenblatt calls 'social energy' (1988, p. 6), they continue to participate in history, doing cultural work, stirring emotions, offering experiences by which humans make and find sense, a degree of coherence, in their lives and circumstances.

Even though – and even while – Shakespeare's plays have been valued as being immutable and fixed, they have changed over time. This book does not provide a full record of the stage history of Shakespeare's Jacobean plays nor of the history of their critical reception and editorial treatment. Instead, in discussions of specific plays, it draws selectively upon those sometimes conflicting, sometimes overlapping histories. A point of particular emphasis is to show how performance tradition, editorial practice, and critical consensus have at given moments obscured, if not obliterated, certain possibilities and facets of Shakespeare's Jacobean plays while endorsing others, presenting as certainties what are in reality alternatives. One example, discussed fully in Chapter 7, is the practice – theatrical as well as critical – of assuming that Camillo and Paulina assent to the marriage Leontes proposes they enter into at the end of *The Winter's Tale* even though both prospective spouses say nothing.

In 1642, as civil war that would topple the British monarchy became imminent, Parliament ordered the closing of all theatres in England. When, eighteen years later, after the restoration of the monarchy in the person of Charles II, James's grandson, the theatres reopened, the theatrical milieu – the conditions and conventions of performance, the kind of stage, the conception of illusion shared by players and audiences – within which and for which Shakespeare's plays were created had been obliterated.

One specific change initiated after the Restoration in 1660 was a casting practice that remains the norm to this day: actresses began playing the women's parts that Shakespeare wrote for performance by the boy actors apprenticed to the all-male Lord Chamberlain's–King's Men. As one example of the effects of that change consider the moment in *Antony and Cleopatra* when Cleopatra describes what awaits her if she believes Caesar's promise of good treatment:

> The quick comedians
> Extemporally will stage us, and present
> Our Alexandrian revels; Antony
> Shall be brought drunken forth, and I shall see
> Some squeaking Cleopatra boy my greatness
> I' the posture of a whore.
>
> (V.ii.215–20)

Cleopatra foresees watching a performance in which a boy plays her, and one reason she chooses to kill herself is to prevent that from happening. However, that is exactly what audiences at performances by the King's Men did see: a boy playing Cleopatra. Under those circumstances, the very process of performance calls into question the totality of the triumph and transcendence she achieves by her suicide. No such questioning occurs, however, if a woman plays Cleopatra. In those circumstances – which have governed perform-ances from the Restoration to the present – no one 'boys' Cleopatra's greatness, and the female body of the actress affirms the fullness of what Cleopatra's suicide achieves.

Performance conditions also changed radically and irreversibly with the use of gas light and lime (calcium) light in the nineteenth century and of electric light in the twentieth century to illuminate both the theatre and the stage. The current practice of having audiences sitting in a darkened area watching performers on a lighted stage is a relatively recent development. Until the late nineteenth century, theatre lighting was uniform, with no sharp difference between the light in which players performed and in which audiences watched. It was also constant, since the technical resources needed to vary the level of lighting at different moments in the performance and at different points on the stage did not exist. The King's Men and their audiences shared the same light – provided by the sun at the open-air Globe and by candles at the roofed Blackfriars. They also shared a conception of 'life-like' imitation that did not require – if only because there were no technical resources to simulate – darkness on-stage as the visual analogue of the night-time darkness in which events such as the murder of Banquo in *Macbeth* and of Desdemona in *Othello* occur.

After the Restoration, Charles II permitted just two commercial theatres to open, and audiences who came to Sir William D'Avenant's in a tennis court building in Lincoln's Inn Fields found themselves in a theatre radically different from any of the Elizabethan–Jacobean era. At the Globe and later at Blackfriars, the King's Men performed on a platform or thrust stage, in front of a façade that included a gallery or balcony and, at the level of the platform, a curtained enclosure used for entrances and exits as well as moments of discovery such as Prospero's revealing of Ferdinand and Miranda playing chess during the final scene of *The Tempest*. Audiences sat and stood on three (perhaps four) sides, possibly even sat on the stage itself – which meant that few large stage properties were used and no elaborate sets. D'Avenant's audiences, however, found themselves positioned solely in front of a stage that had a broad platform akin to the open thrust stages of the Globe and Blackfriars, but at the rear of that platform, where a small inner stage or discovery place had formerly been, there was now a large room, framed by a proscenium arch, to accommodate the moveable painted scenery and stage machines formerly associated with the court masques of James I and Charles I. From D'Avenant's day until well into the present century all theatres have incorporated stages that were variations upon D'Avenant's innovation, the most obvious change being the reduction of the platform in front of the proscenium arch to what is now the few feet in front of the stage curtain.

The domination of the proscenium arch theatre has meant that for most of their history Shakespeare's plays have been performed in circumstances radically alien to those within which they were conceived and first performed – on scenic stages that employ detailed sets and visual illusion to establish place and time rather than on open stages that rely primarily on what audiences hear. When William Poel at the very end of the nineteenth century and Harley Granville-Barker in the first decade of this century began presenting productions in what Poel called the Elizabethan mode, they had to do so on proscenium arch stages. Over the decades since the end of the Second World War, however, the situation has improved, due to the construction of major theatres incorporating open thrust stages derived from those of the Globe and Blackfriars. Because of such playhouses as the Festival Theatre in Stratford, Ontario, the Guthrie Theatre in Minneapolis, the Olivier Theatre within the National Theatre complex in London, and, most recently, the Swan in Stratford-upon-Avon, audiences today can see Shakespearean plays performed on thrust stages that in significant ways are more like those on which those plays first came to life than any since 1642.

1

Shakespeare's Jacobean Plays

The death of Queen Elizabeth I on 24 March 1603 and the accession of King James I were changes of enormous impact in an England already experiencing massive change – political, religious, economic, demographic, technological, cultural – as the late middle ages gave way to the early modern era, and as societal structures and practices as well as systems of personal relationships associated with feudalism gave way to those of nascent capitalism. At her death, Elizabeth had ruled for forty-five years, longer than most of her subjects had been alive. Her dying marked the end of one dynasty, the Tudors, whose rule had lasted for more than a century, and the coming to power of a new dynasty, the Stuarts. With her death the English crown was not simply passing from one monarch to another and one dynasty to another. It was passing to a foreign prince. When Elizabeth Tudor died, James Stuart was already king of Scotland, and in 1603 England and Scotland were distinct nations – and remained so, despite his strenuous efforts to unite them, until 1707. Before travelling from Edinburgh to London after Elizabeth's death, James had never been to England, and about their new king his English subjects knew little beyond the facts that he had a reputation as an intellectual and was the son of Mary, Queen of Scots, whom Elizabeth had kept under house arrest for nearly two decades before authorising her execution in 1587 for plotting to seize the crown.

Any anxieties that the Lord Chamberlain's Men and Shakespeare as their attached playwright may have had about what the change in monarchs would mean for them werre quickly put to rest. One of James's first acts after reaching London in May of 1603 was to change the name of the Lord Chamberlain's Men to the King's

Men.[1] Renaming the company signalled a change in its relationship to the sovereign. As the Lord Chamberlain's Men the patron through whom they were licensed to perform publicly had been a nobleman important enough to be member of the Queen's Privy Council. From May of 1603 on, however, their relationship to the crown was less indirect. Their patron was the king himself, and they were technically his servants and members of his household. That change in the company's relationship to the sovereign was one of a set of changes associated with or occurring after James's accession that altered the circumstances within which Shakespeare's plays came into being and were performed. Those altered circumstances, in turn, had effects on the plays themselves – on their content, their generic identity, their audiences, and their dramaturgy.

The differences between Shakespeare's Elizabethan and Jacobean plays are not absolute or total, but they are significant. Among the most conspicuous of them is a change in the kinds of plays Shakespeare wrote for the King's Men to perform. During Elizabeth's reign the dramatic genres in which Shakespeare worked most frequently were history and comedy, but early in James's reign, he concentrated on tragedies and then, after 1608, in what is regarded as the final phase of his career, shifted his focus again, this time away from tragedy. Only the last of his Jacobean plays, *Henry VIII*, is a history play, and the current consensus is that he co-wrote it with John Fletcher, his successor as the King's Men attached playwright. The first of Shakespeare's Jacobean plays, *Measure for Measure* (1604) is a comedy, but, as Chapter 2 will show, it departs sharply from such romantic or festive comedies as *A Midsummer Night's Dream*, and *As You Like It*. After *Measure for Measure*, Shakespeare worked intensively, perhaps even exclusively, in tragedy, a genre in which he had previously worked only intermittently. During a five-year span (1604–8), he wrote more tragedies – six – than he had during all of his previous career: *Othello, King Lear, Macbeth, Antony and Cleopatra, Timon of Athens*, and *Coriolanus*. Of his twelve Jacobean plays fully half are tragedies, written in a sustained burst, perhaps even in succession. On the other hand, only four of his twenty-five Elizabethan plays are tragedies – *Titus Andronicus* (1593 or earlier), *Romeo and Juliet* (1595), *Julius Caesar* (1599), and *Hamlet* (1601) – written at intervals of two or three years over nearly a decade.

The usual explanation for Shakespeare's concentration on tragedy is a ripening, or a darkening, of his artistic vision, perhaps as a result of his increasing years, perhaps in response to the death of his father in 1601, or of Elizabeth in 1603. 1603 was also the year that Shakespeare turned forty. The evidence available suggests that it is also one of the very few years – if not the only year – up to that point in his career during which he did not provide the acting company whose attached playwright he had been since its founding in 1594 with at least one new play. Some have speculated that during 1603 Shakespeare endured a personal crisis of some sort, perhaps even a nervous breakdown, that kept him from writing and then altered what he subsequently wrote. Such possibilities cannot be ruled out, but at least one alternative explanation, involving professional rather than personal or artistic considerations, is also pertinent. Shakespeare may have written no new play during 1603 because there would have been no opportunity to perform it at the Globe. In the spring of 1603, authorities closed all commercial theatres in the London area because of an outbreak of the plague so severe that the general public was banned from James's coronation (25 July 1603) and his first royal progress through the city was postponed until March 1604. The Globe itself did not reopen until 9 April 1604, having been closed for nearly a year.

Professional considerations may also have been among the factors that led Shakespeare to concentrate, after writing *Measure for Measure* (1604), on providing the King's Men with tragedies. He, unlike most playwrights today, composed his plays for performance by a specific group of actors. He knew as he composed a script who would perform it; the Quarto and Folio versions of some Shakespearean plays have speech headings that give the name of an actor rather than a character, which suggests that he had particular players in mind as he wrote roles. The decision to focus on writing tragedies involving a single character of heroic stature – Hamlet, Othello, Macbeth, Lear – may have been a response to the developing talents of the company, particularly those of Richard Burbage, its leading actor, who first gave those roles life on the stage. A character in a novel may be wholly the creation of the author, but a character in a play is not entirely the creation of a playwright – not a completed entity whom the actor playing the role simply imitates. 'A character in the theater' is, as Michael Goldman explains,

> a self we watch the actor making – or, rather, the self *is* the making. We may be aware that Antony had an historical

existence, we may even entertain some guesses about his nature before he comes on stage, but the Antony we know in the theater is not a figure from the past. The man we are watching is alive now – his character takes shape in an actor's living body. The self we observe is the actor's action. 'Antony' is what the actor is doing now and now and now. (1985, p. 10)

In an important way that the long-dominant conception of artistic creation as the autonomous activity of an extremely gifted individual articulating insights and instincts that are hers or his alone does not accommodate, Shakespeare's great tragic roles and the plays of which they are such crucial parts (in both senses) came into being because of Burbage's creative powers as an actor as well as Shakespeare's as a playwright. What Burbage and Will Kempe and Robert Armin and the other actors of the Lord Chamberlain's–King's Men (including Shakespeare)[2] were capable of doing helped to shape what he wrote for them to play, and what he wrote helped to shape what they were capable of doing. The plays called 'Shakespeare's' emerged, therefore, from a creative process that was collective, interactive, and collaborative rather than wholly individualistic.

Another professional consideration that may help to account for Shakespeare's concentration on tragedy from 1604 through 1608 involves competitive commercial circumstances. From 1599 on, companies consisting exclusively of boy actors added to the competition for London audiences that his acting company already faced from rival companies of mainly adult actors. *Hamlet* offers a glimpse of how devastating the challenge posed by the boys' companies may have been. The actors whom Hamlet uses in an effort to 'catch the conscience of the king' (II.ii.606) have come to Elsinore because the popularity of boy actors – 'little eyases that . . . are now the fashion' (II.ii.339–41) – has driven them from the city, forcing them to tour in order to survive. Shakespeare may have focused his creative energies on writing tragedies so that, during a period when the competition from the boys' companies was particularly severe, the King's Men would have a series of new plays in the genre that allowed them to take maximum advantage of the physical and emotional maturity that set them apart from their pubescent rivals.

After 1608, during what proved to be the final phase of his career, Shakespeare's creative focus shifted again, this time away from tragedy. *Pericles* may have been written after his last tragedy, probably *Coriolanus* (1608), and *Cymbeline*, *The Winter's Tale*, and *The Tempest* certainly were. The generic affiliations of those four plays are complex, but they are certainly not tragedies. No protagonist dies in any of them, and none concludes with the multiple deaths typical of the ending of Shakespearean tragedies. In fact, all four register on virtually all modern editors as so distinct from Shakespeare's comedies, histories, and tragedies that, in most collected editions of Shakespeare's works available today, they are presented as a separate group, sometimes identified as 'romances' or 'tragi-comedies', sometimes called the 'last' or the 'late' plays.

Such groupings are problematic, primarily because there is no basis for them in the First Folio of 1623, the earliest edition of Shakespeare's plays, which two of his fellow sharers in the King's Men, John Heminge and Henry Condell, assembled. *The Tempest* is the first play in the volume and the first of fourteen 'Comedies', the last of which is *The Winter's Tale*. *Cymbeline* is placed among the 'Tragedies' and is the last play in the First Folio. *Pericles* is not among the plays included in the volume, and since it may have been written in 1608 or even earlier, its classification as a 'late' or 'last' play is open to question.

In turning away from tragedy after 1608, Shakespeare may have been responding to events in his personal life, foremost among them the marriage of his daughter Susanna in 1607 and his mother's death in 1608. In each of the 'late' plays, the father–daughter relationship is crucial and the daughter's betrothal or marriage a matter of high importance. Each includes characters who endure the anguish that the loss of a parent or child brings, then experience the joy of learning that those they mourned are alive. In two of them – *Pericles* and *The Winter's Tale* – a mother, either dead or thought to be dead, returns to life.

Shakespeare may also have stopped providing the King's Men with tragedies for what might be called artistic rather than personal reasons. Perhaps, after the sustained engagement with tragedy that saw him write six plays in that genre within five years, his creative energies were waning. Or it may be that the artistic vision that gave rise to those tragedies had developed to the point that he was now capable of including in a single play both the tragic and the comic facets of human experience, capable of embracing both individual mortality and humankind's participation, principally through offspring, in the broad natural cycle of birth, growth, death, and renewal.

The factors that prompted Shakespeare to stop providing the King's Men with tragedies after 1608 may not have been exclusively personal and artistic, however. Although his late plays are unlike his earlier plays, they resemble in important ways plays that dramatists younger than he such as John Marston, Ben Jonson, Thomas Middleton, Francis Beaumont, and John Fletcher were writing for the companies of boy actors against whom the King's Men had been competing since 1599. Those resemblances exist, at least in part, because in the summer of 1608 – the year of Shakespeare's final tragedy – the King's Men took a step that radically changed the circumstances under which they and their attached playwright worked. The company signed a lease to play at Blackfriars, an indoor, artificially lighted 'private' theatre,[3] and they began performing there sometime in 1609, displacing its previous occupants, the Children of the Queen's Revels, a company of boy actors. Blackfriars, located within the city of London but exempt from civic jurisdiction because it was situated in what had once been a monastary for Dominicans, became the King's Men winter playhouse, while their summer playhouse remained the Globe, the open-air 'public' theatre beyond the city limits that had been their principle playing site since 1599.

Acquiring performance rights at Blackfriars signalled the triumph of the King's Men over one of the boys' companies who were among their competitors and, by giving the company access to those who preferred to attend performances at private theatres rather than public theatres like the Globe, offered an opportunity to expand their audience. Performing indoors at Blackfriars during the winter also enhanced the finances of the King's Men, who no longer faced the prospect of losing income during those months when inclement weather was most likely to force cancellation of outdoor performances. The ability to shift between the Globe and Blackfriars from 1609 on gave the King's Men an advantage over their remaining rivals, the adult companies playing only in public theatres and the surviving boys' companies playing only in private theatres. Shakespeare may have stopped writing tragedies because, with the demise of one of the boys' companies and the easing of the commercial threat from that direction, the King's Men had less need for plays in the genre that allowed them to take fullest advantage of their maturity and experience. What the company now needed from him were plays that would allow them to exploit fully the opportunity that playing at both theatres now presented.

Exploiting that opportunity also meant, however, coping with challenges unlike any the King's Men and their attached playwright had faced. From the summer of 1608, Shakespeare found himself called upon to provide, for the first time in his career, plays that the King's Men could perform effectively in either of two London playhouses where the circumstances of performance as well as the composition and expectations of the audiences were sharply different. Against that backdrop, it is not surprising that the plays Shakespeare wrote after 1608 have features that make them distinctly different from those written previously.

The challenges were daunting. Blackfriars held perhaps as many as five hundred spectators – far fewer than the Globe – and admission prices were significantly higher, which meant that its audiences tended to be wealthier, more homogeneous, and less a representative cross-section of the population than audiences at the Globe. The smaller, more socially and economically advantaged Blackfriars audiences constituted a new clientele for the King's Men and their playwright – a select in-group possessing a degree of sophistication (supposedly) lacking in Globe audiences. According to R. A. Foakes,

> the boys, playing and mimicking adults, invited their audiences to be more continuously critical and detached [than audiences at the Globe], and were more stridently anti-mimetic in their frequent mockery of what they portrayed as old-fashioned public-theatre modes of drama or styles of verse (1990, p. 28).

Once they began playing at both the Globe and Blackfriars, the King's Men had to satisfy both their old and their new audiences.

Blackfriars audiences were accustomed to performances that included intervals, perhaps corresponding to act divisions, filled with music and sometimes singing and dancing. Those intervals, which affected the pace and rhythm of a performance, may have been a way of coping with a technical difficulty that did not exist at the open-air Globe: the candles that provided indoor illumination needed periodic trimming during the course of a performance. Once the King's Men commenced playing at Blackfriars, they may have begun using intervals at their Globe performances as well. If so, they had to develop new performance rhythms for all the plays already in their repertory, including Shakespeare's. It is equally possible, however, that they did not, in which case what the company now required from the playwright who had served them since their founding in 1594 were plays capable of accommodating sharply different performance rhythms without losing theatrical effectiveness.

In fashioning plays for performance at both Blackfriars and the Globe, Shakespeare also had to take into account differences in the relationship between stage and audience at each theatre. At Blackfriars, all members of the audience sat, and those seats closest to the stage were the most expensive. At the Globe, on the other hand, some of the audience sat while others stood, and the relationship between proximity to the stage and the price of admission was different. Those who paid least to enter – the 'groundlings' who stood during performances – were nearer to the stage, while those who paid more were farther away, seated in galleries. Differences in the audience–stage relationship affected acting style and technique. Performing at the Globe, the King's Men had to play over the groundlings and to the galleries if they were to have maximum impact on those who paid the most to watch them play, and that in turn required an acting style employing bold gestures and strong delivery of lines. At Blackfriars, however, a smaller theatre where those who paid the most sat nearest the stage, acting of that kind might well have come across as overblown, exaggerated. There 'a more low-keyed and intimate' (Foakes, 1990, p. 31) style was in order – a style that would have been ineffective at the Globe.

For David Daniell, Shakespeare's late plays confirm that 'A very great artist in his last works is usually seen to be taking extraordinary risks: Beethoven springs to mind' (1986, p. 119). They undoubtedly share a dramaturgy that is experimental and risky in its commitment to non-realistic modes and in what it asks its audiences to accept. *Pericles*, for example, asks its audiences to accept that an exceptionally learned physician can restore life to a queen whose coffin washes ashore following her burial at sea in a storm. Audiences of *The Winter's Tale* watch as the statue of a queen dead for sixteen years miraculously comes to life, then learn that, breaking radically with Shakespeare's previous practice, the play has deceived them: she was never dead. *Cymbeline* offers another example of the demands the late plays typically make upon their audiences, both engaging them in and detaching them from events onstage. Awaking beside a headless corpse wearing clothes she recognises as her husband's, Imogen mourns deeply. As she does, audiences find themselves called upon to respond to the intensity of her grief and, simultaneously, to recognise 'the grotesque comedy of her mistake, since in fact she mourns over the corpse of the dead villain, Cloten' (Bliss, 1990, p. 254). To a degree that sets them apart from their predecessors, Shakespeare's late plays insist that audiences acknowledge – and take satisfaction from – their nature as theatrical entities, 'contrived structures that rely on learned conventions and a whole set of social assumptions about the theatre itself' (Bliss, 1990, p. 243). The late plays are experimental and risky, however, not only because the last efforts of 'a very great artist' often are, but also because at least three of them – *Cymbeline*, *The Winter's Tale*, and *The Tempest* – arise from Shakespeare's effort to provide the King's Men with plays that would meet the unprecedented challenges of performing at both Blackfriars and the Globe.

The demise of the Children of the Queen's Revels eased the competitive financial pressure upon the King's Men, but the court masques that James, the company's patron, sponsored exerted a different pressure, dramaturgical rather than financial. A combination of music, dance, drama, and spectacle, the masque was a form of courtly entertainment in which members of the court participated, often taking the roles of classical divinities, while professional actors, including the King's Men, took the other parts. Enormously expensive and highly ephemeral, intended for one or two performances, the masques acted out an idealised vision of the relationships between monarch, court, and society. There had been masques during Elizabeth's reign, but under James they became more frequent, more dazzling, and even more expensive (£3,000 was not an unusual figure). They utilised the talents of men as distinguished as Ben Jonson and the great architect and stage designer Inigo Jones, who collaborated to produce a number of masques during James's first decade on the English throne.

The first masque on which Jonson and Jones collaborated, *The Masque of Blackness*, performed on 6 January 1605, was fundamentally unlike any previous masque in one crucial respect: for it Jones provided moveable scenery – framed by a proscenium arch – that had been painted and arranged in accord with perspectivist principles developed in the fifteenth century in Italy. Those principles, which aimed at the faithful representation of what the eyes see, enabled painters working on a flat, two-dimensional surface to create the illusion of depth by proportionately diminishing the size of objects and figures in the painting. Those watching *The Masque of Blackness* were the first English audience to experience a mode of representation that was scenic and pictorial and thus radically different from the primarily verbal mode of representation upon which performances at commercial theatres like the Globe relied.

At the Globe and later at Blackfriars, audiences were on three (perhaps four) sides, possibly even on the stage itself – which meant that few large stage properties were used and settings could not be elaborate. On those thrust or platform stages, place was established less by what audiences saw than by what they heard. Rosalind's announcement 'this is the Forest of Arden' (II.iv.13) signalled a change in locale to the first audiences watching *As You Like It*, but the stage they looked on as they heard those words had changed little, if at all, from how it had appeared for earlier scenes set outside the forest. No phalanx of potted trees, for example, had been moved on to encourage audiences to 'see' the forest because that would have impeded their view. Rosalind's words summoned the play's first audiences to re-work, to transform, what their eyes saw – to 'see' in a distinctively theatrical way: not just with their eyes but also with their ears and, ultimately, their minds.

Audiences at court masques sat in front of the stage, watching what happened through a wide opening (a proscenium arch) corresponding to the frame of a picture or a window. What they saw through that frame was not possible on the open thrust stages of Blackfriars and the Globe: moveable and elaborately painted scenery carefully proportioned and arranged to establish perspective and thereby intensify the audience's sense that they were actually seeing the place in which the stage action was taking place. The scenery was part of an unified, integrated set. Rapid changes of visually distinct settings signalled changes in locale, and place was a function primarily of what the audience saw. Rosalind had to summon theatre audiences to impose the concept 'forest' upon the open space and relatively unchanged visual features of the Globe stage. The Globe and Blackfriars were not theatres of visual illusionism – settings and scenic machines – but of actors moving and speaking in open spaces given local habitation and a name primarily by what they said and did. Jacobean masques, on the other hand, had the power – like movies and television in this century – to offer their audiences a strikingly engaging visualisation of a forest.

The pressure exerted by the visual illusionism of the Jacobean masque from 1605 on may have begun to register in Shakespeare's plays as early as Edgar's description in *King Lear* (IV.vi.11–24) of the view from the edge of the cliff to which he has supposedly led his eyeless father Gloucester who wants to commit suicide. That description is part of an exceptionally complex theatrical moment, discussed fully in Chapter 4, that invokes the perspectivist mode of seeing in order to take advantage of the distinctive theatrical effects possible on the open stage of the Globe, where what audiences heard determined what they 'saw'. By the time of Shakespeare's last plays, the impact of the masque is indisputable. The stage direction for the appearance of Jupiter in *Cymbeline* suggests that it is an effort to achieve a moment of masque-like spectacle: '*Jupiter descends in thunder and lightning, sitting upon an eagle. He throws a thunderbolt*' (V.iv.92). Contrast that with the appearance of Hymen, another classical deity, towards the end of *As You Like It*, one of Shakspeare's Elizabethan comedies. The stage direction says only, '*Enter Hymen, Rosalind, and Celia*' (V.iv.106). The climactic moment of *The Winter's Tale* – when Hermione's statue, 'stone no more' (V.iii.99), begins to move – involves an adaptation, for use on the commercial stages of the Globe and Blackfriars, of the masque practice of having court ladies pose as statues. *The Tempest* has no play-within-the-play like those in *Hamlet* and *A Midsummer Night's Dream*. Instead, it offers its audiences what Prospero calls a 'vanity of mine Art' (IV.i.41) so much like a masque that critics routinely refer to it as one. Thus, what many regard as the final play Shakespeare wrote singlehandedly associates visionary magic with the masque, not with plays.

* * *

Another major difference between Shakespeare's Elizabethan and Jacobean plays is in how awareness of the sovereign makes itself felt in them. In Shakespeare's plays for the Lord Chamberlain's Men, an awareness of Queen Elizabeth is undoubtedly present – as Leah Marcus (1988), for one, has recently shown – but it manifests itself obliquely, indirectly. In his plays for the King's Men, however, awareness of King James is far more direct and straightforward. Subsequent chapters will consider how that awareness registers in specific plays, but two examples are in order here. A conspicuous difference between James and Elizabeth was that she enjoyed and he intensely disliked making appearances among the people, and the opening scene of *Measure for Measure* – the first Shakespearean play written for the recently renamed King's Men – points to that difference as if voicing, through the figure of the Duke of Vienna, the new sovereign's distaste. The duke insists on leaving Vienna 'privily', without ceremony or public notice, explaining that 'I love the people, / But do not like to stage me to their eyes' (I.i.67–8).

The opening scene of *The Winter's Tale*, one of Shakespeare's 'last' plays, ends with a conversation that glances at a second difference between James and Elizabeth. Unlike the childless Elizabeth, James was the father of a royal family, the begetter of princes and princesses who could carry on the Stuart line. In that conversation, Archidamus, a Bohemian courtier, and Camillo, a Sicilian courtier, discuss how the presence of a young prince satisifies an essential need in a kingdom's people, by giving to even the oldest and most enfeebled of them a revitalising sense of the nation's future:

> ARCH.: You have an unspeakable comfort of your young prince Mamillius: it is a gentleman of the greatest promise that ever came into my note.
> CAM.: I very well agree with you in the hopes of him: it is a gallant child; one that, indeed, physics the subject, makes old hearts fresh: they that went on crutches ere he was born desire yet their life to see him a man.
>
> (I.i.34–40)

Elizabeth, the virgin queen who never married, bore no prince to 'comfort' and 'physic' her subjects when she was of child-bearing age, and during the 1590s, when there was no longer any possibility of her giving birth, Shakespeare provided the King's Men with nine history plays, eight of which (*King John* being the exception) deal with events leading up to the founding of the Tudor dynasty that would end with the death of the now aging queen. Those plays spoke to and arose from a deep cultural anxiety. They provided a means, an opportunity, by which those among Elizabeth's subjects who paid to see them performed might accommodate themselves to what was coming to an end by looking at how it came to be – might cope with uncertainty about England's future by considering crises England had survived in the past.

James brought with him from Scotland what very few English then living had ever seen, a royal family: a wife, two sons, and a daughter. In their new king's princely progeny, especially his sons, James's new subjects could find 'comfort' and 'physic' of a kind their beloved

Elizabeth never gave them – the prospect of a future free of the controversies and uncertainties surrounding the issue of royal succession that had plagued England since the time of Henry VIII and that boiled again in the last decade of Elizabeth's reign as it became clear she would die without bearing an heir.[4]

James regarded the marriages of his children as diplomatic tools to lessen international enmity by establishing what he hoped would be enduring bonds between his kingdom and other European states. In *The Winter's Tale* and *The Tempest* – both among the fourteen plays performed at court during the festivities preceding the marriage of James's daughter Elizabeth to the Elector Palatine on 14 February 1613 – the son of one ruler and the daughter of another become betrothed, establishing the prospect of uniting through their offspring the states their fathers rule separately. James himself was living proof of the reconciliation that could eventually come into being – across what Leontes at the end of *The Winter's Tale* calls 'this wide gap of time' (V.iii.154) – because of a royal marriage. He was the great-grandson of Henry VII's daughter Margaret, who married James IV of Scotland, and that lineage, that blood-line, helped position him to become, in 1603, the first king of both England and Scotland.

James's life also offers evidence of a pattern of events like the one particularly prominent in *Pericles* and *The Winter's Tale*: a ruler's eventual triumph over extreme and sustained adversity. At the end of *Pericles*, Gower, the play's choric narrator, tells the audience that the play confirms the principle that 'Although assailed with fortune fierce and keen, / Virtue [is] preserved from fell destruction's blast, / Led on by heaven, and crowned with joy at last' (V.iii.90–1). James became king of Scotland while still an infant, due to the deposition of his mother Mary Stuart, Queen of Scots, and during his first months as Scotland's putative sovereign, a band of disgruntled noblemen kidnapped him for an extended period. He survived that experience to rule Scotland in his own right. Mary Stuart regarded herself, not Elizabeth, as England's rightful ruler, and in 1587, Elizabeth allowed Mary's execution on the grounds that she had plotted to overthrow her. When, sixteen years later in 1603 – a period equal to the span of time encompassed in *The Winter's Tale* – James became England's king, the crown that Elizabeth had beheaded his mother to keep passed to him.

James's presence on the English throne occasioned a tightening or regularising of the dominant ideology that shaped the controlling conception of social order and relationships. Under Elizabeth as well as James, that conception was profoundly patriarchal: just as God had authority over his human creatures, rulers had authority over their subjects, husbands over their wives, fathers over their children, priests over the laity, masters over their servants and apprentices, the head over the parts of the body, reason over the passions. James invoked that ideology during his first address to Parliament, declaring 'I am the Husband, all the whole Isle is my lawfull Wife; I am the Head, and it is my Body' (McIlwain, 1918, p. 272). During Elizabeth's reign, however, a discernible gap existed between the official conception of the basis of social order and the fact of her rule, between dominant ideology and actual practice. While she ruled, ultimate authority in England rested in the person of a woman. English men, from lowly commoners to the highest lords, were subject to her – precisely the kind of situation that, when James's mother Mary ruled Scotland, John Calvin had denounced as an example of 'the monstrous regiment of women'. Elizabeth's sovereignty constituted a conspicuous and fundamental anomaly at the very apex of the patriarchal system, at the point where state and church in England met in a single head. The fact that that head was a woman, not a man, opened within that system a cultural space that allowed a measure of flexibility, a degree of play, a modicum of freedom.

James's accession gave England a monarch who was male, thereby ending what the era's dominant ideology considered the fundamental anomaly of female rule, closing the cultural space opened by Elizabeth's rule. With James on the throne, the fit between patriarchal theory and actual practice in England was conspicuously tighter. That tighter fit is evident in the differences between Isabella, the heroine of Shakespeare's first Jacobean play, *Measure for Measure*, and Helena, the heroine of what may have been his final Elizabethan play, *All's Well That Ends Well*. Helena is far more active and independent. Isabella must be summoned from the convent by a man to plead for her brother's life, while Helena, pursuing a 'project' (I.i.228) of her own design, sets out for Paris and the French court of her own volition, motivated by her love for Bertram and the desire to use her medical skills to save the diseased king's life. Both women participate in a bed-trick, a manoeuvre in which a woman consents to have sexual relations with a man but then allows another woman to take her place while the man remains ignorant of the switch.

Helena conceives, sets up, and finally implements the bed-trick in which she participates; she takes Diana's place in Bertram's bed. Isabella, on the other hand, participates in a bed-trick that the Duke conceives and oversees, and her role in implementing it is passive; she agrees to tell Angelo she will satisfy his sexual demands and then allows Mariana to take her place. She is – as Helena and such comic heroines as Rosalind of *As You Like It* and Viola of *Twelfth Night* are not – the instrument 'of some more mightier member' (V.i.236). That 'member' is the Duke of Vienna, who, like James himself, the patron of the recently renamed King's Men, is a male sovereign.

As further evidence of the tightening and regularising of ideology following James's accession, one can point to how, in three of Shakespeare's Jacobean tragedies, the androgynous heroines of his Elizabethan comedies are transformed into heroines who, defiant of male authority, incorporate features of the monstrous, unruly 'woman on top'. In *Macbeth, Coriolanus,* and *Antony and Cleopatra,* a woman, employing specifically female forms of power, exercises control over a man who is a warrior, the embodiment of specifically masculine powers and activities. That female dominance is an essential element in the warrior's subsequent destruction, and the unruly women are figures by which a patriarchal culture tried to come to terms with the recent experience of womanly rule under Elizabeth. The feminine features that Rosalind and Viola temporarily cloak in male attire Lady Macbeth tries to extirpate, calling for demonic spirits to 'unsex me here' (I.v.41). In an act that perverts the ideologically correct relation of husband exercising authority over wife, she uses her sexual power over him to bring him to undo his decision not to kill King Duncan. From her Macbeth takes not 'th'milk of human kindness' (I.v.17) but the power to go forward with an act he is not capable of performing on his own, an act that the Elizabethan–Jacobean era regarded as especially heinous: the killing of a king.

A detail that is particularly effective in establishing Lady Macbeth as a monstrous woman is her assertion that even though she knows 'How tender 'tis to love the babe that milks me', she is capable of the shockingly unmaternal act of killing her own suckling infant: 'I would, while it was smiling in my face, / Have pluck'd my nipple from his boneless gums, / And dash'd the brains out' (I.vii.55–8). The capacity to override maternal feelings that Lady Macbeth asserts Volumnia demonstrates in *Coriolanus* when she pleads with her warrior son – 'Thy valiantness was mine, thou suck'st it from me'

(III.ii.129) – to spare Rome, the city he has won fame for defending, that is powerless to resist the army he now leads against it. Consenting at last to the maternal pressures she brings to bear, Coriolanus makes clear that the cost of her placing allegiance to Rome above her maternal feelings for him is likely to be the life of her son:

> O my mother, mother! O!
> You have won a happy victory to Rome;
> But for your son, believe it, O, believe it,
> Most dangerously you have with him prevail'd,
> If not most mortal to him. But let it come.
> (V.iii.185–9)

Antony, the foremost general of his time and ruler of one-third of the Roman world, in *Antony and Cleopatra* finds himself unable and even unwilling to break free of a relationship with Cleopatra that he himself calls a 'dotage' in which he will 'lose myself' (I.ii.114). One feature of that relationship is that it blurs the difference between male and female. Octavius Caesar, Antony's rival, comments that he 'is not more manlike / Than Cleopatra; nor the queen of Ptolemy / More womanly than he' (I.iv.5–7). Cleopatra tells of putting Antony to bed after outdrinking him and then dressing him in 'my tires and mantles' while she, in turn, wears the weapon, 'his sword Philippan' (II.v.22–3), that he carried during his victory over Brutus and Cassius at the battle of Philippi with which Shakespeare's *Julius Caesar* concludes. She insists on taking part in the battle against Octavius even though Enobarbus warns, 'Your presence needs must puzzle Antony, / Take from his heart, take from his brain, from's time, / What should not then be spar'd' (III.vii.10–12). She will, she declares, 'Appear there for a man' (III.vii.18) – a situation that perhaps glances back to the occasion in 1588 when Queen Elizabeth, wearing according to some accounts the armour of a man, reviewed at Tilbury the troops mustered to fight the approaching Spanish Armada. In the speech she gave then, Elizabeth declared,

> I have the body of a weak and feeble woman, but I have the heart and stomach of a king, and of a king of England too; and I think foul scorn that Parma or Spain or any Prince of Europe, should dare to invade the borders of my realm; to which, rather than any dishonour should grow by me, I myself will take up

arms, I myself will be your general, judge, and rewarder of every one of your virtues in the field. (quoted in Marcus, 1988, p. 54)

History does not record what Elizabeth's troops thought of those words, but Antony's soldiers lament that 'our leader's led, / And we are women's men' (III.vii.69–70). That observation and Enobarbus's warning prove true during the ensuing battle at sea. When the ship carrying Cleopatra flees, Antony, the battle-tested warrior, '(like a doting mallard) / Leaving the fight in heighth, flies after her' (III.x.20–1). 'Mine eyes did sicken at the sight', Enobarbus says; Scarus declares, 'I never saw an action of such shame; / Experience, manhood, honour, ne'er before / Did violate so itself' (III.x.17, 22–4). Canididus adds, 'O, he has given example of our flight, / Most grossly by his own' (III.x.28–9). Antony concurs with those judgements: 'I have fled myself, and have instructed cowards / To run, and show their shoulders' (III.xi.7–8).

When Antony, making 'his will / Lord of his reason' and allowing 'the itch of his affection' (III.xiii.3–4, 7) to compromise his generalship, withdraws from the fight and follows the fleeing Cleopatra, he violates those qualities that, from a Roman perspective at least, define a man as great. He not only flees himself, but in the process he also flees from – and loses – himself, ceasing to be a man who possesses a specifically martial and masculine form of greatness. Antony laments that Cleopatra has 'robb'd me of my sword' (IV.xiv.23), and audiences see him complete his own unmanning when he proves incapable of using that sword, with which he once 'Quarter'd the world' (IV.xiv.58), to execute deftly what the play's first audiences regarded as the distinctively Roman action of suicide. Informed that Cleopatra has killed herself, he asks the servant he has freed, appropriately named Eros, to kill him. Instead, Eros turns his sword on himself, dying instantly. Left to follow Eros's example and kill himself with his own sword, the one that Cleopatra spoke of wearing while he slept drunkenly, Antony botches the job, leaving himself mortally wounded but not dead: 'I have done my work ill' (IV.xiv.105). Antony falls short of Eros's example but perhaps the point that most compellingly demonstrates Antony's unmanning is that this renowned general also falls short of the example provided by a teenage girl in another Shakespearean play about a pair of famous lovers, *Romeo and Juliet*. In that Elizabethan tragedy, Juliet accomplishes

what Antony cannot. Alone beside Romeo's corpse in her family's
tomb, she dispatches herself with one thrust of his dagger. Antony's
inability to kill himself with comparable deftness undercuts his dying
claim that his suicide assures him of greatness as the Romans defined
it. He speaks of himself as 'a Roman, by a Roman / Valiantly
vanquish'd' (IV.xv.57–8), but his failure to kill himself cleanly with a
single thrust means that his is not a suicide in what Cleopatra calls
'the high Roman fashion' (IV.xv.87).

Having mis-handled his suicide, Antony lives long enough to learn
that the report of Cleopatra's death was another of her deceptions,
and he asks the Roman soldiers who remain with him to bear him
to her. After the men carrying him arrive at the monument in which
Cleopatra and her attendants have shut themselves, the playtext,
taking advantage of the upper playing level at the Globe, specifies
that '*They heave Antony aloft to Cleopatra*' (IV.xv.38). '*Heave*' registers the
physical effort involved in a sequence of stage business that is
potentially awkward, no matter how often it is rehearsed, and
therefore theatrically risky. Heaved aloft, Antony dies there – not on
the battlefield amongst soldiers but in the womanly company of Cleopatra and her attendants. At his death, Cleopatra praises Antony in
terms that, in a manner she seems not to intend, also summarise his
loss of martial and Roman manliness, of which his isolation among
women (all of them first played by boys) is a visual signal: 'The
soldier's pole is fall'n; young boys and girls / Are level now with
men' (IV.xv.65–6).

Antony is not present when Cleopatra, applying the poisonous asp
to her breast, dies among and with her women, one of whom
precedes her in death, the other of whom follows her. The final
evidence of the effects of what the dominant patriarchal ideology of
the Jacobean era regarded as unnatural female rule is that Cleopatra (and the boy playing her) dominate the play's final act, not
Antony (and the King's Men's foremost tragic actor, Richard Burbage).
After ordering that Cleopatra 'be buried by her Antony', Octavius
declares: 'No grave upon the earth shall clip in it / A pair so famous'
(V.ii.356–8). The fame that history confers on Antony – in no small
measure because of the *Antony and Cleopatra* that Shakespeare and the
King's Men first brought into being – is not his alone, but his *and*
Cleopatra's. He lives through history as Cleopatra's lover, one of 'a
pair so famous'. The cost of that fame, at least from the perspective
of the conception of masculinity associated in this play with Rome,

is that history will always know him as 'her Antony', as a woman's man.[5]

The tightening of patriarchal ideology is not the only way in which *Antony and Cleopatra* discloses how James's presence on the throne that Elizabeth occupied before him made itself felt in Shakespeare's Jacobean plays. As the land battle that will result in Antony's final defeat commences, Octavius declares, 'The time of universal peace is near: / Prove this a prosperous day, the three-nook'd world / Shall bear the olive freely' (IV.vi.5–7). At the start of *Antony and Cleopatra*, authority throughout the 'three-nook'd' Roman world of Europe, Asia, and Africa is divided among three men: Octavius, Antony, and Lepidus. With Octavius's victory over Antony, that authority passes to Octavius alone, whom history has come to know as Augustus Caesar, the first emperor of Rome, whose ascent to power ended the wars, fought since the time of Julius Caesar, over the issues of what form of government Rome should have and who should govern.

Augustus Caesar was one of the models from history most frequently used to mark off James's reign from Elizabeth's – to give it a style that, in contrast to Elizabeth's, is Roman, imperial, and specifically Augustan.[6] For example, James is wished the 'lasting glory' of 'Augustus state' in the entertainment Ben Jonson provided for his official entrance into and procession through London (delayed until 15 March 1604 by a severe outbreak of the plague in the spring and summer of 1603). James presented himself as an *imperial* monarch in ways that Elizabeth did not. In a letter of 28 March 1603, four days after her death, he spoke of London as 'the Chamber of our Imperiall Crowne', and the medal struck to commemorate his accession to the English throne shows him wearing the laurel of a Roman emperor – as he is in Crispin van de Passe's 1613 engraving of him. In Jonson's masque *Hymenaei*, performed on 5 January 1606, 'Augustus, Prince of Peace, is James's identity' (Goldberg, 1983, p. 43). James arrived among his new English subjects as a prince bringing peace. One of his first acts as king was to recall English troops fighting Spanish forces on the continent and declare an end to the hostilities with Spain that had persisted throughout the final fifteen years of Elizabeth's reign. The image of James on the medal commemorating the 1604 Treaty of London, formally establishing peace between England and Spain, shows him wearing the Roman laurel. Thus, in the cultural circumstances within which the King's Men first played it, *Antony and Cleopatra* may have helped to differentiate James's reign from Elizabeth's by allowing audiences to see the final phase of the process by which the Roman empire and its first emperor came into being. James and his realm were, his royal propagandists claimed, the re-embodiment of that empire on British soil.

* * *

The differences between Shakespeare's Elizabethan and Jacobean plays co-exist with similarities, with elements of affiliation and continuity, that are likewise significant. For example, all of Shakespeare's plays – Elizabethan as well as Jacobean – are poetic. Most characters speak most of the time in some form of verse, usually blank verse: lines that do not end in rhyme and consist of ten syllables, grouped into five pairs in each of which an unaccented syllable precedes an accented syllable.[7] Over the course of his career, Shakespeare's blank verse changed, becoming more varied and less regular in form and thus more flexible and conversational. A greater number of lines in his Jacobean plays have fewer or more than ten syllables than in his Elizabethan plays, and the percentage of run-on lines is greater. David Bevington notes that among the most striking changes in Shakespearean blank verse across his career is that he

> increasingly divides a line of verse between two or more speakers. *The Comedy of Errors* and *1 Henry VI* [two of his earliest plays] do so hardly at all, whereas in *Cymbeline* the figures rise to a remarkable 85 percent of all instances in which one speaker stops speaking and another begins; *The Winter's Tale* does so in 87.6 percent of such instances, and *The Tempest* in 84.5 percent. (1992, p. lxxix)

Shakespeare also varied his blank verse by including in his plays both lines of dialogue that rhymed and – with four exceptions, all history plays[8] – passages of dialogue in prose. The dialogue of such early plays as *Richard II* and *A Midsummer Night's Dream* includes among the dominant blank verse a far higher proportion of end-rhymed lines than do his later plays, in which the proportion drops off sharply. Shakespeare did not abandon rhyme over the course of his career – rhyming couplets remain the typical signal of the end of a scene – but he used it less. On the other hand, his use of prose – spoken in his early plays mainly by rustics, servants, and clowns –

generally increased during the 1590s, reaching a peak in *Much Ado About Nothing* and *The Merry Wives of Windsor* – both dated late in Elizabeth's reign – before subsiding in his Jacobean plays.

Blank verse is but one aspect of the pattern of continuity and change shared by Shakespeare's Jacobean and Elizabethan plays. The former routinely re-work, recycle elements of the latter. The blood in which those who have killed Caesar wash their hands in *Julius Caesar*, one of Shakespeare's Elizabethan tragedies, recirculates to become in *Macbeth*, a Jacobean tragedy, the blood of King Duncan that Macbeth and Lady Macbeth try to wash from their hands. *Antony and Cleopatra* ends with Augustus Caesar ruling the entire Roman world, bringing to conclusion events set in motion in *Julius Caesar* when Brutus, Cassius, and the other conspirators assassinate Julius Caesar in order to prevent one-man rule in Rome. Both *Hamlet*, Shakespeare's final Elizabethan tragedy, and *Othello*, his first Jacobean tragedy, begin with a night scene, and both make use of different forms of poison in the ear. The poison that the Ghost of King Hamlet says Claudius poured into his ear as he slept becomes the poison Iago speaks into the ears of Othello. In *A Midsummer Night's Dream*, a comedy of the mid-1590s, Titania dismisses her husband Oberon's accusation of infidelity, declaring, 'These are the forgeries of jealousy' (II.i.81). Such 'forgeries' resurface in both *Othello* and *The Winter's Tale*. Othello murders Desdemona because he believes Iago's forgeries, and in *The Winter's Tale*, Leontes falls victim to his own forgeries, convincing himself that his wife Hermione has committed adultery with Polixenes, his best friend and fellow king.

Refashioning and reforging material is consistent not only with the plays' common authorship but also with a remarkable stability in the core personnel of the Lord Chamberlain's–King's Men from 1594 onwards. Only one of the orginal sharers, Will Kempe, left the company voluntarily, to be replaced by Robert Armin, and several died, but a core group, including Shakespeare and Richard Burbage, remained intact. Re-working is also consistent with similarities in the configurations of the stages on which Shakespeare's plays from 1594 on were written to be played: The Theatre, then, after 1598, The Globe, and, starting in 1609, Blackfriars as well. At all three a curtained recess at the back of the thrust stage that was the main playing area contributes to similarities in three moments from plays written in different genres and at different points in Shakespeare's career: when Prince Hal finds Falstaff asleep in *Henry IV, Part I*, one

of Shakespeare's Elizabethan history plays; when Polonius conceals
himself behind an arras through which Hamlet stabs, mortally
wounding him; and when, near the end of *The Tempest*, Prospero
reveals Miranda and Ferdinand playing chess. *Hamlet* and *Antony and
Cleopatra* contain scenes that exploit the space beneath the thrust
stage. The ghost of *Hamlet*'s father moves from place to place under
it as he seconds his son's command that Horatio, Marcellus, and
Bernardo swear on *Hamlet*'s sword not to disclose what they know.
In *Antony and Cleopatra*, the movement beneath the stage of musicians
playing hautboys signals the departure from Antony of the god
Hercules. A playing level above the thrust stage functions in the same
play as the upper floor or even the top of the monument in which
Cleopatra and her women have taken refuge, and the dying Antony
is hoisted up to them. In *Othello* and *Romeo and Juliet*, written in the
mid-1590s, that upper playing level functions as the balcony of a
house. There Juliet, unable to sleep, first hears Romeo speak of his
love for her and tells him of her love for him, and there, early in
Othello, Desdemona's father enters, awakened by the shouts of
Roderigo and Iago, who tell him she has eloped with Othello.

Shakespeare's Elizabethan and Jacobean plays are different, but
their differences are themselves part of a web of linkages and
affiliations – elements of a pattern of development that is not
straightforwardly linear but a blend of change and continuity, each
important in its own right and in relationship to the other.

2

Measure for Measure: 'A Little Brief Authority'

On 26 December 1604, in the banqueting hall at Whitehall, King James and his court watched a performance of *Measure for Measure*. It followed, by some months, the play's debut at the Globe, which had reopened on 9 April after being closed for nearly a year by an outbreak of the plague so severe that the general public was banned from the new king's cornonation (25 July 1603) and his first royal progress through London was postponed until March of 1604. Performances at the Globe were part of the still relatively new and highly controversial practice of playgoing centred upon the stages of London's public playhouses – structures unknown in England before 1576 – and involving companies of adult actors who earned their livings by performing there before paying audiences as often as six afternoons a week for as long as ten months of the year. During the reigns of Elizabeth and James, the crown and civic officials (particularly in London) jostled to assert their control over playhouses, players, and those who made up their audiences. That manoeuvring was one manifestation of a fundamental struggle under way in early modern Engand regarding the nature, the location, and the scope of ultimate authority – political, religious, economic, cultural. Did it or did it not reside in the person of the monarch? If so, what limits, if any, was the sovereign subject to in exercising that authority, and in what style – by what means and in what manner – should it be exercised?

Censorship, exercised primarily through the office of the Master of Revels, was one tactic by which the crown sought to assert its control over theatrical activity. Another was to make each acting company's licence to perform dependent upon the patronage provided by a great man of the realm, sometimes a member of her Privy Council. By a royal warrant dated 17 May 1603, within three weeks of arriving in London after Elizabeth's death on 23 March 1603, James changed that system. He decreed that only members of the royal family could be patrons of an acting company, and he himself became the patron of that company, previously known as the Lord Chamberlain's Men and now renamed the King's Men, of which Shakespeare was a founding member and for which he had been writing plays exclusively since 1594. By redefining the relationship between the crown and the acting companies, James's modification of the patronage system altered the conditions under which the plays they performed were produced and received. In the case of the King's Men, the changes James instituted made them and their playwright subject in a new, less indirect way to England's sovereign authority. A strong consensus regards *Measure for Measure* as the first play Shakespeare wrote during James's reign. If that consensus is correct, it is the first he wrote after James altered the system of patronage by which the crown had previously sought to exercise its authority over the only three adult acting companies licensed to perform in London's public theatres at the time of his accession.

The players and London playhouses were elements not only of a new cultural practice but also of a new form of mass communication, one made all the more potent by its location in England's population centre. By changing the patronage arrangements within which the acting companies operated so as to assert more directly the authority of the crown over the newest mass medium in English culture, the new king signalled – in effect, if not by design – that his style of exercising authority would be different from Elizabeth's. During the days immediately after Elizabeth's death and before his arrival in London, James used another relatively new form of mass communication to make himself and his ideas about the use of kingly authority better known to his new subjects. Between 24 March and 13 April 1603, London printing presses produced 10,000 copies (eight editions) of *Basilikon Doron*, a book on the theory and practice of kingship that James had written in 1599 in the form of advice to his eldest son, Prince Henry.

A number of issues that James addresses in *Basilikon Doron* are also taken up in *Measure for Measure*, most notably the proper relationship between justice and mercy, and the play offers evidence of the recently renamed King's Men altering their theatrical practices in response to the presence on the throne of England of a man not a woman, of a king rather than a queen, and of a king who is their patron as well as their sovereign. In the cultural circumstances within which the play came into being, its performances – at the Globe and at court – were particular instances of the vast process of accommodation under way across English society as it adapted to the style of Jame's rule, to the forms and modes by which he exercised authority. The first performances of *Measure* were occasions and agents of cultural adaptation, easing the adjustment through which those Londoners who made up the majority of the play's first audiences were passing, by making them more familiar with and responsive to the values and ways of their new sovereign, the first king England had known in over four decades, the first Scots king in English history, and the first sovereign to rule both England and Scotland.

Measure considers the issue of political authority on at least two levels: how those who rule govern their subjects and how those who rule others govern themselves. It establishes a network of correspondences, involving differences as well as resemblances, between Duke Vincentio and King James and between Viennese and Londoners. For example, when Duke Vincentio remarks, 'I love the people, / But do not like to stage me to their eyes' (I.i.67–8), he voices a dislike of public apppearances that came to be a frequently noted point of difference between Elizabeth and James, who shared the Duke's distaste. *Measure* begins with a transfer of sovereign authority; Vincentio designates Angelo as his deputy in his absence: 'In our remove, be thou at full ourself. / Mortality and mercy in Vienna / Live in thy tongue and heart' (I.i.43–5). Most of the rest of the play shows the Viennese adjusting to a new ruler – a situation analogous to that of the English in 1604 as they adjusted to James's kingship.

Such resemblances co-exist with differences that are equally significant. James, who much preferred riding and hunting to the administrative responsibilities of kingship, was frequently away from London, but during his often extended absences, he – in contrast to the Duke – delegated authority to the Privy Council, not to a single deputy, let alone one as untested as Angelo announces himself to be. Another point of difference follows from the fact that in making the severe Angelo his deputy, the Duke hopes to check the disorder he says is rampant in Vienna as the consequence of his own failure to enforce 'strict statutes and most biting laws' (I.iii.19) during the previous years of his reign. The Duke has ruled in a manner at odds with what James recommends in *Basilikon Doron*, where he urges that a new ruler begin his reign by demonstrating his willingness to enforce rigorous justice before showing his capacity for mercy. The ruler who decides instead to show mercy first will find himself, James explains (nominally to Prince Henry), in a predicament:

> For if . . . ye kyth your clemencie at the first, the offences would soone come to such heapes . . . that when ye would fall to punish, the number of them to be punished, would exceeed the innocent: and yee would be troubled whom-at to begin: and against your nature would be compelled to wracke many, whom the chastisement of a few in the beginning might have preserved. (McIlwain, 1918, p. 20)

The situation James describes anticipates the even more extreme dilemma in which the Duke finds himself at the start of *Measure*:

> . . . our decrees,
> Dead to infliction, to themselves are dead,
> And Liberty plucks Justice by the nose,
> The baby beats the nurse, and quite athwart
> Goes all decorum.
> (I.iii.27–31)

He cannot now enforce laws that 'for this fourteen years we have let slip' (I.iii.21) without jeopardising his own standing with his subjects:

> Sith 'twas my fault to give the people scope,
> 'Twould be my tyranny to strike and gall them
> For what I bid them do: for we bid this be done,
> When evil deeds have their permissive pass,
> And not the punishment.
> (I.i.35–9)

The Duke plans to resolve his predicament by (ostensibly) leaving Vienna and conferring sovereign authority on Angelo, who then 'may in the ambush of my name strike home', curbing excesses the Duke's own laxity has fostered, but without compromising the Duke himself: 'And yet my nature never in the sight / To do in slander' (I.iii.41–3).

In *Measure*, the people of Vienna find themselves subject to two extremes, the laxity of the Duke's rule and the absolute rigour of Angelo's. Angelo begins his rule, as James recommends, by demonstrating his willingness to enforce the law – specifically, the 'strict' statute requiring that fornication be punished by death – but he displays no capacity for mercy. On the contrary, stirred by sexual desires he has never before felt, he proves eager to commit, with Isabella, the very crime for which he sentences her brother Claudio to death. What the Duke's subjects do not experience is authority capable of exercising both justice and mercy in accord with the principle of wise moderation, of temperance, that James urges upon Prince Henry in *Basilikon Doron* and, in effect, promises to his new English subjects, from whose ranks came the first audiences of *Measure*. Even at the end of the play, the Duke does not balance justice and mercy. He spares all who are condemned to die, including Barnardine, a convicted murderer whose guilt is 'Most manifest, and not denied by himself' (IV.ii.137). In the cultural circumstances within which the play was composed and initially performed, the various resemblances between the fictional duke and their true king and between Vienna and London perhaps prompted audiences to make comparisons, while the differences probably encouraged many to resolve those comparisons in favour of their new king, who presented himself to his new subjects as a ruler capable, in contrast to the Duke, of enforcing justice and, in contrast to Angelo, of exercising mercy.

James began his rule as England's king by acts that showed him implementing what he said in *Basilikon Doron*. One of the most spectacular demonstrations of his capacity to combine justice with mercy involved his treatment in early December of 1603 of six men convicted of treason and sentenced to die for their roles in a conspiracy called the Bye plot. Three of them were put to death in early December, and the remaining three faced execution on 10 December in Windsor.[1] On that day, in a carefully orchestrated set of manoeuvres that signalled the style with which England's new king was ruling, each of the three was brought separately to the scaffold to face death alone. As the first braced for a death that he declared himself unprepared to meet, a messenger from the king battled through the crowd and, reaching the scaffold at the last moment, halted the proceedings. After speaking with him, the sheriff in charge told the condemned man that he would receive additional time to prepare himself better for death, and he was led away. The second conspirator was then brought alone to the scaffold and, after speaking his final words, was told that the order of the executions had been altered. He too was taken from the scaffold. After the third reached the scaffold and also spoke his final words, the proceedings were once more halted, and the other two condemned men were brought back to the scaffold.

A contemporary account of the reunion of the trio – each thinking the other two already dead and himself about to die – emphasises the theatrical quality of the proceedings. In a letter dated 11 December 1603, Dudley Carleton comments: 'Now all the actors' were 'together on the stage (as use is at the end of a play)' and there they 'looked strange one upon the other, like men beheaded and met again in the other world' (quoted in Mullaney, 1988, p. 106). Assembled on the scaffold, the three traitors, having been brought to the very edge of eternity, then learned they were to be spared. The document granting them life, possibly composed by James himself and delivered by the king's messenger to the sheriff who now read it aloud, prolonged their suspense until its final sentence, which, Carleton reports, called upon the condemned trio – and thus the crowd gathered to witness their executions – to 'see the mercy of your Prince, who of himself hath sent hither a countermand, and hath given you your lives' (quoted in Bernthal, 1992, p. 206). 'There was', the Carleton report goes on to say, 'no need to beg a *Plaudite* of the audience, for it was given with such hues and cries, that it went from the castle to the town, and there began afresh . . .' (quoted in Bernthal, 1992, p. 253, and in Mullaney, 1988, p. 106).

Audiences watching the first performances of *Measure* at the Globe in the spring or early summer of 1604 saw events that strikingly resembled those that had happened at Windsor on that December day. As *Measure* ends, two men brought from prison for what they think will be their execution – Claudio and Barnardine – join a third, Angelo, who thinks Claudio is already dead and who moments before had heard the Duke sentence him to death: 'We do condemn thee to the very block / Where Claudio stoop'd to death, and with like haste' (V.i.412–13). The three then find themselves unexpectedly spared, the beneficiaries of princely mercy that leaves each of them speechless. Another point of similarity is that, like the theatricalized events at Windsor, *Measure* does not 'need to beg a *Plaudite*' of its audiences. Unlike such Elizabethan plays of Shakespeare's as *A*

Midsummer Night's Dream, As You Like It, and *All's Well That Ends Well,* it has no epilogue soliciting applause.

The differences between the events staged at Windsor and those enacted at the Globe are as significant as the similarities. One difference is that James mixed justice with mercy, allowing three of the Bye conspirators to be executed before sparing the remaining three. The Duke, in contrast, permits no executions to occur, exercising mercy that is all-inclusive. He pardons all the condemned men, even Barnardine. A second difference between the fictional duke audiences saw on the Globe stage and the king whose subjects they truly were is the mode of each ruler's participation in events. James was not present at Windsor on 10 December 1603, preferring to exercise his royal mercy at a distance, but the Duke participates directly and personally in shaping the play's final events. Emerging from the friar's disguise in which he has cloaked himself for most of the play, he grants last-minute mercy in his own person. Nor does the Duke's direct and personal involvement end with his acts of life-giving clemency. He also arranges three marriages – between Angelo and Mariana, Claudio and Juliet, Lucio and Kate Keepdown, the prostitute who has borne his child – and, twice, he proposes marriage to Isabella.

* * *

The earliest surviving version of *Measure* is that published in the First Folio of 1623, a collection of Shakespeare's plays assembled after his death by two men who were members of the Lord Chamberlain's–King's Men with Shakespeare. The First Folio classifies *Measure* as a comedy, the type of play that Shakespeare had written most often and regularly during Elizabeth's reign.[2] In each of Shakespeare's eleven Elizabethan comedies, no character whom audiences see dies, and each ends with men and women paired in actual or prospective marriages. These features are typical of a specific kind of comedy, romantic (or festive) comedy, and they are also present in *Measure,* which concludes with the lives of four men sentenced to death spared and with one marriage performed, two pending, and a fourth proposed.

However, while *Measure* includes those features, it also modifies them in ways that point to the play's specifically Jacobean character as a work written to be performed in a culture accommodating itself to the presence of a new form of sovereign authority in England – that exercised by the man who is both the King's Men's new monarch and their new patron. Although no character whom audiences see alive dies in *Measure*, the play's resolution rests on the death by natural causes, 'a cruel fever', of that 'most notorious pirate' Ragozine, a character not even mentioned until his timely demise who, most conveniently, is 'A man of Claudio's years; his beard and head / Just of his colour' (IV.iii.69–72). The Duke hails Ragozine's death as 'an accident that heaven provides' (IV.iii.76). It enables him to deceive Angelo and keep Claudio alive by substituting Ragozine's head for Claudio's – just as earlier, via the bed-trick, Mariana's maidenhead had been substituted for Isabella's.[3] The Provost exits in response to the Duke's command to 'send the head to Angelo' (IV.iii.91), but the play then has him return almost immediately for a brief appearance that is gratuitous in the sense that nothing in the plot requires it. 'Here is the head' (IV.iii.101), the Provost announces when he re-enters, directing the Duke's attention, and the audience's gaze, to what he bears.

The Provost's entrance with Ragozine's head runs counter to the practice in Shakespeare's romantic comedies of keeping death off-stage, out of the audience's sight. In *Loves's Labour's Lost*, for example, audiences know of the death of the King of France only through a messenger's report, and *Measure* could easily have limited its audiences' knowledge of Ragozine's death to the Provost's report. However, by having the Provost enter carrying Ragozine's head, the play goes out of its way to make his death register upon the eyes as well as the ears of its audiences, to give it maximum theatrical impact. In a manoeuvre without precedent in a Shakespearean romantic comedy, *Measure* requires those who watch it being performed – but not those who read it – to *see* either Ragozine's severed head or that in which it is carried, thereby affirming and demonstrating the reach of the Duke's authority, which extends even to the bodies of those who are dead.

Like the romantic comedies that Shakespeare wrote for the Lord Chamberlain's Men during Elizabeth's reign, *Measure* ends with marriages. The marriages in those comedies are explicitly founded upon shared erotic attraction and mutual love. Even individuals who initially do not reciprocate the love that their actual or prospective spouse feels for them ultimately declare themselves willing to accept their mates in good faith. In *As You Like It*, for example, Phebe, manoeuvred by Rosalind into marrying Silvius, whose love she has rejected throughout the play, announces her willingness to accept him as her spouse: 'I will not eat my word, now thou art mine; / Thy faith my fancy to thee doth combine' (V.iv.148–9). Early in *All's Well That Ends Well* – most likely the last of Shakespeare's Elizabethan comedies – Bertram finds himself compelled by his sovereign, the king of France, to marry a woman he does not want as his wife. Obediently submitting but with outspoken reluctance to royal command, Bertram marries Helena in Act II but then refuses to accept his status as her husband. He will not consummmate the marriage and, abandoning the wife he does not want, leaves France to fight abroad. As *All's Well* comes to a close, however, Bertram, the heretofore resisting husband, declares, in the presence of Helena and the king whose authority forced him to marry her, that he is now willing to accept her as his wife: 'I'll love her dearly – ever, ever dearly' (V.iii.317).[4]

Of the four actual or prospective marriages with which *Measure* concludes, however, only one – between Claudio and Juliet – undoubtedly rests upon shared erotic attraction and mutual love. Two others result, as Bertram's did, from the sovereign's command: Angelo's to Mariana and Lucio's to Kate Keepdown. In Lucio's case, marriage to Kate is the only one of the several punishments to which the Duke sentences him that is not remitted, and Lucio's final words make explicit his resistance: 'Marrying a punk, my lord, is pressing to death, / Whipping, and hanging' (V.i.520–1). Angelo, with his last words, asks for death – 'I crave death more willingly than mercy' – but the Duke instead sentences him to marry Mariana, the fiancée he rejected 'five years since' (V.i.474, 216). Brought back onstage as a 'new-married man' (V.i.398), Angelo says nothing to Mariana or anybody else for the rest of the play. Twice the Duke calls upon him to love Mariana. The first call comes after the Duke reveals that Claudio is alive and lifts the death sentence Angelo is under. 'Look that you love your wife', he urges Angelo, 'her worth, worth yours' (V.i.495). He repeats that call before the final exit: 'Joy to you, Mariana; love her, Angelo' (V.i.523). Each time, Angelo says nothing. Remaining silent, he, unlike Bertram, never voices any willingness to love the woman his sovereign has made him take as his wife.

Angelo's silence is open in the sense that the playtext provides no words – including no stage direction or comment by another character – specifying what he feels and does during it. He may indicate his desire to obey the Duke and 'love' Mariana by embracing her or taking her hand or, if he has been keeping himself apart from her, by simply moving to her side. Nothing in the playtext rules out such gestures but, equally, nothing mandates them. Angelo's silence – particularly when set against the example of Bertram's declaration and the Duke's two calls to love Mariana – can signal if not his refusal to 'love' his wife, then his reluctance. Lucio's marriage certainly contradicts the emphasis in romantic comedy on reciprocal love as the basis for marriage, and as it ends, *Measure* allows for the possibility that the life the Duke grants to Angelo is one that he, like Lucio, must live as the husband of a woman he does not love.

In addition to twice urging Angelo to 'love' Mariana, the Duke twice asks Isabella to become his wife. His first proposal is part of a moment that draws upon but also re-works the moment in *All's Well* when the King calls for Bertram to take Helena as his wife:

> KING: Take her by the hand,
>   And tell her she is thine; to whom I promise
>   A counterpoise, if not to thy estate
>   A balance more replete.
> BERTRAM: I take her hand.
> KING: Good fortune and the favour of the king
>   Smile upon this contract . . .
>
> (II.iii.173–6)

Bertram's words make clear that he obediently performs the gesture the King calls for, but they also call attention to what he does not say. He does not 'tell' Helena she is his. The Duke asks Isabella to 'Give me your hand and say you will be mine' (V.i.490). *Measure*, however, provides no indication whether she performs the gesture of assent he seeks, and she, in contrast to Bertram, says nothing at all. Her silence is total. Isabella does not 'say' what the Duke asks her to say, nor does she say anything else.

As *All's Well* concludes, Bertram receives a second chance to declare Helena his, and he responds by expressing sentiments he pointedly refused to speak earlier: 'I'll love her dearly – ever, ever dearly'. *Measure* likewise provides another opportunity for Isabella to 'say' she will be the Duke's wife by having the Duke propose a second time:

Dear Isabel,
I have a motion much imports your good;
Whereto if you'll a willing ear incline,
What's mine is yours, and what is yours is mine.
(V.ii.531–34)

Unlike Bertram, however, Isabella does not speak. She remains silent.

Both of Isabella's silences are, like Angelo's, open. She says nothing to indicate that she accepts or rejects either of the Duke's proposals, and the play provides no stage direction and no statement by another character that specifies what her response is. The combination of her two open silences generates a range of options. She may wordlessly accept the Duke's first proposal by taking his hand or by sharing an embrace or a kiss with him, and she may silently yet clearly reaffirm that acceptance by a similar gesture when he proposes again. *All's Well* suggests a possible variation upon that option. Isabella could respond to the Duke's first proposal by taking his hand in a manner that shows that she, like Bertram when he takes Helena's, is acting out of obedience, not love. If she then responds to his second proposal in a similar fashion, her obedience as the Duke's dutiful subject is further emphasised. If, however, she responds to his second proposal with a more affectionate gesture – an embrace or even a kiss – audiences see an Isabella who is now more than simply obedient, is perhaps even beginning to desire the Duke as her spouse. Isabella's silences allow for additional options. By saying nothing and not offering her hand, she could decline the Duke's first proposal, but she could then consent to the second – perhaps showing her acceptance by this time giving him her hand.

Another option that her silences allow is consistent with the fact that Isabella, whom audiences first see as she is about to join 'the votarists of Saint Clare', an order of religious women she wishes were subject to 'a more strict restraint' (I.iv.5, 4), never says anything that indicates that she has abandoned her desire to become a nun or has developed an amorous interest in the Duke. Isabella may wordlessly but unmistakably declines *both* proposals, perhaps by simply with-holding her hand and saying nothing each time he offers himself as her husband.[5] Such a refusal, particularly if it indicates her resolve to return to the convent from which she was summoned to save the life of a brother sentenced to die for fornicating, would be tantamount to renouncing the sexual energies that, channelled into marriage, Shakespearean romantic comedy celebrates as necessary for the renewal of human life.

Isabella's open silences as well as Angelo's are features of *Measure* by which, as it closes, the play registers, in both its content and its dramaturgy, what Hamlet calls the 'form and pressure' (III.ii.24) of the time, of the particular juncture in the history of England and in the history of English theatre at which it came into being. The Duke's proposals force Isabella to choose between two conflicting conceptions of womanly virtue present in Elizabethan–Jacobean culture, one that prizes virginity, a life of prayer, and withdrawal from the world, and another that prizes wifely chastity and values involvement in the world through marriage. Her silence testifies not only to her difficulty in choosing but also to the balance in the larger culture between those conceptions.

The performance history of *Measure* reveals another way in which the Duke's proposals and Isabella's silences permit the 'form and pressure' of history to mark the play. Even though her silence is open, and thus allows the possibility that she chooses not to become the Duke's wife, there is no record of any production prior to 1970 that ends with Isabella not accepting his proposal. The stage tradition of having Isabella accept the Duke's proposal both reflected and sustained a broad, long-lasting cultural consensus that values the position of wife more highly than that of a nun and links a woman's happiness with marriage.

John Barton's 1970 production broke with that tradition. Isabella did not accept either of the Duke's proposals. She responded to the first by moving away from him and to Claudio. When he proposed again, she remained motionless. After a long silence as the Duke, looking at Isabella, waited for what he hoped would be a positive response, Escalus moved foward and cleared his throat. The Duke then turned from her, spoke the final two lines of the play, and exited. The others followed, with Isabella exiting last and alone. Barton's break with a long-established stage tradition was at least in part a consequence of and a response to changes working their way through the wider culture at that time. One of them was an increasing scepticism about the benevolence of government authority to which the war in Vietnam contributed, and a second was the emergence of a feminist movement challenging the assumption that, given the opportunity, every woman will choose to be a wife.

In early modern England marriage itself was – as it is today – a cultural practice undergoing profound change. Common-law definitions of what constituted a valid marriage varied from locale to locale, and they, in turn, often were at odds with the various definitions of marriage promulgated by the different churches vying for the souls of English men and women of that era: the Church of England, the various denominations grouped under the heading Puritan, and Roman Catholicism. That confusion registers in *Measure* through Claudio's claim that because 'upon a true contract / I got possession of Julietta's bed', 'she is fast my wife, / Save that we do the denunciation lack / Of outward order' (I.ii.134–8). In the England of the early 1600s there was considerable disagreement about what constituted a 'true [valid] contract' of marriage and what 'outward order' was needed to make a man and woman husband and wife. Another index of that era's uncertainties about marriage is Angelo's silence in the face of the Duke's two calls for him to 'love' the woman he has been compelled to marry. His silence poses questions about marriage that Elizabethan–Jacobean culture was in the process of answering. Who decides who should marry whom and who is married to whom? The man and the woman? Their parents? Their church? The state, through its laws? The sovereign? Should marriage be consensual, founded upon the mutual desires of those who become husband and wife? Is love the basis for marriage or that which follows from it?

* * *

In how it departs from the treatment of death and marriage typical of Shakespeare's romantic comedies, *Measure* registers the impact of a different kind of comedy – the disguised-ruler play – that began appearing on the public stages of London during 1604, the first theatrical season of James's reign.[6] In those plays, a governor either deliberately hands over authority or is deposed and then, in disguise, looks on from the periphery as others try to cope in his absence with the responsibilities of rule and with their own desires. The appearance of such plays in 1604 is something more than a coincidence. They demonstrate that London's acting companies – now under the patronage of members of the royal family – and the playwrights, including Shakespeare, who wrote for them were willing to adjust their work to take into account James's presence on the throne of England. James's grandfather, James V of Scotland, reportedly moved frequently in disguise among his subjects, observing without being observed. While there is no evidence that James imitated him in that respect, *The Time Triumphant*, a tract published in 1604, tells of his unsuccessful attempt in March of that year to visit the London Exchange in secrecy so that he might watch the proceedings unobserved. In the tract's dedicatory epistle, Robert Armin – a member of the Lord Chamberlain's–King's Men since 1599 and renowned for his success in roles as a clown or fool – claims to be its author. Rebuking the Londoners who on that occasion rushed to see James with such frenzy that he had to withdraw behind closed doors, the tract calls upon them to behave differently the next time the king comes among them: 'doe as they doe in *Scotland* stand still, see all, and use silence' (quoted in Lever, 1965, p. xxxiv). During the final moments of *Measure*, Shakespeare and the King's Men's 'use silence' in ways that have no equivalent in their earlier work together.

Another feature typical of romantic comedy that *Measure* re-works, in ways consistent with the disguised-ruler plays, is the extent of the sovereign's involvement in and control over the process by which a final order emerges in which deaths are avoided and marriages made possible. Duke Vincentio has counterparts in nine of Shakespeare's eleven Elizabethan comedies, but he alone acts personally and directly to bring about the final order of the play – granting life to those facing death and pairing men and women in marriages. In contrast, his counterparts in Shakespeare's Elizabethan romantic comedies accept a final ordering of events and human relationships brought about by a combination of the activities of others and of fortuitous, happy coincidences that are manifestions of the benevolence of forces – fairies, fortune, providence – beyond the control of any single human character, even a duke or king. *All's Well*, probably the last of Shakespeare's Elizabethan comedies, offers a particularly clear example of the difference between Vincentio's involvement and that typical of the rulers in Shakespeare's romantic comedies. A vital factor in the final order of both plays is a bed-trick, in which a man has sexual intercourse with one woman while believing she is another, who has in fact allowed his actual bedpartner to take her place. In *All's Well*, the King of France is unaware of the bed-trick that Helena sets up and participates in so that she can satisfy the seemingly impossible conditions Bertram has set for accepting her fully as his wife. In *Measure*, however, the Duke conceives of and orchestrates the bed-trick by which Angelo unknowingly satisfies, with Mariana, the fiancée he refused to marry, his lust for Isabella. That sexual union provides the basis for the Duke's subsequent order compelling Angelo to marry Mariana. The King of France – like the other rulers in Shakespeare's Elizabethan romantic comedies – is a monarch who at various points in the play, including the end, knows less about unfolding events than some of his subjects, while Duke Vincentio is a ruler who comes to know more than all of, and any one of, his subjects and uses that knowledge – 'like power divine' (V.i.367) in Angelo's words – to establish his conception of order in Vienna. The play's final words emphasise both the superiority of his knowledge and his control over what others know: 'So, bring us to our palace, where we'll show / What's yet behind that's meet you all should know' (V.i.535–6).

Angelo's words likening the Duke's knowledge of his trespasses to the omniscience of a 'power divine' is one element of *Measure* that has prompted many commentators to see the Duke as a god-like figure – an image, perhaps the personification, of the process by which a Christian God providentially brings order out of the jumble and tumult of human doings and desires. Another is the play's title, which echoes a passage from Christ's Sermon on the Mount: 'Judge not, that ye be not judged. For with what judgment ye judge, ye shall be judged: and with what measure ye mete, it shall be measured unto you again'. A third is the affinities between the Duke and the testing master found in several biblical parables, including those of the talents or pounds and the traveller and his doorkeeper. The Duke manipulates people and events so as to test and temper Angelo and Isabella, the two characters whose sense of virtue is initially most absolute and inflexible and whose tolerance of human frailty, particularly as it manifests itself in sexual drives and excesses, is minimal. Isabella's presence as she pleads for her brother stirs in Angelo urges to which he had thought himself immune – 'Ever till now / When men were fond, I smil'd, and wonder'd how' (II.ii.186–7) – and those promptings propel him to indulge in the same action for which he sentences Claudio to death. All who gather at the gates of Vienna to welcome the returning Duke witness the public disclosure of Angelo's corruption.

When audiences first encounter Isabella, she is about to enter a convent, and she has difficulty even mentioning the deed for which her brother stands condemned when she first pleads for his life. Appalled to discover that Claudio wants her to exchange her virginity for his life, she furiously, perhaps even hysterically, declares him unfit to live: 'Mercy to thee would prove itself a bawd; / 'Tis best that thou diest quickly' (III.i.149–50). However, when the Duke, disguised as a friar, falsely tells her that Claudio has been executed, the desire for revenge upon Angelo flashes within her – 'O, I will to him and pluck out his eyes!' – then subsides into grief so intense that even the flippant Lucio offers words of comfort: 'O pretty Isabella, I am pale at mine heart to see thine eyes so red: thou must be patient' (IV.iii.119, 150–1). In the final scene the woman who earlier resolutely declared, 'More than our brother is our chastity' (II.iv.184), is willing to proclaim, falsely and before the assembled residents of Vienna, that she 'did yield' (V.i.104) that chastity to Angelo in a futile effort to save her brother's life. The Duke's manoeuvrings, which unmask Angelo, place Isabella in a position where, in front of those same residents, she shows herself capable, in response to Mariana's plea, of putting aside her desire for both justice and personal vengeance. The sister who tells her brother that she will 'pray a thousand prayers for thy death; / No word to save thee' (III.i.145–6) calls upon the Duke to save the life of Angelo, whom she holds responsible for what the Duke has led her to believe is that brother's death. For many critics and directors the moment when Isabella must decide how to respond to Mariana's plea is the climax, theatrically and thematically, of the play. Peter Brook's acclaimed 1950 production, for example, stressed that moment by having Barbara Jefford, playing Isabella, hesitate, holding a long and daring pause, neither moving nor speaking, before falling to her knees and pleading for Angelo:

> Most bounteous sir:
> Look, if it please you, on this man condemn'd
> As if my brother liv'd. I partly think
> A due sincerity govern'd his deeds
> Till he did look on me. Since it is so,
> Let him not die.
>
>   (V.i.441–46)

Although Angelo credits the Duke with god-like omniscience, in several respects *Measure* itself presents him as decidedly fallible. As Anne Barton notes, 'If the Duke is an image of Providence, there would seem to be chaos in heaven' (1974, p. 547). The Duke repeatedly overestimates his capacity to impose his designs on what his subjects feel, think, say, and do – to make their lives conform to the patterns he has in mind. Consider his first two times appearances in friar's garb. During the first, Juliet, interrupting him in mid-sentence, cuts short his effort to determine if her penitance for 'the sin you carry' is 'sound, / Or hollowly put on':

DUKE: But as we stand in fear –
JULIET: I do repent me as it is an evil,
  And take the shame with joy.
                    (II.iii.19, 22–3, 34–6)

During the second, he gives his most powerful speech in the play, urging Claudio to 'Be absolute for death' (III.i.5). Claudio, who says he is ready to die before the Duke begins the speech, does not interrupt, and when the Duke finishes he again declares himself willing to die: 'Let it come on' (III.i.43). Whatever success the Duke achieves with his words is very short-lived, however. Once Claudio learns of Angelo's offer to spare his life in exchange for Isabella's virginity, that willingness quickly shrivels. 'Sweet sister, let me live', Claudio pleads, overwhelmed by a profound fear of death – ' 'tis too horrible' – articulated in a speech every bit as powerful as the Duke's calling upon him to face death fearlessly (III.i.132, 127).

The Duke is confident of his ability to apply 'Craft against vice' (III.ii.270) successfully. His plan to expose Angelo, save Claudio, gain a husband for Mariana, and preserve Isabella's virtue rests upon the assumption that Angelo, having had sexual relations with (as he thinks) Isabella, will pardon Claudio. *Measure* shows, however, that the Duke's confidence in his 'craft' is exaggerated. The messenger Angelo sends to the Provost after the tryst does not bear a pardon for Claudio, as the Duke erroneously assumes, but an order commanding that Claudio's execution be carried out speedily and his head be sent to Angelo as proof. The Duke responds to that unanticipated development by adjusting his design. He decides that Angelo will receive Barnardine's head in place of Claudio's, and the scene ends with the Duke's confidence intact. '[A]ll difficulties', he assures the Provost, 'are but easy when they are known. Call your executioner, and off with Barnardine's head' (IV.ii.204–6).

Barnardine, however, frustrates the Duke's scheme. Summoned from his cell, Barnardine clings stubbornly to life and, defiantly,

refuses to 'consent to die this day, that's certain' (IV.iii.55). When
the Duke insists that he 'must' die, Barnardine repeats his defiance
and then, cutting off the Duke in mid-sentence as Juliet did earlier,
departs for his own cell:

> BAR.: I swear I will not die today for any man's persuasion
> DUKE: But hear you –
> BAR.: Not a word. If you have anything to say to me,
>   come to my ward: for thence will not I today.
> *Exit.*
>
> (IV.iii.58–62).

The Duke is even less successful in persuading Barndardine to accept
death than he was with Claudio. With Barnardine's exit, the Duke
finds himself at an impasse, denied the human head he needs as a
substitute for Claudio's. The way out of that impasse comes not as
the result of any 'craft' the Duke exercises but by the very timely
death of Ragozine, a character not previously mentioned, not even
in Pompey's lengthy catalogue of the prison's inmates at the start of
this scene. The combination of Barnardine's refusal to die and Ragozine's highly implausible, extremely fortuitous death – 'an accident
that heaven provides' – accentuates that the Duke's control over
people and events is limited.

Barnardine is not punished for defying the Duke. Instead, *Measure*
shows him being rewarded for it. Had he obediently consented 'to
die this day', he would not have been alive to receive the pardon the
Duke extends to him in the final scene:

> Thou'rt condemn'd;
> But for those earthly faults, I quit them all,
> And pray thee take this mercy to provide
> For better times to come.
>
> (V.i.480–3)

Barnardine accepts 'this mercy' in silence – speaking no words of
remorse or repentance for the murder he has committed, stating no
desire to reform, voicing no gratitude for the clemency he has
received. Nor does the play offer any indication by way of a stage
direction or comment by another character of how Barnardine reacts.
His silence – open like Angelo's and Isabella's – does not rule out the

possibility that by a gesture such as falling to his knees he speechlessly expresses gratitude, repentance, and a desire to reform too over-whelming to be expressed by words, but nothing in the playtext mandates such a gesture, thus leaving open the possibility that, incorrigible, he is capable of killing again. 'Mercy is not itself, that oft looks so; / Pardon is still the nurse of second woe' (II.i.280–1), Escalus comments, and Barnardine's silence, depending on what the actor playing him does upon being pardoned, can prompt audiences to question the prudence of the Duke's mercy towards him and thus at least one element of the final order the Duke achieves.

Pardoning Barnardine is also at least potentially problematic because it confirms the equation that Angelo establishes when justifying his resolve to carry out Claudio's execution for fornication. He argues that the act of illicitly begetting a human life is legally and morally equivalent to murder, the act of illicitly ending a human life. 'It were as good', he reasons with Isabella,

> To pardon him that hath from nature stolen
> A man already made, as to remit
> Their saucy sweetness that do coin heaven's image
> In stamps that are forbid.
>
> (II.iv.42–6)

In granting life to both Barnardine, a murderer, and Claudio, sentenced to die for illegitimately fathering a child, the Duke also equates their offences. For Angelo, murder and fornication are acts that merit death; for the Duke they are acts that call forth mercy.

Lucio is still another means by which *Measure* establishes resistance to the Duke's design. The Duke's disguise as a friar compels him to listen to Lucio describe him as a ruler who, preferring to have 'dark deeds darkly answered', would have spared a fornicator like Claudio because 'He had some feeling of the sport; he knew the service; and that instructed him to mercy' (III.ii.171, 115–17). 'He would be drunk, too', Lucio adds, before declaring the Duke a 'very superficial, ignorant, unweighing fellow' (III.ii.124, 136). The point is not simply whether Lucio's characterisation of the ruler he calls 'the old fantastical duke of dark corners' (IV.iii.156) is accurate or inaccurate, but that Lucio's remarks make clear the Duke's limited ability to make what his subjects think and say about him conform to his conception of himself as a man endowed with the personal qualities a ruler needs:

He who the sword of heaven will bear
Should be as holy as severe:
Pattern in himself to know,
Grace to stand, and virtue, go:
More nor less to others paying
Than by self-offences weighing.
                                     (III.ii.254–9)

The Duke denounces what Lucio says about him as 'slandering a prince' (V.i.521), but Lucio's presence in the play ensures that the Duke's vision of himself and his deeds is not the only one presented to the audience.

Lucio's resistance to ducal authority includes during the final scene his frequent interruptions of the trial that the Duke, while disguised as a friar, has arranged for Isabella to set in motion by calling for 'Justice! Justice! Justice!' (V.i.26). In his capacity as a friar, the Duke can convince Isabella to speak 'indirectly' (IV.vi.1), falsely accusing Angelo of fornication with her, and he can persuade her and Mariana to orchestrate their charges against Angelo so that they contradict one another. He cannot, however, control Lucio's voice, not even when he appears in his own person. Lucio repeatedly speaks up during the judicial proceedings, despite the Duke's repeated commands that he be silent, and his refusal to stop speaking accentuates, by contrast, Barnardine's silence when the Duke pardons him, Angelo's when the Duke twice calls upon him to 'love' his wife Mariana, and Isabella's when the Duke twice asks her to marry him.

The Duke has, and exercises, the power to spare Barnardine's life, but the silence with which Barnardine responds to the Duke's mercy can raise questions about the wisdom of extending mercy to a convicted murderer who speaks no words of thanks, repentance, remorse, or reformation. The Duke also has, and exercises, the power to compel Angelo to take Mariana as his wife, but Angelo's enduring silence in response to the Duke's calls for him to 'love' her raises the issue of whether love – as distinct from the institution of marriage – is subject to ducal dictate. When Mariana asks Isabella to join her in pleading for Angelo's life, she stresses that Isabella need not speak: 'Sweet Isabel, do yet but kneel by me; / Hold up your hands, say nothing: I'll speak all' (V.i.435–6). Isabella chooses to speak on his behalf, and that choice contrasts directly with the one she makes when the Duke first proposes: 'Give me your hand, and say you will be mine'. Earlier, Isabella, in obedience to the friar whom she did not know was the Duke, was willing in full public view to speak falsely and accuse Angelo of subjecting 'my chaste body / To his concupiscible intemperate lust' (V.i.100–1). When the Duke asks her to 'say you will be mine', she chooses to say nothing. Isabella may signal her acceptance of the proposal by taking the Duke's hand or sharing an embrace or a kiss. Alternatively, she can refuse his proposal, a development that would open a gap between what the Duke hopes to achieve and what he in fact accomplishes. Whether Isabella accepts or rejects the Duke's proposal, the fact is that she does not *say* she will be his. She remains silent, which also means that the last words audiences hear her speak are those that end her appeal for Angelo's life. They, significantly, speak of a realm into which the Duke's authority does not extend: 'Thoughts are no subjects; / Intents, but merely thoughts' (V.i.451–2). The Duke who cannot silence Lucio also cannot bring the woman he wants as his wife to say she will be his. The silences of Barnardine, Angelo, and Isabella – of the murderer the Duke pardons, of a man he has made a husband, and of the woman he asks to be his wife – signal limits in the application, effectiveness, and scope of the Duke's authority.

Their individual silences overlap and interlock, generating a network of silences that has no equivalent in any other Shakespearean play. Individually and collectively, the silences in *Measure*, in addition to marking the limits of political authority, illustrate with unusual clarity the difference between seeing a performance of a play and reading the words that constitute a playtext. Characters who cease speaking slip beyond the frame of attention established by the process of reading, which, by concentrating on and thus privileging words and their speakers, downplays the non-verbal facets of a given theatrical moment. During performances of *Measure*, however, Isabella, Angelo, and Barnardine remain visible to audiences and are capable, therefore, of being the focus of attention and thus potentially vital factors in shaping the meaning and impact of the theatrical moments, and the play, of which they and their silences are elements.

Those silences also raise questions about the nature of theatrical authority. Who determines what happens during the performance of a play, who decides what audiences hear and see? The usual answer is that theatrical authority belongs to the playwright, who exercises it through the words of the playtext much as James exercised his sovereign authority over the three Bye conspirators through the words of the document his messenger brought on 10 December 1603 to the scaffold at Windsor as they thought themselves about to die. That answer is inadequate historically because it is at odds – as Chapter 1 explains – with what is known today of the circumstances within which Shakespeare worked, but its inadequacy is also theoretical. It cannot accommodate moments, such as the open silences at the conclusion of *Measure*, when the playtext provides no words through which the authority conventionally assigned to the playwright can make itself felt. Who decides how Barnardine responds when the Duke spares his life? Who decides if audiences see in Angelo a sign that he is willing to love the woman whom the Duke has forced him to marry? Who decides whether Isabella accepts either, both, or none of the Duke's proposals of marriage? In such instances does theatrical authority belong to the actor or actress playing the individual part, to the star performer, to the director? Or is theatrical authority collective, shared by the playwright and those who, at various points in history from the spring of 1604 to the present, perform the play? It is tempting to endow Shakespeare, as playwright, with a theatrical sovereignty analogous to the Duke's political sovereignty, but the open silences that are such distinctive elements of the dramaturgy of *Measure* establish that while his control over what happens during performances is – like the Duke's over what his subjects think, feel, say, and do – considerable, it is also less than complete, less than total, less than absolute.

3

Othello:
'A Pageant to Keep Us in
False Gaze'

Othello is both Shakespeare's first Jacobean tragedy and the first of six tragedies written in a concentrated burst between 1604 and 1608, perhaps even in succession. Like three other tragedies among those six – *Macbeth*, *Coriolanus*, and *Antony and Cleopatra* – its protagonist is an acclaimed warrior whose relationship with a woman (wife, mother, lover) is of crucial importance. In that respect, *Othello* marks a departure from *Hamlet*, Shakespeare's last Elizabethan tragedy. *Hamlet* has never led men in battle, and the military funeral that Fortinbras orders for him at the end of the play acknowledges the warrior he might have become, not the warrior he was.

Like *Hamlet*, *Othello* begins at night, and much of it takes place in darkness that comes to signify error, incomprehension, and delusion. In that darkness, the play explores the processes of cognition and the movement from knowing to doing, from judgement to action. Act I, Scene iii begins with the Venetian Senate assembled in emergency night session, evaluating 'disproportion'd' (I.iii.2) reports that give conflicting estimates of the size of a Turkish fleet but concur that it is bound for Cyprus. When a report arrives that the fleet has altered direction and now heads towards Rhodes, the First Senator observes: 'This cannot be / By no assay of reason . . . 'tis a pageant, / To keep us in false gaze' (I.iii.17–19). The Duke subsequently agrees: 'Nay, in all confidence, he's not for Rhodes' (I.iii.31). Their judgements are quickly vindicated when a messenger reports that the Turkish fleet has met another fleet and 'now they do re-stem / Their backward course, bearing with frank appearance / Their purposes towards Cyprus' (I.iii.37–9). The Duke and Senate succeed in sifting through a welter of contradictory reports and interpreting the 'pageant' so as to deduce the designs of the Turkish fleet, and by demonstrating the human capacity to discriminate accurately between what seems to be and what is, that success establishes a norm for cognition.

How the duke and senators of Venice deduce what the Turkish fleet is doing corresponds to how audiences know during a performance of *Othello*. In the Venetian Senate as in the London playhouses of the early 1600s (and those of today), the exercise of an individual's powers of perception and judgement occurs within and as part of a process that is also – and essentially – collective, corporate, and communal. What happens during the Senate scene after Brabantio and *Othello* enter affirms that cognitive norm by demonstrating the triumph, over private desires and impulses, of rationality functioning in a collective setting. Brabantio is himself one of the Senators, and his lament that his daughter 'is abus'd, stol'n from me and corrupted, / By spells and medicines bought of mountebanks' prompts the Duke to respond:

> Whoe'er he be, that in this foul proceeding
> Hath thus beguil'd your daughter of herself,
> And you of her, the bloody book of law
> You shall yourself read, in the bitter letter,
> After its own sense, though our proper son
> Stood in your action.
>
> (I.iii.60–1, 65–70)

His words are both a statement of consolation and a pledge of impartial justice; the wrongdoer will be punished, no matter who he is.[1] Brabantio's identification of the wrongdoer – 'Here is the man, this Moor' (I.iii.71) – begins what is in effect the first of a series of trials in the play. Othello is the defendant, Brabantio the plaintiff, and the issue is whether Othello has stolen Desdemona from her father or properly won her. As they did earlier when evaluating reports of the Turkish fleet, the Duke and the Senators must sift, weigh, and interpret divergent testimony.

Brabantio charges Othello with withcraft: 'with some mixtures powerful o'er the blood, / Or with some dram conjur'd to this effect, / He wrought upon her' (I.iii.104–6). The Duke's response emphasises the distinction between accusation and evidence that is the basis for reasoned judgement: 'To vouch this is no proof, / Without more

certain and more overt test' (I.iii.106–7). He and the Senators then
turn to hear Othello, who testifies how he came to 'thrive' in Desdemona's love by telling her 'the story of my life' (I.iii.129) 'This only,'
he insists, 'is the witchcraft I have us'd', and, as Desdemona enters,
he calls upon the Senate to 'let her witness it' (I.iii.169–70). Her
testimony, before the Duke and Senators, convinces Brabantio that
'she was half the wooer', and he declares, 'God bu'y, I ha'done'
(I.iii.176, 189). He then formally and publicly acknowledges the
marriage, which, he makes clear, he wishes he could have thwarted:

> Come hither, Moor:
> I here do give thee that, with all my heart,
> Which, but thou hast already, with all my heart
> I would keep from thee.
>
> (I.iii.192–5)

His words are part of complex theatrical moment. It suggests the
point in the traditional Christian wedding ceremony when the bride's
father presents his daughter to the man who will shortly become her
husband, often by giving him her hand. Thus, the moment echoes
the secret wedding between Othello and Desedemona that the play's
audiences never see and from which Brabantio, the bride's father,
was excluded. He is doing now, before Duke and Senate (and the
theatre audience), what he had no opportunity to do then: transfer-
ring his rights in his daughter to her husband. At the same time,
however, Brabantio's words make clear how different this moment is
from the ceremony it suggests. The man to whom he gives his
daughter is *already* her husband, and that giving is tantamount to a
rejection of Desdemona. Brabantio gives her to Othello 'with all my
heart' because he no longer wants anything to do with her. Brabantio distorts the father's act of free giving signified by the ceremony
into an act of repudiation. His actions can further accentuate the
difference between what is happening 'here' and the ideal of the
father who gives his daughter freely. For example, in John Neville's
1987 production at the Stratford (Ontario) Festival, Brabantio placed
Desdemona's hand in Othello's, but then, as he finished saying 'with
all my heart / I would keep from thee', he thrust their hands apart,
turning away in bitter anger.

The outcome of Othello's trial confirms the capacity of Venice's
deliberative processes to produce a decision that, whatever the

frailties of the individuals participating in it, is both rational and
accurate. The processes that enabled the Venetians to discern the
direction and the designs of the Turkish fleet now bring everyone,
including Brabantio – initially distraught and still bitterly unrecon-
ciled to the marriage – to the realisation that love, not witchcraft, is
responsible for Desdemona's marriage to Othello in defiance of their
differences in age, culture, and race. The trial frustrates Iago's effort
to act out his malevolence towards Othello by using Brabantio to
disrupt the marriage. The combination of Othello's 'trial' and the
deliberations regarding the Turkish fleet affirms the power of reasoned judgement exercised collectively to understand events and
persons accurately. As the authorised representative of Venice –
presented, Alvin Kernan points out, as 'a form of *The City*, the ageless
image of government, of reason, of law, of social concord' (1970,
p. 353) – Othello carries that norm to Cyprus, 'a town of war, / Yet
wild' vulnerable to attack by 'the general enemy' of Christian
civilisation, the Ottoman Turks (II.iii.204–5; I.iii.49).[2]

The shift of action from city to beleaguered outpost corresponds
to the shift in locale – out of a city or court into a forest – typical of
the romantic comedies Shakespeare wrote during the last decade of
Elizabeth's reign, and it is one of the features associated with them
that *Othello* re-works into a tragic configuration. *Othello* also begins as
they typically end – with a marriage. The marriage of Desdemona
and Othello takes place without her father's knowledge or approval,
which makes them the tragic cousins of Bianca and Lucentio of *The
Taming of the Shrew* and Anne Page and Fenton of *The Merry Wives of
Windsor* – couples who, eluding parental control, enter into marriages
with mates they have chosen for themselves, in accord with the
imperatives of erotic desire. Like Egeus of *A Midsummer Night's Dream*,
Shylock of *The Merchant of Venice*, and Page of *The Merry Wives of
Windsor*, Brabantio is a blocking father, but he struggles to undo,
rather than prevent, his daughter's marriage to the husband she
wants. In comedies a tricky servant often helps his young master to
defeat the father's designs and marry the girl. In *Othello*, however,
Iago works to destroy his general's marriage. Like Shylock's Jessica,
Desdemona elopes from her father's house, but she and Othello
remain in Venice after their marriage – in contrast to Jessica and
Lorenzo who must flee Venice in order to be married. In *Dream*, the
Athenian legal process supports the father and obstructs the marriage
of Lysander and Hermia. They must seek a place where 'the sharp

Athenian law / Cannot pursue us' after Theseus, the Duke of Athens, warns her

> To fit your fancies to your father's will;
> Or else the law of Athens yields you up
> (Which by no means we may extenuate)
> To death, or to a vow of single life.
>   (I.i.162–3, 118–21)

The Venetian legal process, in sharp contrast, subjects Brabantio's charges of witchcraft and theft to reasoned scrutiny and ultimately confirms the validity of the marriage between Othello and Desdemona.

Othello also has affiliations with *Measure for Measure*, the comedy written directly before it. The process of substitution – of replacing and of changing places – is important in both. At the start of *Measure*, the Duke publicly designates Angelo as his deputy, his substitute, and the Duke's scheme to save Claudio and expose Angelo succeeds because Ragozine's head is substituted for Claudio's and Mariana takes Isabella's place as Angelo's sexual partner. In *Othello*, Iago's malevolence towards Othello arises in part because Othello has not made him his 'lieutenant', an officer who acts as a deputy for, in place of, his superior. Before the assembled Venetian Senate, Desdemona tells her father that her husband Othello now fills what was formerly his place as her 'lord of all my duty' (I.iii.184), and what triggers Othello's murderous jealousy is the conviction that Cassio has functioned as his sexual lieutenant, substituting for him in Desdemona's bed.

Othello itself changes places, moving from Venice to Cyprus at the start of Act II, which opens with an account of the storm that has wrecked the Turkish fleet. That storm, suggestive of disruptive forces beyond human control, is the backdrop to the happiest moment that audiences see Othello and Desdemona share: their joyous reunion after sailing to Cyprus on separate ships. Their love has survived the storm as it earlier survived Iago's malevolence, Brabantio's fury, and the Senate's scrutiny, but as they kiss, Iago's bitter aside signals the imminence of another threat, the approach of a different storm: 'O, you are well tun'd now, / But I'll set down the pegs that make this music, / As honest as I am' (II.i.199–201).

Iago begins again to act out his enmity for Othello by getting Cassio drunk. Cassio's nearly instantaneous transformation from a Venetian gentleman and officer to a drunken brawler prefigures the less rapid but still swift transformation in Othello. The wine Iago persuades Cassio to drink has an effect on him like the effect on Othello of the venomous words Iago pours into his ear. Under the influence of those words, the commanding general to whom Venice entrusts the defence of Cyprus becomes a man driven by jealousy to murder his innocent wife. Using Cassio's drunkenness, Iago triggers a nightime mêlée, the noise of which awakens Othello. Once that 'barbarous brawl' (II.iii.163) is stilled, Othello, the defendant during the play's first trial, conducts a second trial, acting, as the Duke did earlier, as the judge. In that capacity he tries to understand what has happened, which is in fact 'a false pageant' orchestrated by Iago analogous to that of the Turks, which the Duke and Senators accurately deciphered. The playtext makes sure that audiences become aware of anger seething in a man whose self-control and calm poise never so much as wavered in Venice. 'Now, by heaven,' Othello declares, his efforts to clarify the incident frustrated, 'My blood begins my safer guides to rule, / And passion having my best judgement collied / Assays to lead the way'. (II.iii.195–8). This momentary lapse anticipates a later, more sustained, and more disastrous failure in his 'best judgement'.

The awakening of Othello parallels that of Brabantio during the play's opening moments, and that parallel gives substance to the correspondence between husband and father that Brabantio, bitterly, warned about with the last words audiences hear him speak: 'Look to her, Moor, have a quick eye to see: / She has deceiv'd her father, may do thee' (I.iii.292–3). Othello's reply – 'My life upon her faith' (I.iii.294) – declares his confidence in Desdemona's fidelity, but it is also, in ways he does not know, a prediction and summary of what will ensue. Events confirm the correspondence between husband and father that Brabantio posits and Othello denies. Aroused by Iago, each becomes convinced that he has 'lost' Desdemona, and each attempts to make up for that loss by seeking what he regards as justice. The heart of the correspondence between Brabantio and Othello is that each – in ways consistent with dominant Elizabethan–Jacobean attitudes towards the relationship between fathers and daughters and between husbands and wives – regards Desdemona as property, a possession of extraordinary value.

Iago, having seen Cassio leaving Desdemona seconds before, takes advantage of this and begins the process that will plunge Othello into emotional and cognitive chaos by asking a question:

IAGO: My noble lord, –
OTH.: What does thou say, Iago?
IAGO: Did Michael Cassio, when you woo'd my lady,
  Know of your love?

> (III.iii.94–6)

Some two hundred lines later, the connection between love and the concept of property becomes manifest in Othello's response to what he now accepts is the possibility that the woman he has taken as *his* wife has been unfaithful. 'O curse of marriage,' he laments,

> That we can call these delicate creatures ours,
> And not their appetites! I had rather be a toad,
> And live upon the vapour in a dungeon,
> Than keep a corner in a thing I love,
> For others' uses. . . .

> (III.iii.272–7)

His words, Karen Newman notes, show that, like Brabantio, he 'perceives of his love and indeed his human, as opposed to bestial, identity as depending on property rights, on absolute ownership' (1987, p. 150).

Within one hundred and fifty lines Othello accepts Desdemona's infidelity as an established truth, a fact beyond questioning: 'Now do I see 'tis true; look here, Iago, / All my fond love thus do I blow to heaven, / 'Tis gone' (III.iii.451–3). The speed with which Othello becomes fully convinced of Desdemona's adultery is often taken as evidence of his gullibility and naivete, if not of his stupidity. Trusting Iago, he does not even question either Desdemona or Cassio before determining their guilt, and he ignores a basic fact: there has been no opportunity for Desdemona to commit adultery with Cassio.[3] Othello's gross errors in judgement are necessary elements of the play's emphasis upon the irrationality of jealousy, on the degree to which Iago succeeds in his scheme to stir in Othello 'a jealousy so strong, / That judgement cannot cure' (II.i.296–7).

The process by which Othello comes to be certain of Desdemona's adultery is tantamount to a third trial. Othello and Iago see Cassio leave Desdemona as they approach. Iago testifies to the meaning of what they have seen when Cassio leaves Desdemona, and Othello evaluates that testimony and reaches a judgement. Unlike the first two trials – Othello's before the Senate and Cassio's after the brawl – this one takes place in private, and Desdemona, the accused, is tried *in absentia*. Typically, the scene is set in a room that suggests Othello's office or study and, thus, rationality. Another possible setting is a garden, which would encourage audiences to connect what happens here to what Iago tells Roderigo about the relationship between body and will, sensuality and reason directly after the trial that validates the marriage of Othello and Desdemona. When Roderigo laments that it is 'not in my virtue' to cease behaving foolishly because of his love for Desdemona, Iago replies,

> Virtue?[4] a fig! 'tis in ourselves, that we are thus, or thus: our bodies are gardens, to the which our wills are gardeners . . . If the balance of our lives had not one scale of reason, to poise another of sensuality, the blood and baseness of our natures would conduct us to most preposterous conclusions. (I.iii.318, 319–30)

During the 'trial' of Desdemona, Othello, the balance between his reason and passion upset by what Iago says, comes to a 'most preposterous' conclusion: she is guilty of sexual infidelity.

The vehemence with which Othello demands indisputable proof gives audiences a sense of the irrationality gathering in him: 'Make me to see 't, or at the least so prove it, / That the probation bear no hinge, nor loop, / To hang a doubt on: or woe upon thy life!' (III.iii.370–2). The homicidal impulses building in him can flare out in actions that, posing physical threats to Iago's life, anticipate either the murder of Desdemona or Othello's suicide. In David William's 1973 production at the Stratford (Ontario) Festival, for example, Othello forced Iago to his knees, throttling him with the same hands that later strangle Desdemona. Ronald Eyre's 1979 production for the Royal Shakespeare Company enacted a different possibility: Othello held against Iago's throat the knife with which he later kills himself.

After denying the possibility of 'ocular proof' – 'Would you . . . Behold her topp'd?' (III.iii.401–2) – Iago offers two bits of evidence: his account of Cassio's dream and his claim that Cassio possesses Desdemona's handkerchief. They are two of the 'trifles light as air' that, Iago comments immediately after seizing the handkerchief from Emilia, 'Are to the jealous, confirmations strong / As proofs of holy writ' (III.iii.327-9). They complete the process by which Iago elaborates a 'pageant' – akin to that faced by Duke and Senators of Venice immediately before Othello's trial – calculated to keep Othello in 'false gaze'. Othello is their representative on Cyprus, and, like them, he proceeds to interpret the 'pageant' and form a judgement: 'Now do I see 'tis true' (III.iii.451). With that judgement, Othello falls.

When Iago urges him to 'be content', Othello, kneeling (according to a stage direction found only in the Quarto version[5]) calls for 'blood, Iago, blood' (III.iii.458). He rejects Iago's suggestion that 'your mind perhaps may change'. 'Never, Iago,' he insists and, in lines found only in the Folio version, compares his implacable movement towards revenge to the irreversible flow of water from the Black ('Pontic') Sea, through the Hellespont, into the Aegean Sea:

> ⟨ Like to the Pontic sea,
> Whose icy current, and compulsive course,
> Ne'er feels retiring ebb, but keeps due on
> To the Propontic, and the Hellespont:
> Even so my bloody thoughts, with violent pace
> Shall ne'er look back, ne'er ebb to humble love,
> Till that a capable and wide revenge
> Swallow them up. Now by yond marble heaven, ⟩
> In the due reverence of a sacred vow,
> I here engage my words.[6]
>
> (III.iii.460-9)

Othello's elaborate simile has echoes of the eloquence with which, after professing himself 'Rude . . . in my speech' (I.iii.81), he spoke before the Duke and Senators of Venice during his 'trial'. Thus, the very quality of the language with which (in the Folio) he vows vengeance upon Desdemona links this moment with the earlier moments when he spoke movingly of how he won her love.

Stage directions present only in the Quarto specify that first Othello and then Iago kneel. Iago's statement 'Do not rise yet' (I.iii.469) occurs in both versions of the play, and in the Folio, which has no explicit stage directions indicating that either man kneels, it establishes that Othello is not standing erect. It does not, however, establish exactly what Othello's posture is. He may be kneeling, but he might also be prostrate on the ground, or he might be crouching or squatting or doubled over in anguish. If – as the Quarto requires –

Othello does kneel, how does he kneel? In a fashion that is recognisably Christian? Or, with his forehead touching the ground, in a manner that would register as non-Christian and suggest reversion to rites he practised before converting to Christianity?

The sight of Iago standing over Othello, whatever his posture, conveys visually the domination Iago has achieved over his commanding officer. If Othello is kneeling upright, that sight encourages audiences to juxtapose the moment when Othello vows revenge upon Desdemona with the moment when she too kneels in Iago's presence, calling upon him to assist her: 'Good friend, go to him, for, by this light of heaven, / I know not how I lost him. Here I kneel' (IV.ii.152–3). If, however, as the absence of explicit stage directions in the Folio permits, Othello is lying prostrate, the visual link is with the moment when Iago stands over Othello, who has slumped to the floor in a fit or trance, and exults: 'Work on, / My medicine, work' (IV.i.44–5).

A stage direction present only in the Quarto specifies that after Othello vows his revenge Iago also kneels and pledges total loyalty:

> Witness that here Iago doth give up
> The excellency of his wit, hand, heart,
> To wrong'd Othello's service: let him command,
> And to obey shall be in me remorse,
> What bloody work so ever.
>
> (III.iii.472–6)

By having the two men kneel together – one pledging, the other accepting faithful service – *Othello* (in its Quarto version) inverts the Christian marriage ritual in which husband and wife pledge fidelity to one another. Like the moment when Brabantio says that he gives Othello the daughter he wishes he could keep from him, this moment both invokes and distorts the marriage ceremony uniting Othello and Desdemona. The play does not allow its audiences to see that ceremony, but it does shows them this moment when, kneeling with Othello, Iago displaces Desdemona as the person whose love Othello most values. Othello disavows the bond uniting husband and wife, commiting himself instead to Iago and to specifically masculine forms of bonding: between male friends, between master and servant, and – relationships with which his military life has made him more familiar – the bond between general and subordinate officer as well as the comitatus bond shared by men who together have faced death

in battle. Laurence Olivier, in the 1965 film of *Othello*, directed by
Stuart Burge, uses Othello's sword to convey both the specifically
martial bonding and the distortion of Christian ceremony: as the two
men kneel together, they swear upon Othello's sword, which, its
point held upwards, became an inverted cross. The exchange that
ends the scene signals the triumph of masculine and martial bonds
over those that are marital. 'Now art thou my lieutenant,' Othello
tells Iago, whose reply echoes and mocks the conventional pledges of
undying, total commitment exchanged by men and women in love:
'I am your own forever' (III.iii.485–6).

The moment marks the subversion not only of marriage, the
traditional form of ordering relationships between men and woman,
but also of the male bonds that Iago invokes and Othello embraces.
Iago, who declares himself Othello's 'own for ever', is one of those
who 'Keep yet their hearts attending on themselves' (I.i.51). The man
whom Othello here accepts as his 'honest' friend, trusted servant, and
loyal lieutenant acts 'not . . . for love and duty, / But seeming so, for
my peculiar end' (I.i.59–60). As one who serves no one 'but myself'
(I.i.58), Iago epitomises a ruthlessly self-serving individualism destructive of all modes of human relationship. The accelerating crumbling
during the Elizabethan–Jacobean period of social structures and
modes of personal relationships associated with feudalism heightened
the era's fascination with and fear of rampant, unchecked individualism. Iago is but one of the villains – among them Edmund in *King Lear*
and Richard III – through whom Shakespeare's plays tapped into that
deep cultural anxiety. He is also the only one alive at the play's end.

* * *

Othello's exit with Iago seeking 'some swift means of death' (III.iii.484)
for Desdemona is followed – in a striking juxtaposition typical of
Shakespearean drama – by the entrance of the Clown, who is cut
from what are arguably the two most widely seen productions of
Othello in history, the Olivier movie and Jonathan Miller's 1981
production for BBC-TV. Here, as during his only other appearance
(III.i), the Clown assists in arranging a meeting between Cassio and
Desdemona, but his two appearances involve more than advancing the
plot and providing comic relief. In a play concerned with the act of
forming accurate judgements, the Clown's dialogue with Desdemona is
riddled with puns that draw attention to the ambiguity inherent in

language. His banter verges on the inscrutable. 'Can any thing be made of this?' Desdemona wonders on hearing his answer to her question whether he knows 'where the Lieutenant Cassio lies' (III.iv.8, 1). The Clown's talk is the extreme instance of a process at work throughout *Othello*: the abuse of language as a means by which humans know accurately.

The punning on 'lie' that dominates the Clown's dialogue with Desdemona comes directly after Othello becomes convinced of the truth of the lie that Desdemona has been unfaithful with Cassio, and the play again directs attention to the multiple meanings of 'lie' at a critical moment – immediately before Othello's collapse. Othello asks Iago to tell him what Cassio has said:

> IAGO: Faith, that he did . . . I know not what he did.
> OTH.: But what?
> IAGO: Lie.
> OTH.: With her?
> IAGO: With her, on her, what you will.
> OTH.: Lie with her, lie on her? – We say lie on her, when
>   they belie her, – lie with her, zounds, that's fulsome!
>   (IV.i.32–6)

The correspondence has another dimension. Othello's words here are, James Calderwood points out (1987, p. 294), the first he speaks that are not in blank verse but in prose, which is how the Clown always speaks. As Othello spirals towards unconsciousness, his sentences distintegrate, deepening a process of lingual disorder signalled the first time audiences see Othello with Desdemona after he becomes convinced of her infidelity. They witness the breakdown of conversation, of the process of verbal exchange and sharing. While Desdemona insistently pleads on behalf of Cassio, Othello, just as insistently, demands that she speak of 'The handkerchief! . . . The handkerchief! . . . The handkerchief!' (III.iv.89–94). What is supposed to be dialogue between two people breaks down into two monologues running concurrently side-by-side.

The word 'lie' points to the important relationship between the Clown's talk and what happens in *Othello*. Brabantio, embittered, responds to the Duke's maxims on patience with a maxim stressing the inability of language to affect how one feels: 'But words are words; I never yet did hear / That the bruis'd heart was pierced through the ear' (I.iii.218–19). The course of the play refutes Brabantio's maxim. Iago occasions Othello's destruction by using language to 'pour this pestilence into his ear' (II.iii.347), wielding it so that it distorts rather than clarifies reality. 'It is not words that shake me thus',[7] Othello insists before falling to the ground unconscious – a posture that points to still another meaning of 'lie'. But it *is* words, primarily Iago's words, that shake him 'thus', stirring an emotional storm so severe that it short-circuits his mental processes and momentarily obliterates his consciousness.

What occurs after Othello regains consciousness demonstrates how his certainty that Desdemona has been unfaithful skews his knowledge of the people and events around him. He overhears the conversation between Iago and Cassio and sees Bianca return Desdemona's handkerchief, but what he sees and hears becomes in effect 'a pageant' that keeps him 'in false gaze' as he misconstrues the testimony of his own senses. He takes Cassio's references to Bianca as references to Desdemona, and the sight of Bianca and Cassio with the handkerchief that Desdemona could not show him in the previous scene gives Othello 'ocular proof' of her waywardness.

This process of (mis)interpretation affirms the power of language, and it does so in ways that draw upon the theatrical conventions that governed the first performances of the play. As Othello witnesses what Cassio, Iago, and Bianca do and say, he is an (onstage) audience of one, and the words Iago has poured into his ears shape how he construes what he sees and hears. For the initial audiences of *Othello*, language shaped the theatrical frame of reference in a similarly powerful way. Gathered in the Globe, those audiences saw actors speaking and moving before them on a stage that made little effort to offer the theatrical equivalent of 'ocular proof' by deploying stage properties and scenery to create the visual equivalent of the place in which or even the time of day at which events were occurring. On the relatively bare stage of the Globe, the primary means for establishing place and time was verbal rather than visual. At the opening of *Othello*, for example, Jacobean audiences learned where the action was set more by what they heard than by what they saw: 'Here is her father's house.... this is Venice' (I.i.74, 105). They watched actors moving and speaking before them in full daylight, but they (mis)construed the daylight their eyes registered and accepted that what they were seeing took place at night primarily because they heard so many references to darkness. What Iago's language does to

Othello's perceptions – especially as he sees and hears the interactions of Cassio, Iago, and Bianca during Act IV, Scene i – is analogous to how the language of *Othello* shapes and transforms the perceptions of its audiences, especially when performed on a non-illusionistic stage like that of the Globe. Iago is a surrogate playwright – a figure through whom the play presents the negative possibilities inherent in the processes by which illusion, including the illusion upon which performance depends, is generated and sustained.

The presence of Bianca compounds the process of misinterpretation. She is in fact what Othello now thinks Desdemona is – a whore. As Othello equates Desdemona and Bianca, an important similarity between Bianca and Othello takes shape. Just as Othello takes Cassio's possession of Desdemona's handkerchief as evidence of Desdemona's infidelity, Bianca takes Cassio's possession of it as evidence that his appetites have strayed. Drawing on the same piece of evidence, the general and the whore reach the same conclusion – infidelity – but apply it to different people.

After Cassio exits in pursuit of Bianca, Othello agrees to Iago's suggestion that he kill Desdemona, not by poison, but by strangling her 'in her bed, even the bed she hath contaminated': 'Good, good, the justice of it pleases, very good' (IV.i.203–5). A trumpet anouncing the arrival of Lodovico, an emissary from Venice, cuts short their deliberations. That arrival, timed to occur immediately after Othello determines how he will murder Desdemona, invokes the values associated with Venice – social concord, reason, law, civility – and accentuates their absence from Cyprus. As Othello reads the document appointing Cassio his successor, his attention flits between what he reads and Desdemona's conversation with Lodovico. Enraged at overhearing Desdemona speak of 'the love I bear to Cassio' and say she is 'glad on't' that Cassio will replace him, Othello strikes her and calls her 'Devil!' (IV.i.228, 233, 235). His language zigzags erratically between abuse aimed at Desdemona and the formal, polite address, proper to the governor of Cyprus welcoming an official representative of the state he serves, he uses when speaking to Lodovico:

> Concerning this, sir, – O well-painted passion! –
> I am commanded here: . . . get you away,
> I'll send for you anon . . . Sir, I obey the mandate,
> And will return to Venice: . . . Hence, avaunt!
>   [*Exit Desdemona.*

Cassio shall have my place; and, sir, to-night,
I do entreat that we may sup together,
You are welcome, sir, to Cyprus . . . Goats and monkeys!
                                               (IV.i.253–9)

Olivier's Othello paused noticeably after 'Cassio shall have my',
before, with a near sob, saying, 'place'. For Othello, the 'place'
referred to was not only his official position as governor of Cyprus
but also his place in Desdemona's bed and affections.

* * *

The climax of Othello's confusion is his murder of Desdemona. He
enters *'with a light'*[8] – a detail that accentuates the magnitude of his
error. As he puts out 'the light' (V.ii.7) that was the breath of life in
Desdemona, he acts in cognitive darkness that is total. Precisely how
he kills her is not specified by the Quarto or the Folio, thus leaving
open a range of performance possibilities. As a result, the choice of
a specific method becomes an index to how perspectives of Othello,
of the conceptions of the tragic hero and tragic decorum, and even of
Desdemona and notions of approriately 'feminine' behaviour shift or
persist from era to era. Does Desdemona try to escape? Does she
physically resist Othello, and if so, does the ensuing struggle both
mimic and distort the sexual embraces audiences have not seen them
share? Does a production play down the combination of eroticism
and violence her killing can embody by having her die passively,
yielding one last (and fatal) time to a cultural tradition that expects
obedience and submission of women and of wives?

Does Othello strangle her with his bare hands and in a way that
registers on the audience as barbaric, savage, African? Or do his hands
on her throat signify the absolute perversion of the caresses they have
shared? Does he use something to strangle her, perhaps ensuring that
they are not touching as she dies – as if trying to keep himself free of
the pollution he thinks she embodies? If so, what does he use? His belt
or some other item of his attire that conveys visually the outraged
masculinity and pride expressed in his earlier cry, 'I will chop her into
messes . . . Cuckold me!' (IV.i.196)? Does he use something of hers – a
piece of her clothing perhaps – as if to signal his belief that she is
responsible for his killing her? Does he rip off a piece of the bedsheet
and strangle her with it, thus tightening the circle of 'justice' Iago

invokes when he recommends strangling her 'even in the bed she hath contaminated?' Othellos in most eighteenth- and nineteenth-century productions smothered Desdemona with a pillow, according to James R. Siemon (1986, p. 46), as if too refined to kill her barehanded, and the 1930 London production starring Paul Robeson is evidence that the use of a pillow persisted into the twentieth century.

When, as Emilia calls offstage, Othello realises that Desdemona is 'not yet quite dead', he completes the murder: 'I that am cruel, am yet merciful, / I would not have thee linger in thy pain, . . . / So, so' (V.ii.87–90). Does he finish her off by resuming what he has been doing or does he change technique? If he was strangling Desdemona barehanded, does he now resort to his belt or to a piece of her apparel or to a strip of sheet or to a pillow? Or does he put by whatever object he has been using, and use his hands for the first time?

Nearly two-thirds of the last scene of *Othello* takes place after Desdemona's death (at line 126), and most of those final 245 lines involve discovering and describing what has happened. As exposition, they are superfluous, for they repeat what audiences already know. Through them, however, the play re-establishes the cognitive norm, bringing Othello to more accurate knowledge of himself and his deed and exposing Iago's plot, in its many turnings, to the people of Cyprus and to the representatives of Venice. The play's final moments close the gap between what the characters know and what audiences know, and they take the form of a trial-like process, during which – as during Othello's earlier 'trial' in Venice – events and people are found out and judged.

Emilia is the first to begin paring away the confusion. She rejects Othello's charge that Desdemona 'was a whore. . . . and false as water', asserting to his face that 'she was heavenly true' (V.ii.133–6). Her disbelieving repetition of 'My husband' (V.ii.141–53) as Othello justifies the killing accentuates her refusal to submit to her husband's authority and be silent. When Iago commands, 'charm your tongue', she replies, 'I am bound to speak' (V.ii.184–5). After Othello offers as proof of Desdemona's adultery the fact that he saw Cassio with the handkerchief he had given her as a 'recognizance and pledge of love', Emilia again refuses Iago's command to 'hold your peace': 'Let heaven, and men, and devils, let 'em all, / All, all cry shame against me, yet I'll speak' (V.ii.215, 219, 222–3).

Emilia's insistence on testifying on Desdemona's behalf violates the ideal of wifely obedience, of which, ironically, Desdemona herself is the paragon, remaining obedient even after Othello hits her in Act IV, Scene i. ' 'Tis proper I obey him,' Emilia says as Iago tries to silence her, 'but not now' (V.ii.197). Earlier, by keeping the handkerchief Desdemona dropped and then, despite her dismay, not telling her what had become of it, Emilia had valued her husband's wishes more than her duties to her mistress. Now, she reverses those priorities, subordinating her duties as wife to her obligations as Desdemona's serving lady. She will 'speak true' (V.ii.251) and thus be true to, faithful to, Desdemona, even if that means violating, being false to, her duties as Iago's wife. By subordinating her marriage to Iago to her relationship with the lady she serves, Emilia (unknowingly) repeats the realignment of priorities that Othello carries out when he subordinates his marriage to Desdemona to his relationship with Iago, who (ostensibly) serves him with total loyalty. In each instance, the bond between two members of the same sex overrides the bond between husband and wife. Othello comes to value his lieutenant more than his wife, Emilia her mistress more than her husband. What Emilia does in her final moments is also a variation of what Iago pledges when he vows absolute loyalty to Othello: she gives herself totally to 'wrong'd' Desdemona's 'service'. In *Othello* both the murder of Desdemona and the full disclosure of it require violating the marital bond. On one level, that is proof of the havoc Iago has wrought in perverting relationships. On another, it is evidence of the limits of and contradictions in the ideal of wifely fidelity.

Desdemona's dying words also illustrate those limits and contradictions. When Emilia asks, 'O, who has done this deed?' Desdemona answers: 'Nobody, I myself, farewell: / Commend me to my kind lord, O, farewell!' (V.ii.124–6). Those words are her final expression of her love for Othello, but they are also a distortion of what audiences have seen happen. Rather than name Othello as her killer, Desdemona claims total responsibility for her death, concealing her husband's guilt. In contrast to Emilia, who persists in speaking 'true" no matter what the consequences for her husband, Desdemona dies conforming to the ideal of the wife faithful to the point of subordinating all to her husband's welfare. What she declares before the Senate when asking to accompany Othello to Cyprus remains true even now: 'My heart's subdued / Even to the utmost pleasure of my lord' (I.iii.250–1).[9] More true to her 'kind lord' than to the facts of her own murder, she is, even with her last breath, an examplar of wifely fidelity. In an irony that makes excruciatingly clear the limits and contradictions of such fidelity, Othello takes Desdemona's last words protecting him as proof that she is the false wife he has killed her for being. He insists on telling (what he thinks is) the truth: 'She's like a liar gone to burning hell, / 'Twas I that kill'd her' (V.ii.130–1).

Through Emilia and Desdemona, the final moments of *Othello* set in conflict two kinds of truth, two kinds of fidelity: to one's husband and to the facts as one knows them. Desdemona is true to the former, Emilia, ultimately, to the latter. Perhaps the most telling critique the play offers of the ideal of wifely fidelity is that both Desdemona, the wife who is true to her husband, and Emilia, the wife who insists on speaking 'true' even if that means being false to her husband, die murdered by their spouses. Neither form of truth enables either wife to survive. Their shared victimage receives visual emphasis if Emilia's request after being mortally wounded is fulfilled: 'O lay me by my mistress' side' (V.ii.238). In fact, however, it rarely (if ever) happens in a production that her corpse is placed on the bed beside Desdemona's[10] – a pattern that has interesting cultural implications. Not granting Emilia's dying wish deflects and blunts the challenge that her final allegiance to Desdemona poses to the notion – deeply embedded in English-speaking cultures over the centuries *Othello* has been performed – that marriage has primacy among the relationships humans form.

Emilia's testimony about the handkerchief breaks down Othello's defence that Desdemona was an adulteress, driving him to despairing recognition of his crime. Convinced that his soul will not, and should not, come to bliss, he declares as he looks on Desdemona's corpse, 'This look of thine will hurl my soul from heaven, / And fiends will snatch at it.' (V.ii.275–6). His despair arises not only from what he regards as the fact of his own damnation but also from his conviction that he is separated from Desdemona forever. Unlike Romeo killing himself beside what he thinks is Juliet's corpse, Othello envisages no reunion with his beloved beyond death.

At the conclusion of the scene that includes Othello's 'trial' before the Venetian Senate, Iago exults as he anticipates how what he has in mind will be converted into action: 'Hell and night / Must bring this monstrous birth to the world's light' (I.iii.401–2). Othello's 'trial' after Desdemona's death brings 'that monstrous birth' to light in another sense: by making Iago's plot known to those on Cyprus. Through Othello's 'second trial' the play reaffirms the cognitive norm established during his first; people succeed in knowing 'what hath befall'n'.

That affirmation is steeped in pain and loss, however, and it emerges from blood, fatal error, and evil successfully practised. Lodovico, recently arrived on Cyprus as the emissary of Venice, brings the 'trial' to what he thinks is its conclusion by relieving Othello of 'your power and your command', installing Cassio as his successor, and specifying that he will 'close prisoner rest, / Till that the nature of your fault be known / To the Venetian state' (V.ii.332, 336–8).

Othello asks to speak 'a word or two', and what he says concentrates less on matters of guilt or innocence than on influencing what will be spoken or written – the stories that will be told – about 'these unlucky deeds' and about himself (V.ii.339, 342). He asks those who will report to the Senate to be accurate and objective, to speak of him as

> one that lov'd not wisely, but too well:
> Of one not easily jealous, but being wrought,
> Perplex'd in the extreme; of one whose hand,
> Like the base Indian,[11] threw a pearl away,
> Richer than all his tribe: of one whose subdued eyes,
> Albeit unused to the melting mood,
> Drops tears as fast as the Arabian trees
> Their medicinal gum.
>
> (V.ii.345–52)

Othello, who won Desdemona's love by telling 'the story of my life' (I.iii.129), ends his testimony by telling another story about himself:

> in Aleppo once,
> Where a malignant and a turban'd Turk
> Beat a Venetian, and traduc'd the state,
> I took by the throat the circumcised dog,
> And smote him thus.   [*Stabs himself.*
>
> (V.ii.353–7)

By killing himself, using the dagger that, in some productions, he also uses to menace Iago, Othello, who previously acted as Desdemona's judge, jury, and executioner, acts as his own judge, jury, and executioner.

The presentation of Othello's suicide draws attention to and makes use of the feature that most fundamentally distinguishes drama from

narrative: drama consists of actions performed in the present. As he
stabs himself, Othello shifts from narration to enactment, from talking about past actions to performing present deeds, from talk of
stabbing a 'malignant and a turban'd Turk' to stabbing himself
'thus'. As he tries, by means of that shift, to align his sense of the
man he was with his sense of the man he is now, his past with his
present, Othello equates himself with that Turk. He ends 'as both
the Turk and the destroyer of the Turk, the infidel and the defender
of the faith' (Kernan, 1970, p. 359) – a status that details of performance can both anticipate and reinforce. For example, in Hands's
1986 production for the Royal Shakespeare Company, Othello made
his first entrance, wearing, like the 'malignant' Turk he tells of killing, a turban, and the weapon audiences saw him carrying was not
a sword but a scimitar.

Othello addresses his final words not to those who will tell his story
and report to Venice but to Desdemona's corpse: 'I kiss'd thee ere I
kill'd thee, no way but this, / Killing myself, to die upon a kiss'
(V.ii.359–60). Does he in fact die, as his words indicate he wants to,
upon the kiss he longs to give her, and does his corpse lie with or
even on hers on the bed? Or do audiences see what Roderigo says
of Iago prove true of Othello in his last seconds: 'your words and
performance are no kin together' (IV.ii.184–5)? Neither the Quarto
nor the Folio enables us to determine whether there is a gap between
the death Othello envisages for himself and what occurs. The stage
direction in the former is simply '*He dies*', and in the latter it is, even
more simply, '*Dyes*'. Their imprecision generates a field of possibilities
to which different eras have responded differently. Eighteenth- and
nineteenth-century productions, Siemon reports (1986, pp. 49–50),
almost always denied Othello the death he desires; he regularly died
struggling to reach Desdemona, never dying on the bed with her and
rarely managing to give her the kiss he wants to die upon. Audiences
at such productions whose eyes obeyed Lodovico's call to 'Look on
the tragic lodging of this bed' (V.ii.364) saw Desdemona's corpse
alone, in isolation, distanced from Othello's body on the floor. That
sight confirmed Othello's failure to perform the act that would be his
final affirmation of his love for her.

What audiences of those earlier eras never saw has beome routine
during this century, perhaps in part because of an increasing taste
for mixing eroticism and violence: Desdemona and Othello together
on the bed and in death.[12] When Othello dies on the bed with Des-

demona, what audiences see – two bodies together – emphasises their
unity in death. Such a sight mitigates, if it does not cancel, the
prospect of unending separation that Othello voices when he envisages his soul hurled from heaven and calls for what he considers just
punishment:

> Whip me, you devils,
> From the possession of this heavenly sight,
> Blow me about in winds, roast me in sulphur,
> Wash me in steep-down gulfs of liquid fire!
>   (V.ii.278–81)

Together on the bed, the two corpses take on an emblematic quality.
On the one hand, they offer visual evidence of enduring differences:
black/white, male/female, older/younger. On the other, they affirm
a desire – frustrated in this instance – to move past such differences,
to become one with the other who is one's beloved.

The question of where Othello lies as and after he dies is not
unlike the question Desdemona puts to the Clown at the start of the
scene directly after Othello, having judged her false, accepts Iago as
'my lieutenant' 'forever'. 'Do you know sirrah,' she asks, 'where the
lieutenant Cassio lies?' (III.iv.1). The Clown's answer plays upon two
different meanings of 'lie' – resting or reclining, and speaking
untruths. Before collapsing in Act IV, Scene i, Othello fastens upon
the phrases 'lie on her' and 'lie with her', in which the meanings of
falsification and sexual intercourse overlap. If in death Othello lies
on Desdemona or with (beside) her, that sight provides one last
variation, this time in visual form, of the play's punning exploration
of the word 'lie'.

* * *

Several features set *Othello* apart from Shakespeare's other tragedies,
Elizabethan as well as Jacobean. One is that Othello's death has no
major impact on the world of which he has been a part. Hamlet's
death, in the tragedy Shakespeare wrote before *Othello*, completes the
extinction of a dynasty, opening the way for a foreigner to rule in
Denmark. In *King Lear*, usually regarded as the Shakespeare tragedy
written after *Othello*, the deaths of King Lear and Cordelia leave the
survivors to face the problem of deciding who will rule over and

sustain a Britain so damaged by what has happened that one of them refers to it as 'the gor'd state' (V.iii.319). In contrast, the Turkish threat to Cyprus and ultimately to Venice that Othello is charged with repulsing is dispelled early in *Othello* by the non-human agency of the storm, and Venice remains intact and secure, ungored by events that Lodovico, with the play's last words, undertakes to 'relate' 'to the state' (V.ii.371–2). Even the deaths of Romeo and Juliet – in some respects the teen-age equivalents of Othello and Desdemona – have a societal impact greater than the deaths of the Moor and his wife. Their dying brings to an end the feud that has long plagued Verona.

Another feature that sets *Othello* apart is the racial identity of its protagonist. The great voyages of discovery around Africa and to the New World during the fifteenth and sixteenth centuries brought the English into contact with races they had never before encountered directly. Those voyages and the travel literature they generated help to spur a re-examination of what it meant to be English and, more broadly, to be human – a re-examination in which skin colour became a critical factor. The first performances of *Othello* participated in and contributed to that re-examination. 'At an historical moment when the only roles blacks played on stage was that of a villain of low status' (Newman, 1987, p. 157), Shakespeare and the King's Men took the risk of presenting a black man as a tragic protagonist – of calling upon *Othello*'s first audiences, and audiences since, to attend to and respond to what a black man thinks, feels, says, and does.

A third features that distinguishes *Othello* is the attention given during its final moments to the motives of its villain. Othello asks Cassio, 'Will you, I pray, demand that demi-devil / Why he hath thus ensnar'd my soul and body?' (V.ii.302–3). Iago replies, 'Demand me nothing, what you know, you know, / From this time forth I never will speak word' (V.ii.304–5). Othello dies without receiving any answer to his question. Iago is the only Shakespearean tragic villain who is alive at the end of the play, and with the silence he vows to keep, *Othello* establishes a limit upon cognition: those on Cyprus come to know 'what hath befall'n' but not why. By having Othello seek (but not receive) an explanation of why Iago has 'ensnar'd' him, the play explicitly raises the issue of Iago's motivation. Certainly Iago reveals to audiences and readers information about his motivation of the kind that he will not disclose to the characters who question him as *Othello* ends. Audiences and readers learn of his anger at not being appointed Othello's lieutenant, of his 'suspicion' (I.iii.387) that 'the lustful Moor / Hath leap'd into my seat' (II.i.290–1) and slept with Emilia, of his own desire to sleep with Desdemona, not simply out of lust but also to be 'even with' Othello, 'wife, for wife' (II.i.294), and even of his resentment of Cassio, who 'has a daily beauty in his life, / That makes me ugly' (V.i.19–20).

Some commentators find in one or more of the motives Iago mentions satisfactory explanation of why he destroys Othello. Others regard the fact that Iago talks about a variety of motives, as suspicious, noting that the more motives he mentions, the less convincing any one of them is. A number of those who reject the motives he explicitly discusses try to deduce what they think are adequate ones, including motives of which he may not be consciously aware. A representative sample would include Iago's virulent racism, or his suppressed homosexual love for Othello, or the pleasure he takes in exercising power, particularly the power to hurt others, or the profound self-hatred that he displaces onto those around him, against whom he then lashes out. Others regard the fact that Iago talks about a variety of motives as the basis for arguing that he has none. Coleridge, for example, spoke of the 'motive-hunting of motiveless malignity' (1930, p. 49).

The debate over Iago's motive(s) is an extension, and a consequence, of the play's concern with the issue of how well, how accurately, one person can know another. All claims regarding Iago's motives, even the claim that he has none, rest upon a confidence that one person can accurately know another's innermost self – a confidence that the play itself both indulges and calls into question. Such claims presume that the cognitive limits *Othello* posits for its characters do not extend to its audiences, yet they, like the play's characters, must rely on what they see Iago do and hear him say as they try to discern his motives. They must rely upon appearances, and appearances, *Othello* demonstrates, are radically unreliable. Indeed, performances of *Othello* consist of such appearances; audiences take what actors say and do onstage to be the words and actions of persons they know the actors are not. The actors present, and audiences participate in, 'a pageant / To keep us in false gaze'. The fact that questions arise about Iago's motive(s) is proof of the force such appearances, such a 'pageant', have. The long-running debate over Iago's motivation arises from, and continues to demonstrate, the desire – perhaps even the need – to be convinced that we have the power to know accurately the inner workings of another person and to find comfort in the security such power gives. Most plays, even most Shakespearean plays, satisfy that desire and offer that security. *Othello*, however, seems to expose and question it, by presenting the *possibility* that we who are the play's audiences and readers know its characters, primarily Iago, only slightly better than those characters know one another. That possibility raises another that is even more unsettling: we know one another no better than we know them.

4

King Lear: 'O! See, See'

At its Greek root, the word 'theatre' means 'seeing place', and *King Lear*, more audaciously than any other Shakespearean play, challenges the capacity of those who watch it to bear up under the kinds of seeing in which audiences engage during performance. That challenge involves both what they see and how they see. Characters in *Lear* speak often of seeing. Goneril, for exmple, begins the competition to gain the largest dowry by declaring that she loves Lear 'Dearer than eyesight' (I.i.55). When Kent tries to prevent Lear from dividing the realm and disowning Cordelia, Lear orders, 'Out of my sight', and Kent responds, 'See better, Lear, and let me still remain / The true blank of thine eye' (I.i.156–8). After the King of France accepts Cordelia as his wife, Lear finalises his rejection of the daughter he most loves, vowing never to see her again: 'we / Have no such daughter, nor shall ever see / That face of hers again' (I.i.261–3). There is talk of seeing as *Lear* ends. Albany interrupts his own effort to restore political order and, calling, 'O! see, see!' (V.iii.303), directs the gaze of characters and audience alike to the sight of Lear with the corpse of his beloved Cordelia. Lear's last words, according to the Folio version that most modern editors follow, also call for acts of seeing: 'Do you see this? Look on her, look, her lips, / Look there, look there!' (V.iii.309–10).

Those and the many other verbal references to sight in *Lear* are important, not least because they link the physical ability to see with the capacity to understand one's self and others and to feel with and for them, but full force of those references rests upon their relationship to acts of seeing in which audiences watch characters engage during performance. After hearing Kent call for Lear to 'see better', audiences, but not readers, then see Lear look on Kent, disguised as

Caius, and fail to perceive his identity. They also see Gloucester, even before losing his eyes, fail to recognise Edgar beneath his disguise as Poor Tom. Only after his eyes are destroyed does Gloucester learn to 'see better' in the sense that he realises how he has misjudged Edgar, but audiences never see him understand that the man ministering to him is Edgar. They watch Edmund in the final scene accept a challenge to single combat from an adversary whose face he cannot see and whose identity he does not know. Only after his defeat does Edmund learn that the man who has mortally wounded him is 'Edgar, and thy father's son' (V.iii.168). Audiences who hear Kent ask to 'remain the true blank' of Lear's eye subsequently see Glocester's eyesockets made blank because, defying the orders of Cornwall and Regan, he remains true to Lear. When eyeless Gloucester and mad Lear meet, audiences see Lear himself look upon the true blank of what were Gloucester's eyes. 'Dost thou know me?' Gloucester asks, and Lear responds, 'I remember thine eyes well enough' (IV.vi.134–5). When Lear is reunited with Cordelia, who implores him to 'look upon me, Sir' (IV.vii.57), audiences see – as readers do not – Lear fix his eyes upon the face he had vowed never to see again.

The plot of Gloucester and his sons is based upon an episode in Sir Philip Sidney's *Arcadia*, in which the son equivalent to Edgar tells another character how his brother has deprived their father of his sight. What *Arcadia* narrates the King's Men and Shakespeare present to the eyes of their audiences, calling upon them to watch an act that goes beyond depriving a man of his sight. They are challenged to look on with their eyes while Gloucester's are gouged out. *Lear* confronts its audiences with the sight of a Gloucester who is not only blind like his counterpart in the *Arcadia* but is also, horrifyingly, eyeless.

Two productions directed by Peter Brook show how seeing Gloucester's blinding enacted is an experience crucially different from reading about it. In his 1962 production for the Royal Shakespeare Company, Brook placed the intermission immediately after Gloucester's blinding and signalled the intermission by bringing the house lights to full intensity with a speed that dazzled the audience's eyes, momentarily hurting them. In his 1971 film based upon that production, Brook positioned the camera so that the audience saw what was happening as if looking through Gloucester's eyes. The spoon that Cornwall plunged into Gloucester's remaining eye seemed to come through the camera lens into the audience's eyes, and the screen went black. Briefly, the audience, like Gloucester, could see nothing. Taking advantage of the different visual possibilities offered by stage and film, Brook made the blinding of Gloucester register not just upon the sensitivities of his audiences but also upon their eyes.

By enacting the blinding of Gloucester, *Lear* tests what its audiences will bear to see, but it also challenges its audiences in precisely the opposite way: by not letting them see what they have been expecting to see, the climactic battle. Stage directions at the start of Act V, Scene ii in both Quarto and Folio, specify that audiences see the forces of Lear and Cordelia pass over the stage:

> *Alarum. Enter the powers of France over the stage, Cordelia with her father in her hand.* [Quarto]

and

> *Alarum within. Enter with Drumme and Colours, Lear, Cordelia, and souldiers, over the Stage, and Exeunt.* [Folio].

That, however, is the only sight of the battle that either version of the play gives audiences, who then watch Gloucester waiting, alone, to learn the outcome of a battle he cannot see. It is also a battle that they cannot see. *Lear* places all combat offstage, out of their sight, while what they are allowed to see is a character who cannot see. In effect, the play forces them to see through the eyes Gloucester does not have. While the battle rages, they are, like the eyeless old man they watch, dependent solely upon what they hear. The sounds that reach his ears also reach theirs, but those signals for '*Alarum*' and '*retreat*' give no certain clues to the progress of the unseen battle. Audiences learn the outcome by the same non-visual means that the sightless Gloucester does, when Edgar enters crying, 'Away, old man! give me thy hand: away! / King Lear hath lost, he and his daughter ta'en' (V.ii.5–6). Gloucester's exit with Edgar ends a scene in which the King's Men and their playwright took the risk of subjecting those who watched their *Lear* to the theatrical equivalent of blindness.

Another, considerably more complex example of how *Lear* manipulates its audiences' capacity to see occurs when Edgar brings his father to a spot that is, he says, the very edge of a towering cliff at Dover. By including this scene, *Lear* asks its audiences to watch events that have no equivalent in the *Arcadia*. There the faithful son who is Edgar's counterpart refuses to take his father to the top of the rock from which he wants to leap to his death, but Edgar as Poor Tom does not refuse. He takes Gloucester to 'th' extreme verge', then uses the fact that Gloucester survives what he thinks is his suicidal leap from 'the dread summit of this chalky bourn' to 'cure' him of the despair that drove him to want to end his life (IV.vi.26, 57, 34). 'Thy life's a miracle', Edgar insists, altering his voice and pretending to be a fisherman at the bottom of the cliff from which Gloucester has jumped, and Gloucester resolves to continue living: 'henceforth I'll bear / Affliction till it do cry out itself / "Enough, enough", and die' (IV.vi.55, 75–7). While audiences may be moved by and even rejoice in Gloucester's renewed determination to 'bear affliction', *Lear* forces them to see that his will to go on living rests upon deception. Not only is there no 'miracle', there is not even a cliff.

Gloucester is not the only one deceived during those moments. *Lear* presents Edgar's 'miracle'-like deception of Gloucester in a way that exploits the specific kinds of theatrical seeing in which audiences at the Globe engaged. All theatre audiences engage in a process of complicit miscognition, agreeing for the duration of the performance to accept, among other things, that a given actor represents ('is') a character they know he or she is not and that the playing area they are looking upon now in this theatre in this city or town 'is' (represents) a different place: a nunnery or a prison in Vienna while watching *Measure for Measure*, for example, or, during a performance of *Othello*, the Senate chamber of Venice and a bedroom on Cyprus. The particular form that such misrecognition and representation take, however, varies according to the theatrical conventions functioning at a given moment in history – the terms of reference shared by audiences, playwright, and players that enable a performance to take place. According to the theatrical conventions at the Globe, the principal means for representing locale was what audiences heard the (actors playing) characters say on the subject of place, not what they saw, which was a stage, generally devoid of scenery and employing few props, that provided little, if anything, in the way of visual signals to indicate the specific site of the events being represented. At the Globe, 'place' rested upon a process of miscognition and representation requiring audiences to engage in a particular kind of theatrical seeing that disregarded what their eyes actually saw. In matters bearing upon locale, they subordinated the testimony of their eyes to that of their ears, doing in effect what mad Lear calls upon eyeless Gloucester to do: 'Look with thine ears' (IV.vi.149).

When the two members of the King's Men playing Gloucester and Edgar entered to begin the scene, the play's first audiences, seeing two figures moving across a bare, flat stage, would have had to determine the locale of the action being played on the basis of the words spoken. Initially, what Edgar and Gloucester say provides guidance of the kind Globe audiences expected. Gloucester asks, 'When shall I come to th' top of that same hill?' from which he wants to leap to his death, and Edgar says, 'You do climb up it now; look how we labour' (IV.vi.1–2). However, the dialogue then jars the convention for establishing place in the Globe by having Gloucester question Edgar's account of where they are. 'Methinks the ground is even' (IV.vi.3), he says, a comment that accurately describes the slope of the stage upon which audiences at the Globe saw them standing. 'Horrible steep' (IV.vi.3), Edgar replies, insisting on the accuracy of what he has said about the slope of the 'ground' over which they are moving. The exchange would have left Globe audiences without any certain way of deciding which character's account of where they are is accurate and thus no way of being certain whether, in a play that had already asked them to see a man's eyes put out, they were now about to see Gloucester commit suicide assisted by the son he foolishly rejected.

The dramaturgy of the scene subjected those who watched the earliest performances of *Lear* at the Globe to a form of theatrical disorientation – a combination of uncertainty and suspense – as they found themselves unable to know for sure where the actions being played on the stage were occurring. Were they or were they not watching characters climbing a hill towards the edge of a cliff? If they were, would Edgar permit Gloucester to jump to his death? If they accepted that the level stage they in fact saw was to be construed as 'ground' 'horrible steep', then they were relying, even more than eyeless Gloucester, upon what they hear Edgar say for their sense of place. On the other hand, if they trusted the testimony of their own eyes and accepted that the 'ground' was 'even', they were, in effect, aligning their sense of place with Gloucester's, and he has no eyes to show him where he is.

The scene intensifies that experience of disorienting uncertainty. Globe audiences would have heard Edgar declare that he has brought Gloucester to the edge of the cliff – 'Come on, sir; here's the place: stand still' (IV.vi.11) – and then describe what he sees when he looks down. He begins by stressing the vertigo he experiences: 'How fearful / And dizzy 'tis to cast one's eyes so low' (IV.vi.11–12). He ends with the same emphasis: 'I'll look no more, / Lest my brain turn, and the deficient sight / Topple down headlong' (IV.vi.22–4). The 'deficient sight' of which Edgar speaks is a reference to what he says is his own vertiginous disorientation, but it also refers to the eyeless Gloucester, who soon will throw himself off what he thinks is the cliff on which he stands. In addition, 'deficient sight' glances at how, during performances at the Globe, audiences were called upon to accept that in matters of locale what their eyes see is 'deficient'.[1]

The description Edgar proceeds to give of the birds, the man gathering samphire, the fishermen on the beach, and the ship at anchor, was written to be spoken by an actor standing on a flat stage in a theatre without the capacity to offer its audiences visually compelling signs of a cliff-top location. What he says is exactly what, given the form of miscognition upon which performance at the Globe depended, audiences there would have taken as a signal that the character speaking is (to be construed as) standing on the edge of a cliff. Edgar's words convince·Gloucester, who asks, 'Set me where you stand', and Edgar complies: 'Give me your hand; you are now within a foot / Of th'extreme verge: for all beneath the moon / Would I not leap upright' (IV.vi.24, 25–7). They are also false. '[Had] he been where he thought', Edgar says after watching Gloucester throw himself forward off what he thinks is a cliff to what he hopes will be his death, 'By this had thought been past' (IV.vi.44–5). Where Gloucester thinks he is is where the play, relying most on Edgar's compelling description, encouraged its first audiences to think he is. By proving that description false, *Lear* completes an extremely risky dramaturgical manoeuvre that involves turning the primary means by which place was signified at the Globe against itself. That manoeuvre undercuts the very processes of misrecognition and representation upon which performances there relied. What Globe audiences would have seen with their own eyes – a flat surface that in no way resembles the edge of a cliff – proves to be a more accurate guide to the site of events than what they hear a character say. Like Lear, they came to learn that they cannot always rely on the words they hear, not even in the theatre. The bond linking them with players and playwright during performance turned out to be as vulnerable to exploitation and abuse as that between father and child.

Edgar's description of what he sees as he looks down from a cliff on which he is not standing discloses the impact upon Shakespeare and the King's Men of what was in England a radically new technique of stage representation. The earliest performance of *Lear* of which any mention survives is that mentioned on the title page of the 1608 Quarto. That performance, before James and his court on 26 December 1606, opened that year's round of the festivities traditionally associated with the twelve days after Christmas, and the current consensus is that Shakespeare wrote the play earlier that year or in 1605. The Twelfth Night festivities two years earlier had ended, on 6 January 1605, with James and his court watching *The Masque of Blackness* – a form of royal entertainment, involving both professional actors like the King's Men and members of the court, that combined music, dance, and drama. Masques were an established form of royal entertainment in England dating back to the reign of Henry VIII, but *The Masque of Blackness*, the first on which Ben Jonson and Inigo Jones collaborated, was fundamentally unlike any previous masque in one crucial respect: for it Jones provided moveable scenery, framed by a proscenium arch, that had been painted and arranged in accord with perspectivist principles developed in fifteenth-century Italy. Those principles, which aimed at the faithful representation of what the eyes see, enabled painters working on a flat, two-dimensional surface to create the illusion of depth by proportionately diminishing the size of objects and figures in the painting. Those watching *The Masque of Blackness* were the first English audience to experience a mode of representation and miscognition that was pictorial rather than verbal. Because it relied primarily upon what those watching saw to establish locale, that mode was radically different from the mode upon which performances at commercial theatres like the Globe relied.

Since the King's Men regularly performed in the court masques, they and their playwright certainly knew of this new scenic technique, but they could not use it at the Globe, where audiences stood and sat on at least three sides of the stage and perhaps on the stage itself. That arrangement created sightlines incompatible with deploying painted scenery framed by a proscenium arch, which required an audience gathered in front of the performance space. Edgar's description of what he sees when he looks down from a cliff on which he does not stand is evidence of how, to the extent possible at the Globe, Shakespeare and the King's Men drew upon the new mode of representation. As Edgar describes what he sees from the cliff, he 'paints' with words a picture for Gloucester and for audiences that conforms to perspectivist principles. The farther from Edgar the things he reports he sees supposedly are, the more they seem to have shrunk proportionately in size. Birds 'that wing the midway air' seem the size of 'beetles', while 'fishermen who walk upon the beach / Appear like mice' (IV.vi.13–18). A ship at anchor shrinks to the size of her cockboat, itself the size of a 'buoy / Almost too small for sight' (IV.vi.19–20).

From 1605 on, pictorial representation was an alternative, and a challenge, to the mode of representation that was the basis for performances at the commercial theatres of London, including the Globe. The two modes co-existed in their separate domains until 1642, when, as civil war was about to break out, Parliament ordered all theatres in England to be closed. Following the restoration of the monarchy in 1660, Charles II authorised two men, William D'Avenant and Thomas Killigrew, to establish acting companies, but by then the Globe and the other commerical theatres in which the King's Men and their rivals once played had been demolished. With their passing the mode of theatrical representation within and for which Shakespeare wrote plays for performance by the King's Men disappeared. D'Avenant and then Killigrew proceeded to build theatres designed to take full advantage of the techniques of scenic illusion that, before 1642, had been confined to the court masques of James I and Charles I. Restoration audiences sat in front of a stage that included at its rear, where there had been the fixed façade of the Globe, a large room, framed by a proscenium arch, in which painted scenery could be set. The dominance that the pictorial mode of theatrical representation achieved after the Restoration went unchallenged during succeeding centuries, and until after the mid-point of the twentieth century, the theatres constructed, including both the Shakespeare Memorial Theatre at Stratford-upon-Avon in 1879 and in 1932 its successor, the Royal Shakespeare Theatre, were essentially variations upon the proscenium-arch model of D'Avenant and Killigrew.

What many continue to call the 'cliff' or 'suicide' scene is a particularly clear instance of the impact of that dominance. The uncertainty about locale that audiences at the Globe experienced watching the first moments of this scene being played on an open, bare stage cannot be generated if what and how audiences see

involves pictorial conventions of staging. Audiences watching according-
ing to those conventions expect to see compelling visual signs of a
specific locale, but in the case of Edgar bringing Gloucester to what
he says is the edge of a cliff at Dover, such signs are not possible
because that is not where in fact they are. If, for example, a specific
locale is established, audiences see immediately that it is not a cliff-
top. If, on the other hand, the set used for the scene leaves the locale
indeterminate, audiences will not take it to be the edge of a cliff of
which they see no evidence. In either case, audiences watching
performances based upon pictorial representation know from the
moment they see Gloucester and Edgar enter what their counterparts at the Globe, relying primarily on what they heard to establish
locale, had to learn during the ensuing moments: Gloucester is in no
danger, for Edgar and he are not at the top of a cliff, never 'within
a foot / Of th' extreme verge'.

The dominance of the proscenium-arch theatre is a major reason
why early in the nineteenth century *Lear* came to be regarded as a
play whose greatness exceeded the capacity of any performance. *Lear*
is best appreciated, critics of that era such as Samuel Taylor Coleridge and Charles Lamb insisted, when it is read, not seen in performance, and John Keats's great sonnet of 1818 – 'On Sitting Down to
Read *King Lear* Once Again' – concentrates on his experience as a
reader, not a spectator:

> once again, the fierce dispute
> Between damnation and impassion'd clay
> Must I burn through; once more humbly assay
> The bitter-sweet of this Shakespearean fruit.

Early in this century, A. C. Bradley put the case for reading *Lear*
rather than seeing it performed in a way that remains powerfully
influential. Many, he noted, consider *Lear* to be 'Shakespeare's
greatest work, the best of his plays, the tragedy in which he exhibits
most fully his multitudinous powers', yet compared with his other
major tragedies – *Hamlet, Othello,* and *Macbeth* – it is the one 'least
often presented on the stage, and the least successful there' (1904,
p. 200). That is so, Bradley explained, because *Lear* is 'Shakespeare's
greatest achievement' but '*not* his best play' (p. 201). 'There is', he
said, 'something in its very essence which is at war with the senses,
and demands a purely imaginative realization' (p. 204). For Bradley,

Lear is 'too huge for the stage' (p. 203), but that assertion must be weighed against the fact that 'the stage' upon which he – as well as Lamb, Coleridge, and most audiences over the centuries – have seen *Lear* played involved a mode of theatrical representation fundamentally different from that within which the King's Men and Shakespeare worked and *Lear* came into being.

In fact, from 1681 until 1823 all who saw performances of *Lear* watched an adaptation by Nahum Tate that, among other changes, omitted the Fool and ended with Lear and Cordelia triumphant and Cordelia and Edgar betrothed. Thus, for a period of almost one hundred and fifty years – nearly half the life of *Lear* – the response to the challenge of *Lear* was to alter what audiences saw. During that span, actors performed and audiences preferred an ending less heartrending than *Lear* provides. That long-enduring preference for playing Tate's adaptation testifies to a deep cultural consensus expressed in responses such as that voiced in 1765 by Samuel Johnson, one of the first editors of Shakespeare's plays: 'I was many years ago so shocked by Cordelia's death, that I know not whether I ever endured to read again the last scenes of the play till I undertook to revise [re-read] them as editor'.

Tate's adaptation and the triumph of the pictorial mode of representation forcefully demonstrate that what and how audiences see during performances of *Lear* has changed over the centuries. Amidst such vast changes, however, certain facets of the theatrical experience *Lear* provides have remained constant. The reader reads alone. 'Once again, this fierce dispute . . . Must I burn through', Keats says. '*I*', not 'we'. Theatre audiences, on the other hand, consist of individuals, each watching with his or her own eyes, who see together, in one another's presence. *Lear* draws upon the fact that today, as when the King's Men first played it, theatrical seeing is communal, collective. *Lear* emphasises that the capacity to bear the agonies living brings is greater when suffering is shared – when 'grief hath mates, and bearing fellowship' (III.vi.105) – and it offers examples of such 'fellowship'.

The Fool and Kent elect to stay with Lear even during the night storm on the heath, and audiences see them bear what he bears. They also see Edgar choose to accompany his maimed father – 'Give me thy arm: / Poor Tom shall lead thee' (IV.i.77–8) – and bring him to the point where, at the imagined bottom of what is not a cliff at Dover, Gloucester is willing to continue to 'bear' the afflictions from which, an instant before, he sought release in suicide. Lear, reunited with Cordelia, says to her, 'You must bear with me . . . I am old and foolish' (IV.vii.83–4). His words ask her not only to put up with him as one who is 'old and foolish' but also to share with him what comes of, and with, being 'old and foolish'. He faces without despair the defeat of Cordelia's army precisely because he envisages that he and she – 'We two alone' (V.iii.9) – will, together, endure whatever comes. Unlike Gloucester, Lear never contemplates suicide. What loosens his grip on life is Cordelia's death and with it the prospect of having to endure without her.

Lear also uses the process of performance to bring such 'fellowship' of 'bearing' into being. Those who watch it performed enter into that fellowship as, together, they bear what the play calls upon them to feel and see. That, the play's final words insist, is less than what they have watched others endure: 'The oldest hath borne most: we that are young / Shall never see so much, nor live so long'. Since the Second World War, *Lear* has been performed with greater frequency than in previous eras, perhaps because such horrors as the forced collectivisation of the Soviet peasantry, the death camps of Nazi-dominated Europe, the air raids that incinerated Hamburg and Dresden, the nuclear bombings of Hiroshima and Nagasaki, and the killing fields of Kampuchea have made audiences more willing than earlier generations to face and endure, together, what the play demands of them. Indeed, it may be displacing *Hamlet* as the Shakespearean play that sees most deeply and profoundly into the human predicament. In 1990 *Lear*'s theatrical vitality reached a zenith; three major British acting companies mounted concurrent productions: the National Theatre, the Royal Shakespeare Company, and the Renaissance Company.

Differences between the earliest surviving versions of *Lear* – the Quarto of 1608 and the Folio of 1623 – suggest that changes in what audiences see were already occurring during the first decades of the play's existence. Quarto presents what it calls the '*True Chronicle Historie . . . of King Lear and his three daughters*' and claims it to be a record of a specific performance: 'As it was played before the Kings majestie at Whitehall upon S. Stephans night in Christmas Hollidayes' (26 December 1606). Folio, on the other hand, changes the genre, calling the play '*The Tragedie of King Lear*', and claims to offer it, not as it was performed on a given occasion, but as Shakespeare 'conceived' it. Audiences, like those on St Stephen's Night, 1606, who watch performances based on Quarto hear speeches and see actions and events not present in Folio, and vice versa. For example, the prophecy of the Fool that concludes Act III, Scene ii of Quarto is not present in Folio, and nor is the episode (III.vii) in which Lear, in his madness, imagines he is trying Goneril and Regan before a court composed of the Fool, Edgar disguised as the lunatic Poor Tom, and Kent disguised as Caius. Nearly three hundred lines that are present in Quarto *Lear* are not in Folio, while one hundred in Folio *Lear* are not in Quarto. Most editions of *Lear* widely used today follow the long-established practice of combining Quarto and Folio into a single composite playtext.[2] Such conflated editions in effect lift *Lear* out of time by denying the changes it underwent during its first years.

The opening moments of Quarto and Folio *Lear* offer clear examples of how differences between them affect what audiences see during a performance. In each, the dialogue that begins the play is cut short by Gloucester's announcement, 'The King is coming' (I.i.32). Quarto audiences see Lear and his court enter in the following fashion: '*Sound a Sennet, Enter one bearing a Coronet, then Lear, then the Dukes of Albany, and Cornwall, next Gonorill, Regan, Cordelia, with followers*'. The corresponding stage direction in Folio is significantly different: '*Sennet. Enter King Lear, Cornwall, Albany, Gonerill, Regan, Cordelia, and attendants*'. The most conspicuous difference involves the coronet, soon to be the centre of the audience's attention when Lear calls upon Cornwall and Albany to split it: 'This coronet part between you' (I.i.138). Quarto registers its importance by making it visually prominent; audiences see it, '*then Lear*', and '*next*' those that follow in his wake. Folio, however, does not. It makes no mention of the coronet.[3]

In both Quarto and Folio, Kent challenges Lear's decision to renounce Cordelia and divide what would have been her share of the kingdom between Albany and Cornwall. Lear, enraged, threatens Kent with physical violence, perhaps even drawing his sword to strike him. In Folio, two characters protest at what Lear is about to do, calling on him to 'forbeare':

LEAR: O Vassal! Miscreant.
ALB., COR:. Dear Sir forbeare.
KENT: Kill thy Physition, and thy fee bestow
    Upon the foule disease. . . .

Albany and the other character – Cornwall? Cordelia?[4] – may even take physical action, possibly interposing themselves between Lear and Kent or even holding Lear back. Lear, checked by their intervention, regains his composure and, reminding his outspoken counsellor of his allegiance, silences him by banishing him on pain of death. In Quarto, however, no onlookers intervene on Kent's behalf:

> LEAR: Vassall, recreant.
> KENT: Doe, kill thy Physician,
> And the fee bestow upon the foul disease.

Lear checks himself, perhaps in response to Kent's defiant willingness to die rather than stop telling Lear 'thou dost evil' (I.i.165), and – as in Folio – proceeds to order Kent's banishment.

Kent avoids injury on this occasion, but *Lear* subjects its characters to suffering that is not only emotional and mental but also – as the destruction of Gloucester's eyes demonstrates most appallingly – corporeal, inflicted upon and felt by their bodies. The degree of bodily anguish *Lear* makes its characters endure and its audiences witness sets it apart from Shakespeare's other plays, most specifically *Othello*, its immediate predecessor, and *Hamlet*, which vies with it for the status of Shakespeare's greatest play. Othello becomes metaphorically blind to the truth of Desdemona's love and fidelity, much as Lear refuses to see Cordelia's love and loyalty; Gloucester, manoeuvred by Edmund much as Othello is manoeuvred by Iago, loses sight of Edgar's love and loyalty. Othello, however, endures no physical hardship like Lear's exposure on the heath to the raging night storm and no ocular maiming like that inflicted on Gloucester. Hamlet speaks of the world in which he finds himself as 'an unweeded garden / That grows to seed' (I.ii.135–6) and as a 'sterile promontory' in a 'firmament' that is 'nothing . . . but a foul and pestilent congregation of vapours' (II.ii.295–9). Characters in *Lear*, by contrast, use comparisons that stress the pain of being in and of this world, pain to which humans instinctively respond, Lear tells Gloucester, by wawling 'the first time that we smell the air. . . . When we are born, we cry that we are come / To this great stage of fools' (IV.vi.177–81). Awakened from what in his confusion he thinks is the sleep of death, Lear says, 'I am bound / Upon a wheel of fire, that mine own tears / Do scald like molten lead' (IV.vii.46–8). Kent, speaking in the presence of Lear's corpse and Cordelia's, likens what

Lear has endured to being stretched 'upon the rack of this tough world' (V.iii.313). A moment during Lear's reunion with Cordelia provides a pointedly non-metaphorical illustration of the significance of physical pain. Disoriented after being awakened, Lear seeks to determine whether he is alive or dead: 'let's see; / I feel this pin prick' (IV.vii.55–6). That self-inflicted prick confirms that, in the universe *Lear* asks audiences to look upon, what distinguishes the living from the dead is the capacity to feel pain.

The pinprick that (the actor playing) Lear (seemingly) inflicts on his own flesh is one example of how *Lear* takes advantage of the fundamental theatrical fact that during performance audiences (but not readers) see living actors using their bodies – facial expressions, gestures, voices, movements, posture – as part of a process of representation that is not only verbal but also corporeal. *Lear* audiences repeatedly see characters injure their own flesh and blood – both metaphorically in what they do to those who are their parents, childrens, or siblings, and literally in the damage they inflict upon their own bodies. To make his design to displace and destroy his brother Edgar more effective, Edmund wounds his own flesh, commenting derisively, 'I have seen drunkards / Do more than this in sport' (II.i.34–5). To save his life, Edgar, who disguises himself by removing, rather than changing, clothing, does to his bare flesh what the 'Bedlam beggars' he seeks to imitate do to theirs: 'Strike in their numb'd and mortified bare arms / Pins, wooden pricks, nails, sprigs of rosemary' (II.iii.14, 15–16). Lear's words to Goneril make explicit the fact that parent and child are of one flesh, one blood:

> . . . thou art my flesh, my blood, my daughter;
> Or rather a disease that's in my flesh,
> Which I must needs call mine: thou art a boil,
> A plague-sore, or embossed carbuncle,
> In my corrupted blood.
>
> (II.iv.219–23)

Eyeing Edgar disguised as nearly-naked Poor Tom, Lear links their predicaments – 'What! has his daughters brought him to this pass?' – and pronounces what Edgar has done to his body to be 'Judicious punishment' because ' 'twas this flesh begot / Those pelican daughters' (III.iv.62, 73–4). Later in the scene, Lear tries to inflict equally 'judicious punishment' on his own flesh by stripping off his royal attire and exposing his body, like Edgar's, to the storm and the cold: 'Off, off, you lendings! Come; unbutton here' (III.iv.106–7). The final scene drives home the correspondence between self-inflicted injuries and the wrongs that brothers and sisters, as well as parents and children, do to (those who are) their own flesh and blood. Audiences see one brother mortally wound another and learn that one sister has fatally poisoned another, then killed herself.

By interweaving the stories of Lear's family and Gloucester's, *Lear* establishes that what transpires, which includes acts of extraordinary malevolence and of equally extraordinary love, has origins not simply in the individual personalities of family members but also in the very structure of the family, in the relationships that constitute it. The play insists upon a terrifying truth at the core of the relatedness that helps make us human. We are most vulnerable to those from whom we most want to receive and to whom we most want to give love, to those whose flesh and blood we share: our parents, our children, our brothers and sisters, our spouses. Our vulnerability to them is, simultaneously, a vulnerability to ourselves – to our need for love and our appetites for power and pleasure.

The situations in *Lear* are archetypal, capable of stirring the deepest reverberations: vicious, ultimately mortal sibling rivalry, wilful rejection by an all-powerful parent, malevolent mistreatment in old age by one's own children. Lear's rebuke of Cordelia, for example, makes explicit the grounds for parental rejection that, psychiatrists and psychologists tell us, is among our most profound childhood fears: 'Better thou / Hadst not been born than not t' have pleased me better' (I.i.232–3). The play also has elements of a folktale or a parable: two wicked older sisters stand juxtaposed to a good youngest sister, an older and virtuous son to an evil and illegitimate younger half-brother, whom Folio's speech-headings, after the first scene, identify simply as '*Bastard*'. *Lear*'s demonstration of the human capacity for evil is among the most striking that Western art has produced, yet the play also offers equally striking demonstrations of the human capacity to do good, to act virtuously.

Even as it presents compelling examples of those antithetical capacities, *Lear* insists that they overlap and interpenetrate, complicating and challenging the moral clarity of folk-tale and parable. Cordelia, the faithful daughter, says, 'Nothing, my lord' (I.i.86) when her father asks what she will say to gain her share of the kingdom, and Edmund, the malevolent son, begins implementing his wicked plan with the same words, replying 'Nothing, my Lord' when his father asks what he has been reading (I.ii.31). Lear, the rejecting father, echoes Cordelia's 'nothing' when, rejected by Goneril and Regan, he is exposed on the heath to the fury of the storm: 'I will be the pattern of all patience; / I will say nothing' (III.ii.37–8). Edmund sighs 'like Tom o'Bedlam' (I.ii.133) to convince Edgar of his sincerity, and Edgar, to survive the mortal danger in which Edmund's duplicity puts him, disguises himself as a Bedlam beggar named Poor Tom. Gloucester wrongs his son Edgar yet is capable of exemplary fidelity to 'the King, my old master', whose plight he is determined to relieve even if 'I die for it' (III.iii.17–18). It costs him his eyes.

Wronged by his father, Edgar nevertheless comes to his aid after Regan and Cornwall have maimed him. However, even after hearing Gloucester say, 'Oh! dear son Edgar . . . Might I but live to see thee in my touch, / I'd say I had eyes again' (IV.i.21–4), Edgar does not disclose his identity. By continuing to pose as Poor Tom, Edgar denies Gloucester the kind of seeing he longs to have now that Cornwall and Regan have destroyed his eyes. Thus, *Lear* compels audiences to look on as the faithful son who truly loves Gloucester keeps him from having his 'eyes again' and, in the very act of helping his father, metaphorically blinds him. Edmund's impulse to do 'some good' by saving Cordelia and Lear further demonstrates the perplexing conflation of goodness and evil in *Lear*. It comes as, dying himself, Edmund looks upon the corpses of Goneril and Regan, and it springs from the knowledge that both sisters loved him: 'Yet Edmund was belov'd' (V.iii.238). The love that prompts him to do good, however, is, in Goneril's case especially, far from virtuous. Her love for him is not only adulterous but also murderous and suicidal: 'The one the other poison'd for my sake, / And after slew herself' (V.iii.239–40).

For many who across the centuries have seen *Lear* performed, or read its words, Cordelia epitomises the faithful daughter who serves and loves her father despite his mistreatment of her. Lear wilfully rejects her, yet she comes to his aid with an army. Reunited with the father who vowed never to look upon her again, she forgives him without reservation, insisting she has 'No cause, no cause' (IV.vii.75) to revenge the wrongs he now acknowledges he has inflicted upon her. For those who see Cordelia in such exemplary terms, the bond that forms between father and daughter during their heartbreaking reunion and makes itself felt even after her death in the grief that wracks Lear, is a profoundly moving affirmation of the extraordinary power of human love – of its capacity not only to withstand and transcend but even to redeem what the world inflicts on humankind and what humans inflict on one another, especially those whom they most love and by whom they most want to be loved.

If *Lear* offers such an affirmation, however, it comes about in a way that blurs what Cordelia insists is a fundamental difference between her and her sisters. 'Why', she asks Lear, 'have my sisters husbands, if they say / They love you all?', then adds, 'Happily, when I shall wed, / That lord whose hand must take my plight shall carry / Half my love with him, half my care and duty' (I.i.98–101). She concludes by declaring confidently, 'Sure I shall never marry like my sisters, / To love my father all' (I.i.102–3).[5] That, however, is exactly what comes to pass. She accepts the King of France as her husband in the opening scene, but audiences never again see them together. Her efforts to assist Lear involve her in events that overwhelm any effort to balance her obligations and affections as wife and as daughter. Lear becomes the focus of 'all' Cordelia's 'care and duty' once they are reunited. Unlike her sisters, Cordelia refuses to give Lear the words he wants to hear, refuses to tell him she loves him 'all', but she gives her life for him. In death, she gives Lear 'all', not 'half', her love. Audiences and readers alike mourn for her not as France's wife but as the most loving and most loved of her father's daughters.

When Lear enters '*with Cordelia dead in his arms*', he is howling in grief. 'She's gone for ever', he declares, 'She's dead as earth', but then, struggling to cope with the agony of his loss, he tries to convince himself that she is not dead: 'This feather stirs; she lives! if it be so, / It is a chance which does redeem all sorrows / That ever I have felt' (V.iii.258–60, 264–6). But it is no 'so'. Although Lear repeats that process of insisting upon and then denying the reality of Cordelia's death, she 'never' returns to life, and his sorrows remain unredeemed. At one point, Lear, perhaps bending down to her, asks, 'What is't thou say'st?' then praises her voice as one that 'was ever soft, / Gentle and low, an excellent thing in woman' (V.iii.271–2). His words accentuate the fact that audiences do not now hear the voice he praises. They twice heard her say 'Nothing' in the opening scene when Lear looked for words from her lips, but now hear her say nothing at all. She is, and she remains – despite her father's anguished hopes – speechless, 'dead as earth'. In *Othello*, Desdemona revives momentarily and, by claiming with her last words that she alone is responsible for her own death, provides a final demonstration

of her love for and fidelity to Othello. Cordelia, however, does not
revive, not even long enough for audiences to have the satisfaction
of hearing her exchange words of love and farewell with the father
who pleads for her to 'stay a little' (V.iii.30–2). 'Why', Lear asks,
'should a dog, a horse, a rat, have life, / And thou no breath at all?'
(V.iii.305–6). No one even tries to voice an answer.

The presence of Cordelia's corpse and what Lear says about it
pose still another challenge to how theatre audiences see. The
'corpse' they look upon is actually the living body of an actress (in
Jacobean times a boy actor), who cannot maintain the absolute
stillness of a corpse, if only because she (he) must breathe. Audiences
typically engage in miscognition that allows them to disregard such
signs of vitality, but Lear's words direct attention to them. Lamenting
that Cordelia is 'dead as earth', he looks for breath that will mist a
mirror or move a feather and, in Folio, for something from her lips.
Thus, all in the audience have their attention drawn to those signs
of vitality, and at least some in the audience (but no reader) will see
in the performer playing Cordelia the signs of life that Lear seeks.
Those who do must discount the testimony of their eyes if they are
to accept what the play insists is its truth: Cordelia is dead. They
must deny the life they see in the performer as they watch Lear
struggle to deny the death he sees in his most beloved daughter.

Lear's death is among the most moving moments in all of Shakespeare's plays, but it is sharply different in Quarto and Folio versions
of the play. In both, Lear insists that Cordelia is dead and will 'come
no more' and then drives home the point by repeatedly saying 'never'
– three times in Quarto, five times in Folio. He asks, 'pray you undo
this button', and thanks whoever carries out that request: 'thanke you
sir'. In Quarto, he then faints, groaning – 'O, o, o, o'. When Edgar
tries to revive him, Lear, with his final words, asserts his desire to
die: 'Breake hart, I prethe break'. In Folio, however, Lear does not
faint after thanking whoever has undone the button. Instead, he continues speaking: 'Do you see this? Looke on her? Looke her lips, /
Looke there, looke there'. Those words are followed by the stage direction '*He dies*'. In Folio, which is the version most modern editions
follow at this point, Lear, unlike his counterpart in Quarto, expires
with his attention focused upon Cordelia, still looking, perhaps, for
evidence of life in her and convinced, possibly, that he sees it.

The deaths of Lear and Cordelia are parts of an ending that sets
Lear apart from all other Shakespearean tragedies, in which the

survivors carry on in a society where lines of authority are clear and firm and the basic institutions and fundamental structures of political order are intact. *Hamlet*, for example, ends with the entire royal family of Denmark dead but with the institution of kingship intact; Fortinbras, a foreign (Norwegian) prince, claims the vacant throne of Denmark for himself. At the end of *Othello*, *Lear*'s immediate predecessor, Cassio is in place as Othello's successor as 'lord governor' (V.ii.368) of Cyprus, and Iago, defiantly silent, is in his custody. Lodovico, the emissary of Venice, is about to sail from Cyprus in order to 'relate' 'to the state' what has happened. The deeds he will report may appall the Duke and Senators of Venice, but, confined to the island outpost of Cyprus, they pose no threat to Venice itself. The end of *Macbeth*, written directly after *Lear*, stresses the restoration of a proper political order. Not only is the regicidal Macbeth dead, but '*All*' now hail as the new 'King of Scotland' (V.ix.25) Malcolm, the oldest son of the man Macbeth killed to become king.

Lear, in contrast, calls upon its audience to watch events that end with what Albany calls 'the gor'd state' (V.iii.319) damaged to such an extent that neither the structure nor the location of political authority is fixed or firm. The scene in which Gloucester loses his eyes powerfully demonstrates the systemic breakdown of social and political order. Regan and Cornwall declare Gloucester a traitor because he succours 'the King my old master' in violation of their command forbidding him to 'in any way sustain him' (III.iii.5–6). In the divided Britain over which Lear has chosen not to rule, loyalty to the king has become grounds for treason, and the judicial processes emphasised in *Othello* are trampled upon. *Lear* audiences see Gloucester, bound to a chair, tortured, interrogated, and hideously maimed, not tried in accord with what Cornwall dismissively calls 'the form of justice' (III.vii.25).[6] Cornwall and Regan violate the code of hospitality, which Gloucester futilely invokes when Regan yanks hairs from his beard: 'I am your host: / With robbers' hands my hospitable favours / You should not ruffle thus' (III.vii.39–41). As Cornwall moves to put out Gloucester's remaining eye, one of his own servants tries to stop him, violating the principle of subordination to one's master. In the ensuing struggle, audiences see that unnamed servant mortally wound his master, a prince of the realm who rules half of Britain. They also see Regan, not Cornwall, slay the rebellious servant, stabbing him with the sword of one of the male bystanders, none of whom moves to intervene. She is the only Shakespearean woman who kills unassisted and with her own hands.

The 'future strife' that Lear seeks to forestall in the opening scene by making public 'now' 'our daughters' several dowers' (I.i.43–4) comes to pass in the last act, which includes a battle that combines elements of a civil war and a foreign invasion. As that battle begins, Edgar tells Gloucester to 'pray that the right may thrive' (V.ii.2), but for that to happen Cordelia's French forces fighting on Lear's behalf must defeat a British army – a situation that sets nationalistic values in opposition to moral values. 'Right' does not thrive, however; Cordelia's army is defeated, and she is hung. Albany offers to return to Lear the 'absolute power' (V.iii.299) that he now wields as sole survivor of those commanding the victorious army and of those among whom Lear initially divided his united kingdom, but Lear, his attention fixed upon Cordelia's corpse, does not respond.

Even after Lear dies, Albany does not assume 'absolute power'. Instead, repeating Lear's earlier division of the kingdom, he seeks to divide royal authority in Britain, calling for Kent and Edgar to rule jointly: 'Friends of my soul, you twain / Rule in this realm [Quarto: kingdom], and the gor'd state sustain' (V.iii.318–19). Kent refuses, insisting in both playtexts that his obligation is not to the state but to his 'master' (V.iii.321), whom he must join in death. In Quarto, Edgar says nothing in reply to Albany's offer. Faced with that silence, Albany speaks the final words of the play:

> The weight of this sad time we must obey;
> Speak what we feel, not what we ought to say,
> The oldest have borne most, we that are young,
> Shall never see so much, nor live so long.

Edgar's silence in the Quarto is open. It does not rule out the possibility that, with an appropriate gesture, he wordlessly accepts responsibility for 'the gor'd state', but, equally, it does not make his acceptance a certainty.

Folio ends with virtually the same words – 'The oldest have borne most' becomes 'Hath borne most' – but it is Edgar, not Albany, who voices them. What the Folio has Edgar say, however, is as open to different possibilities – as ambiguous – as his silence in Quarto. Is Edgar voicing a reluctant willingness to accept the responsibility of rule when he speaks of obeying the time? Is he calling for Albany himself to 'obey' the time and accept, not shirk, the responsibility that is solely his now that – with the deaths of Cornwall, Regan, Goneril, Cordelia, and Lear – 'absolute power' has passed into his hands? Or, given the repetition of 'we', is Edgar calling for the two of them to share that responsibility? Spoken by Albany as Quarto specifies, the last words of *Lear* are equally ambiguous. When he speaks of obeying the time, he may be voicing his own acceptance of responsibility he prefers not to have and has tried to shun, but can no longer avoid. He may also be re-stating his call for the silent Edgar to rule the realm. Or, again because of the repeated 'we', he may be offering to share the responsibility with Edgar. In each instance, Edgar remains silent.

Does *Lear* end with a single person ruling the realm – and if so, is that person Edgar or Albany? Does it end with those two men sharing power and thus prolonging the division Lear inflicts on a united Britain? Does it end with no one willing to assume responsibility for 'the gor'd state'? Different productions of *Lear* across the centuries have answered such questions differently, with a good number opting to end with Edgar reluctantly accepting 'absolute power'. The noteworthy point, however, is that no other Shakespearean play even poses such questions, even asks its audiences to face events so cataclysmic, so apocalyptic that there is even a possibility that the structures of political authority do not survive.

If any political order exists at the end of *Lear*, it is not one that – as in *Othello* – has survived intact the storms loosed upon it but one that must be reconstructed from the debris of a shattered state. That reconstruction, if it occurs, is not presented as the re-emergence of an underlying natural order as in *Macbeth* or as the fulfillment of an overarching providential design as in *Hamlet*. It is the product of pained human choice and weary effort. There is no sense at the end of *Lear* of the start of a new and better era. No one proclaims, 'peace lives again' (V.v.40) as Henry Tudor does at the end of *Richard III* after triumphing in a battle that concludes two generations of civil war. No one declares, as Macduff does at the end of *Macbeth*, following a campaign in which foreign (English) troops have joined Scotsmen to overthrow Macbeth, 'the time is free' (V.ix.21). What one hears instead in the final words of *Lear* – whoever speaks them and whatever they mean – is deep exhaustion and the strain of turning to face the future: 'we that are young / Shall never see so much, nor live so long'. Audiences at performances of Peter Brook's 1962 production

for the Royal Shakespeare Company heard something else as well:
the faint rumble of thunder as a new storm gathered.

To some, if not many, in the Globe audiences who first saw *Lear*
performed, its ending must have been especially shocking because
the events they found themselves watching contradicted the outcome
of the story of Lear and his daughters as they already knew it in a
variety of modes: historical, poetic, and theatrical.[7] In all of the many
earlier versions of that story, Cordelia's forces win the climactic battle
and Lear regains the throne of a reunited Britain. More familiar than
later generations with those other versions, Jacobean audiences were
in a position to register the extent to which the ending of *Lear* is
gratuitous, even arbitrary, in the sense that nothing in the Lear story
as it came down to the King's Men compelled them to have their play
end with Cordelia and Lear defeated and dead. In effect, the King's
Men and their playwright chose to make that story their own by
doing violence to its ending so that it became something fundamentally different from what it had been. They fashioned that story into
a play that the Folio could call a tragedy. Many are prone to denounce the changes Tate made in *Lear* as violations, but his changes
are no more extreme than those that *Lear* inflicts upon its sources.
Ironically, in resisting the challenge that *Lear* poses and fashioning a
happy ending, Tate's adaptation proved (perhaps unknowingly) less
untrue to the play's sources than *Lear* itself.

The ending of *Lear* may be the result of Shakespeare's individual
genius or even of the collective genius of the King's Men, but it may
also reflect the impact of a major controversy during the early years
of James's reign as king of England. Among his first acts after
ascending the English throne in 1603 was to issue a 'Proclamation
for the uniting of England and Scotland', a union he saw as already
implicit in his person as the king of both nations, and in a speech to
his first Parliament, James declared,

> I am the Husband and the whole Isle is my lawfull Wife; I am
> the Head, and it is my Body . . . I hope therefore no man will
> be so unreasonable as to think that I . . . should be a polygamist
> and husband to two wives; that I being the Head should have a
> divided and monstrous body. (McIlwain, 1918, p. 272)

In the same year, he assumed the title 'King of Great Britain'. James
envisaged a single kingdom arising from the union of Scotland and

England that would restore the legendary kingdom of Britain and undo its subsequent fragmentation into Wales, Scotland, and England. His cherished Project for Union met resistance in both England and Scotland, and during 1606, the year in which *Lear* was played before James and his court at Whitehall on St Stephen's night, the king several times rebuked the English Parliament for not moving swiftly to implement the union of the kingdoms. In the cultural circumstances within which *Lear* came into being and was initially played (at least once before James himself[8]), it may well have functioned as a 'dramatization of the perils of division' (Marcus, 1988, p. 148). By ending with Lear and Cordelia dead and with the issue of who, if anyone, will rule the realm not clearly resolved, the *Lear* of Shakespeare and the King's Men emphasises the difficulty and uncertainty of re-establishing unity once it is shattered. Subsequent history attests to that difficulty. James's Project for Union was stalemated, and within two decades of his death in 1625, England was 'gor'd' by civil war. England and Scotland remained distinct until 1707 when, with the Act of Union, they became a united kingdom like the one that James sought and Lear fractured.

5

Macbeth: 'Double, Double'

Macbeth, the shortest of Shakespearean tragedies, begins unlike any other. It opens not with an entrance followed by a chorus or dialogue but with stage effects, '*Thunder and lightning*', that have far greater impact on theatre audiences than on readers. Amidst those stage effects, audiences see three figures enter – as they do in the opening moments of *King Lear*, which begins, far more typically, with Kent, Gloucester, and Edmund entering unaccompanied by any stage effects. The three figures who enter in *Macbeth*, however, are witches, not two earls affiliated with Lear's court and the illegitimate son of one of them.

Like *King Lear*, which may have been its immediate predecessor among the series of six tragedies Shakespeare provided for the King's Men from 1604 through 1608, *Macbeth* takes advantage of the seeing in which theatre audiences engage during a performance. It denies them any sight of the killing of Duncan, thereby forcing them to envisage for themselves what is happening behind the door leading to the chamber where Duncan sleeps. In effect, the play uses their powers of imagination to implicate them in the assassination. The combat in which Macduff kills Macbeth is another example of how the play exploits theatrical seeing. In four of Shakespeare's six Jacobean tragedies, the protagonist is a warrior, but, unlike Othello, Antony, and Coriolanus, Macbeth alone dies fighting: 'before my body / I throw my warlike shield: lay on, Macduff; / And damn'd be him that first cries, "Hold, enough!" ' (V.viii.32–4).

The presentation of the ensuing combat is even more unusual than the opening of the play. Stage directions specify that audiences should see Macbeth and Macduff engaging in two distinct sequences of fighting, not one continuous sequence: '*Exeunt, fighting. Alarums. Re-enter fighting, and Macbeth slain.*' The dramaturgy of this stage combat

108

takes the risk of requiring audiences to look at a stage empty of all
characters while '*Alarums*' sound – an interval of unspecified duration
that can vary from sustained to brief. Taking that risk in order to
have audiences see two fight sequences when one would have
sufficed is the most extreme example of the importance in *Macbeth* of
the phenomenon of doubleness. Doubleness manifests itself not only
in the presentation of Macbeth's death but also in the words characters speak and their tellingly equivocal meanings, in correspondences
between characters and events, in the casting practices of the Jacobean era, and in how audiences perceive and respond to the play.

The word 'double', in its various forms, appears more often in
Macbeth than in any other play we call Shakespeare's. The bleeding
Captain uses it first while reporting how Banquo and Macbeth
reacted to the Norwegian king's 'fresh assault': 'they were / As can-
nons overcharg'd with double cracks; / So they / Doubly redoubled
strokes upon the foe' (I.ii.33, 36–9). 'Double' occurs again in the
duplicitous welcome Lady Macbeth extends to Duncan. 'All our
service,' she says,

> In every point twice done, and then done double,
> Were poor and single business to contend
> Against those honours deep and broad wherewith
> Your Majesty loads our house . . .
>
> (I.vi.14–18)

'Twice done, and then done double', by echoing the Captain's
'doubly redoubled', aligns the battlefield where blood has been shed
to keep Duncan king with the castle in which his blood will be shed to
make Macbeth king. Lady Macbeth's welcome is also 'double' in that
it is simultaneously both sincere and insincere. It is insincere because,
far from being the gracious hostess, she is resolved that Duncan will
not leave the castle alive: 'O! never / Shall sun that morrow see!'
(I.v.60–1). It is sincere because she is indeed delighted by 'the fatal
entrance of Duncan / Under my battlements' (I.v.39–40).

Macbeth himself uses the word 'double' on several occasions.
During the scene immediately after Lady Macbeth welcomes Duncan as a guest, he hesitates to shed Duncan's blood, in part because

> He's here in double trust:
> First, as I am his kinsman and his subject,

> Strong both against the deed; then, as his host,
> Who should against his murtherer shut the door,
> Not bear the knife myself.
>
> (I.vii.12–16)

After the first appparition warns, 'beware Macduff', Macoeth takes comfort in the second apparition's revelation that 'none of woman born / Shall harm Macbeth' (VI.i.71, 80–1). 'Then live, Macduff: what need I fear of thee?' he reasons, before, using 'double' a second time, he resolves to kill him anyway: 'But yet I'll make assurance double sure, / And take a bond of Fate: thou shalt not live' (IV.i.82–4). Macbeth uses 'double' a final time after Macduff reveals that he was 'from his mother's womb / Untimely ripp'd' (V.viii.15–16). Now aware of how the apparitions' revelations can be true in ways he had not foreseen, Macbeth declares, 'And be these juggling fiends no more believ'd, / That palter with us in a double sense' (V.viii.19–20).

Just as Lady Macbeth speaks 'doubly' when welcoming Duncan, so the witches, through the apparitions, speak 'doubly' to Macbeth, using words that convey truths other than or in addition to those that seem most obvious. They do so, fittingly, in a scene during which they themselves use the word 'double' in the twice-repeated refrain of the chant with which they prepare the cauldron and its loathsome ingredients: 'Double, double toil and trouble: / Fire, burn; and, cauldron bubble' (IV.i.10–11, 20–1, 35–6).

Speaking 'in a double sense' is akin to 'equivocation', a species of duplicity involving statements worded ambiguously enough to be true (and not true) in different, even contradictory ways. The messenger's report that as he 'look'd toward Birnam ... The wood began to move' (V.v.34–5) drives Macbeth to reconsider what he took to be the witches' assurance of his invulnerability: 'I pull in resolution; and begin / To doubt th'equivocation of the fiend, / That lies like truth' (V.v.42–4). Macbeth's reference to 'equivocation' echoes the Porter who, wakened by knocking, imagines himself welcoming men to hell, among them 'an equivocator, that could swear in both the scales against either scale; who committed treason enough for God's sake, yet could not equivocate to heaven: O! come in, equivocator' (II.iii.8–12).

When *Macbeth* was first played, probably in 1606, 'equivocation' was very likely a highly charged issue for its initial audiences because of the word's association with the Gunpowder Plot of 5 November

1605, which aimed at killing in a single massive explosion not only King James and the entire royal family but also what James himself, addressing Parliament, called 'the whole Body of the State in general': 'the whole Nobilitie, the whole Reverend Clergie, Bishops and most part of the good Preachers, the most part of the Knights and Gentrie . . . the whole Judges of the land, with most of the lawyers and the whole Clerkes' (McIlwain, 1918, p. 282). One of those charged with treason in the Plot, a priest named Garnett, justified the lies he was caught in by insisting that he had the right to equivocate. Garnett may have been the 'equivocator' original audiences thought of when the Porter welcomes one to hell.

More than the Gunpower Plot binds *Macbeth* to James, England's Scottish king, one of whose first acts on the English throne was to make Shakespeare's acting company his by renaming them the King's Men. In 1600 James had narrowly escaped an attempt on his life by the Earl of Gowrie, his host, and he traced his lineage back to Banquo, of whom the witches prophesy, 'Thou shalt get kings, though thou be none' (I.iii.67).

From the moment of its atypical opening, *Macbeth* gives the witches a prominence that is consistent with James's own interest in witchcraft. In the early 1590s he authorised a series of trials in Scotland to root out witches, and his writings include a work on witchcraft, *Daemonologie* (1599). The witches in *Macbeth* serve several functions. One is that, affiliated with all that is considered unholy, ungodly, and unnatural, they embody the spectre of a world in which women rule over men (as Elizabeth did in England from 1558 to 1603).

They also serve, however, to define and legitimate the male-dominated social and political order of which they are the antithesis – one in which a king possesses power and authority, ruling over his subjects as God rules over his creatures, fathers rules over their families, and husbands over their wives. The final apparition the witches summon for Macbeth is '*A show of eight Kings, the last with a glas in his hand*; BANQUO *following*' (IV.i.111). That '*show*' foresees the fulfillment of the prophecy that Banquo will beget kings. Macbeth's fear that the line of Banquo's royal progeny will 'stretch out to th' crack of doom' (IV.i.117) alludes to what James emphasised as a major difference between the childless Elizabeth and himself: his potency in siring sons and thus beginning a line of kings who would prevent disputes over succession like those that had troubled England under Elizabeth. Some of the monarchs reflected in the '*glas*' (mirror) carried by the eighth king hold 'two-fold balls and treble sceptres' (IV.i.121), thus signifying the double kingship James gained when, with Elizabeth's death in 1603, he became the first person to be sovereign of England as well as Scotland.

Their '*show*' completed, the witches disappear from the play, and Macbeth later denounces the 'equivocation' by which they 'lie like truth', but for the play's first audiences, James's kingship demonstrated the truth in history of what the witches prophesy about Banquo's progeny and what they show to Macbeth. Thus, in the early Jacobean era, the witches functioned as figures that affirm the providential validity of the rule of the King's Men royal patron, James VI of Scotland and James I of England. The '*glas*' carried by the eighth king in the witches '*show*' allows Macbeth to see into a future that has not yet come into being, and those who watched the first performance of *Macbeth* found themselves looking into a theatrical mirror that allowed them to see far back into 'the seeds of time' (I.iii.58), to see what was to be their own present under James first coming into being.

The witches also function – much like the Prologue-Chorus of *Romeo and Juliet* – to accentuate the issue of the relationship between fate and choice in human affairs. Does Duncan's murder follow from a decision Macbeth is free to make, or is it an element in a predetermined pattern of events? Does the witches' prophecy of Macbeth's kingship instil desire for the crown that was not previously present, converting what has been true loyalty into treason, or does the prophecy voice a desire already lurking in a warrior and thane who only seems loyal? There was no agreement on the answers to such questions in the Jacobean era, when people were caught up in the debate between Catholics and Protestants over the role of free will and predestination in salvation, and there is none now among commentators on *Macbeth*. Agreeing on answers to them is less important than recognising that *Macbeth* poses them by means of a medium – theatrical performance – that is itself radically enmeshed in issues of freedom and predeterminism. Robert Hapgood notes that 'The illusion that the life of the play is, like real life, taking place before our eyes, at that very moment, is one of the most powerful of dramatic appeals' (1988, p. 33). What characters say and do and the events that unfold seem spontaneous and accidental, immersed in the flow of life in the very process of being lived. On the other hand, the playing that generates that illusion includes words, gestures, and actions that have been predetermined to the fullest extent that the script and rehearsals make possible. The fullest extent possible is not, however, total. Precisely because it involves living actors playing in the presence of living audiences, every theatrical performance, no matter how carefully rehearsed, has a capacity for the unexpected and unforeseen – for freedom and for change – that asserts itself via an improvised gesture or a spur-of-the-moment change in how a line or speech is delivered or even an actor's failure to remember his lines.

The issue of speaking 'in a double sense', of equivocating, surfaces in a more problematic form in the lament Macbeth voices after seeing Duncan's corpse for what he wants everybody to think is the first time:

> Had I but died an hour before this chance,
> I had liv'd a blessed time; for, from this instant,
> There's nothing serious in mortality;
> All is but toys: renown, and grace, is dead;
> The wine of life is drawn, and the mere lees
> Is left this vault to brag of.
>
> (II.iii.89–94)

The issue comes into focus if one asks whether Macbeth's words are true in the sense of expressing emotions he genuinely feels, arising from the moral revulsion he had to overcome in order to kill his king. If they are true, their truth is one element in a larger process of deception in that they foster the illusion that Macbeth is not the murderer, and that deception is, ironically, all the more effective because they are true. If, however, the words of Macbeth's lament are false, then they are a lie that, whether or not Macbeth realises it, becomes profoundly 'like truth'. Falsely uttered, his words speaking of the bitter emptiness of the days that lie ahead, of the worthlessness of continuing to live after Duncan's death, uncannily anticipate what he says and feels when told of his wife's death:

> To-morrow, and to-morrow, and to-morrow,
> Creeps in this petty pace from day to day,
> To the last syllable of recorded time;
> And all our yesterdays have lighted fools
> The way to dusty death. Out, out, brief candle!

> Life's but a walking shadow; a poor player,
> That struts and frets his hour upon the stage,
> And then is heard no more: it is a tale
> Told by an idiot, full of sound and fury,
> Signifying nothing.
>
> (V.v.19–28)

If Macbeth is lying in his lament for Duncan, it is a lie that is also, as Kenneth Muir comments, 'a precise description of the truth about himself . . . a brilliant counterpart to the equivocation of the fiend that lies like truth: it is the equivocation of the murderer who utters truth like lies' (1972b, p. xxviii). If false, Macbeth's words are part of a larger truth; if true, part of a larger falsehood. In either case, and in both cases, they have 'a double sense'.

The emotions Macbeth feels in response to his wife's death can vary widely both within the speech and from one production to another. Numbness, indifference, resignation, bitterness, love, despair, futility, grief, exhaustion, anger – those are among the more obvious possibilities. The moment can be extremely intense – so much so that it is often played (and referred to) as a soliloquy even though no stage direction calls for Seyton to exit after telling Macbeth, 'The Queen, my Lord, is dead' (V.v.16). At the same time, Macbeth's use of the metaphor of the world as a stage – 'Life's but a walking shadow, a poor player' – suffuses the moment with a specifically theatrical species of doubleness. The metaphor accentuates and takes advantage of what Stephen Booth terms 'the double experience of the audience, which always sees two things at once, actors on a stage and characters in a story' (1983, p. 92). The theatrical moment of which the metaphor is part involves audiences in a process of double awareness, double perception. As they attend to Macbeth speaking of himself as 'a poor player' on the stage of the world, they attend also to the actor playing him on the stage of the theatre in which they have gathered to watch a performance. If that theatre were the Globe, which reputedly displayed above its entrance the motto *totus mundus agit histrionem*, the circumstances of performance fostered that double awareness, emphasising that, as Michael Goldman puts it, 'a character in a play is something an actor *does*' (1985, p. 149). In contrast to the current practice of having audiences in relative darkness watching actors on a stage illuminated more fully, lighting at the Globe was uniform, shared alike by actors and audiences, who watched from three, if not four, sides of the thrust stage and perhaps sat on the stage as well. In such circumstances, anyone looking at the actor playing Macbeth, probably Richard Burbage, the star of the King's Men, would have seen others in the audience also looking at him.

The specifically theatrical mode of doubleness accentuated during Macbeth's response to Lady Macbeth's death also has a bearing on his lament at Duncan's murder. If that lament is false, audiences witness Macbeth, like a player, performing the part of the shocked, grieving thane loyal to the assassinated king whose bloodied corpse he has just beheld for the first time. If that lament is true, its truth registers in performance only to the extent that the actor playing Macbeth – to whom Duncan means no more than Hecuba does to the First Player in *Hamlet* – succeeds so well in feigning grief and shock in Macbeth that he convinces the audience of their validity.

A more straightforward example than that lament of Macbeth's capacity to lie 'like truth' is his explanation for killing the grooms attending Duncan:

> Who can be wise, amaz'd, temperate and furious,
> Loyal and neutral, in a moment? No man:
> Th'expedition of my violent love
> Outrun the pauser, reason.
>
> (II.iii.106–9)

The words are false. Killing the grooms, which completes the cover-up, is not an irrational act arising from Macbeth's uncontrollably 'violent love' for Duncan. However, the instantaneous movement, unchecked by rational thought, from impulse to act that Macbeth claims overwhelmed him on seeing Duncan's blood-stained grooms turns out to be precisely the mode of action he will commit himself to on two subsequent occasions. The first comes after Banquo's ghost has disrupted the banquet; 'Strange things I have in head,' Macbeth confides to his wife, 'that will to hand, / Which must be acted, ere they may be scann'd' (III.iv.135–9). Macbeth resolves a second time to 'outrun the pauser, reason' when, following his final encounter with the witches, he learns that Macduff has fled to England:

> Time, thou anticipat'st my dread exploits:
> The flighty purpose never is o'ertook,
> Unless the deed go with it. From this moment,

> The very firstlings of my heart shall be
> The firstlings of my hand. And even now,
> To crown my thoughts with acts, be it thought and
>   done. . . .
>
> (IV.i.144–9)

Since the Elizabethan–Jacobean era regarded reason as the faculty that defined humanity's distinctiveness as a species, Macbeth's twice-stated determination to convert his thoughts instantaneously into acts, his impulses immediately into deeds, violates that conception of human nature.

Macbeth's rejection of reason begins before the murder of Duncan, which he scrutinises with careful rationality. 'If it were done, when 'tis done, then 'twere well / It were done quickly,' he reasons, setting aside the claims of an after-life ('the life to come') and assessing the murder he is contemplating solely in terms of this temporal life, 'this bank and shoal of time' (I.vii.1–2, 7, 6). 'If' – a word all the more prominent because it begins both the scene and the soliloquy – establishes Macbeth's awareness that the deed will not in fact be completed ('done') when it is performed ('done'). 'Success', he knows, will not come with Duncan's 'surcease', and the 'blow' that kills him will not 'be the be-all and the end-all' (I.vii.4, 5). Even *if* that were not true, Macbeth continues, murdering Duncan makes no sense because whoever kills his king to become king offers 'Bloody instructions' teaching others to slay him in turn (I.vii.9). Thus, 'even-handed Justice', built into the very calculus of events, ensures that 'We still have judgment here' in this life even if, hazarding eternal damnation, 'We'd jump the life to come' (I.vii.10, 8, 7). Macbeth goes on to specify other reasons for not killing Duncan, including the 'double trust' upon him as Duncan's kinsman, subject, and host as well as Duncan's exemplary conduct as king:[1] 'his virtues / Will plead like angels, trumpet-tongu'd, against / The deep damnation of his taking-off . . .' (I.vii.12, 18–20).

Macbeth's soliloquy, like the action he analyses during it, is never 'done' in the sense of reaching completion because Lady Macbeth's entrance cuts it short, but Macbeth tells her the conclusion towards which his reasoning has led him: 'We will proceed no further in this business' (I.vii.31). The speech is also never 'done' in a second sense. Lady Macbeth talks him out of implementing it. It is not 'thought and done'. Macbeth's inability on this occasion to 'crown' what are rational 'thoughts with acts' leads to a murder whose consequences include the massacre of Macduff's family that occurs when Macbeth, implementing his resolve to obliterate his rationality, does 'crown my thoughts with acts'.

The scene ends with Macbeth assuring his wife, 'I am settled, and bend up / Each corporal agent to this terrible feat' (I.vii.80–1). Lady Macbeth moves him to undertake an act at odds with his reason (and his moral sensibility) principally by calling his manliness into question. 'From this time / Such I account thy love,' she tells him, then poses a question that associates his passion for her with his desire for the crown: 'Art thou afeard / To be the same in thine own act and valour, / As thou art in desire?' (I.vii.38–41). To his answer, 'I dare do all that may become a man; / Who dares do more is none', she counters,

> What beast was't then,
> That made you break this enterprise to me?
> When you durst do it, then you were a man;
> And, to be more than what you were, you would
> Be so much more the man.
>
> (I.vii.47–51)

Two meanings of 'man' overlap here; a 'man' is a human being, and a 'man' is a male. The exchange crystallises and juxtaposes two conflicting conceptions of what it means to be masculine (and therefore virile and courageous) and of what it means to be human – conceptions that different cultures reconcile differently and that a given culture reconciles differently at various moments in its history. One, voiced by Macbeth, equates being 'a man' with accepting and acting in accord with the norms and values that fix what actions are appropriate for a 'man' in either sense of the term. To do what does not befit ('become') a 'man' is to cease being one. The other, voiced by Lady Macbeth, equates being 'a man' with the willingness to violate those values and norms. To act 'to be more' than what one is is to be 'so much more the man' – more fully masculine and more fully human.

Within the dominant ideology of Shakespeare's time, which stressed the primacy of reason over passion and of husband over wife, Macbeth in this scene fails to be 'a man' in both senses of the term. He subverts the 'proper' relationship between spouses by allowing his wife to bend his actions to her will; and in permitting passions she arouses in him to override what reason tells him to do, he blurs the distinction between himself as a man endowed with reason and a 'beast' that has none. Ironically, by agreeing to perform the 'terrible feat' of murdering Duncan, Macbeth begins a process that will make him into the 'beast' Lady Macbeth accuses him of being after he resolves to 'proceed no further in this business'.

* * *

The murdering of Duncan points to another species of doubleness in *Macbeth*: the pairing of characters in partnership. Macbeth is paired with two 'partners', one male, the other female. The first, whose initial appearance in the play is also Macbeth's, is his fellow general Banquo, who, speaking to the witches, refers to Macbeth as 'my noble partner' (I.iii.54). The second is Lady Macbeth, whom Macbeth addresses as 'my dearest partner of greatness' (I.v.11) in his letter telling of the witches' predictions. Macbeth and Banquo are partners in defending Duncan, Macbeth and Lady Macbeth in killing him. Just as defending Duncan requires both Banquo and Macbeth, so murdering him is an act that neither Macbeth nor Lady Macbeth can carry out single-handedly. Left to himself, Macbeth would not do it; left to herself, Lady Macbeth could not do it, because, she says, the sleeping Duncan resembled her father. Each requires the other to kill Duncan, and doing it requires the two of them. Killing Duncan is a deed 'done double' in the sense that for it to be done, they must do it together, in tandem.

Macbeth proceeds to separate himself from both partners – a development that illustrates how the killing of the king puts all bonds between humans at risk, including, even, those that bind Macduff to his wife and children, whom he leaves defenceless when he flees to England. Macbeth arranges Banquo's murder in an effort to frustrate the witches' prediction that he will beget kings. The murder of Duncan makes Lady Macbeth her husband's partner in blood as well as 'greatness', but under the pressure of ensuing events and his own anxieties, Macbeth isolates himself from her. She has no role in Banquo's murder nor in the slaughter of Macduff's wife and family. When her husband and co-murderer enters after having arranged Banquo's murder, she asks, 'How now, my Lord? why do you keep alone . . . ?' (III.ii.8), and after Macbeth's response to the presence of

Banquo's ghost has disrupted the banquet, he vows, 'For mine own good, / All causes shall give way ...' (III.iv.134–5). Everything will be subordinated to '*mine* own good', not their mutual good. 'All causes' includes their relationship. Audiences never again see them onstage together.

The precise distribution of power, responsibility, and initiative between Lady Macbeth and Macbeth within the partnership that enables them to kill Duncan is the major variable that most clearly shows the impact on the play of changes in cultural values, especially those that, at a given moment, define what is appropriately masculine and feminine behaviour. The post-1660 conviction that heroes possessed an essential nobility and decency meant that the Macbeths of David Garrick and John Kemble were sympathetic figures driven to do evil by external influences. Each was paired with a Lady Macbeth – Mrs. Pritchard and Sarah Siddons, respectively – who was correspondingly fierce, cruel, ruthless. Marvin Rosenberg points out that 'one stage direction, in Garrick's edition, for his first meeting with her in I,v, has her *Embracing him*; what else we know of their relationship suggests that she must have collared the little man' (1978, p. 68). Nineteenth-century Macbeths were more resolute and villainous – men who freely chose to do murder of their own will – and their Lady Macbeths conformed to the prevailing Victorian conception of the wife as loving helpmate. According to Benedict Nightingale, that trend peaked in the 1880s when Ellen Terry 'seemed not merely to be voicing the unspoken wishes of Henry Irving's Macbeth but self-sacrificially taking from him the responsibility for Duncan's murder' (1988, p. 5).

Productions of the 1970s and 1980s, responsive to the sexual revolution of those decades, tended to make prominent the sexual elements in the bond between the Macbeths. In Trevor Nunn's 1974 production for the Royal Shakespeare Company, Helen Mirren's hold over Macbeth (Nicol Williamson) was 'unambiguously erotic':

> For her regicide was not just titillating in itself but a test of his virility. For Williamson, a prim counselor with an insecure male ego, it meant continued access to her favors. So, Lady Macbeth's first line after the killing, 'My husband!', was a cry of sexual jubilation. (Nightingale, 1988, p. 38)

Jane Lapotaire's Lady Macbeth in Jack Gold's 1983 production for the BBC-TV series 'The Shakespeare Plays' made her sexual power over Macbeth (Williamson again) especially vivid. Wearing a close-fitting gown, she lay on a bed during the 'unsexing' speech, writhing in arousal, and when she told Macbeth to 'Leave all the rest to me' (I.v.73), she pulled him to her on the same bed. The 1988 *Macbeth* starring Christopher Plummer and Glenda Jackson – in which three directors were involved at different times – combined eroticism and a measure of sexual equality. He seized her breasts and they kissed passionately when he entered in Act I, Scene v. However, Jackson's Lady Macbeth, unlike Mirren's, withered as events unfolded not simply because she was sexually isolated from Macbeth but also because she, Macbeth's 'dearest partner in greatness' who had been fully his equal in carrying out the murder, became less and less his full partner as he executed his subsequent plots.

The concept of partnership might well be relevant to how *Macbeth* came into being. Only one version of the play has come down to us from Shakespeare's era – that published in the 1623 Folio assembled by John Heminge and Henry Condell, fellow shareholders with Shakespeare in the King's Men. Over the centuries since then, various parts of the play, including the Porter Scene, have been attributed to playwrights other than Shakespeare and judged 'spurious'. The current consensus is that those parts of the play in which Hecate appears[2] are not Shakespeare's work, since they include two songs from *The Witch*, by Thomas Middleton, whom we know wrote plays performed by the King's Men. If the consensus is correct, then the *Macbeth* that Heminge and Condell chose to have published is itself the result of a collaborative effort and has its origins in a species of doubleness.

Macbeth also illustrates the advantages arising from another form of doubling: the practice of 'doubling' parts by casting the same actor in two (or more) roles. Ralph Berry points out that 'full casting – a different actor for each part – was an indulgence of the Victorian / Edwardian London stage, a demonstration of lavish production values' (1981, p. 204), which remains the norm in today's theatre. However, as Berry notes, 'Given a company of 15–16, the assumed strength of [the King's Men], extensive doubling was inevitable' (p. 204). Revived by Peter Brook in his 1970–1 production of *A Midsummer Night's Dream* for the Royal Shakespeare Company, 'doubling' parts has now, as it had in Shakespeare's day, the economic advantage of reducing the number of salaries to be paid as well as the logistical advantage of minimising the number of people involved when a company tours – as Shakespeare's did periodically, particularly when outbreaks of plague prompted authorities to close the London theatres.

While practical considerations may require that parts be doubled, doubling also offers what might be called theatrical advantages. It enables the most highly skilled actors to play not only major parts but also small parts, giving them status and impact they might otherwise not have. In addition, by encouraging audiences to perceive relationships between and among the different characters they see the same actor playing, doubling can 'inform, comment on, and, perhaps, augment the events enacted' (Booth, 1983, p. 134). Thus, the actor playing, say, Duncan, who, last seen entering Macbeth's castle, disappears from *Macbeth* even before his murder, could also play a number of other characters, including Siward, the general leading the English forces against Macbeth.

As one example of the advantages that doubling offers, consider what develops if the roles of Duncan and the Scottish doctor who observes Lady Macbeth as she walks in her sleep are doubled. Doubling those parts can make the sleepwalking scene all the more intense by encouraging audiences to associate the man who witnesses Lady Macbeth's guilt-ridden re-enactment of Duncan's murder with the king who was her victim. 'The old man' who 'had so much blood in him' (V.i.37–8) would be obliquely present, through the doctor, to the audience as he is to Lady Macbeth's troubled mind. Doubling Duncan and the Scottish doctor has the additional advantage of visually reinforcing the symmetry linking her last words and last appearance with the final words and final appearance of the king she helps to kill. Duncan's final lines in the play, spoken to Lady Macbeth, begin 'Give me your hand . . .' (I.vi.28), and her final lines, spoken as she walks in her sleep, include exactly the same words: 'Come, come, come, come, give me your hand' (V.i.63).

Macduff's entrance with Macbeth's severed head signifies the ending, the curing, of the agony inflicted upon Scotland when Macbeth metaphorically beheaded it by striking down Duncan. Separating Macbeth's head from his body frees the Scottish body politic of its tyrannical head and allows Macduff to salute Malcolm as the new head of state: 'Hail, King! for so thou art. Behold, where stands / Th'usurper's cursed head: the time is free' (V.ix.20–1). '*All*' then join in proclaiming Malcolm 'King of Scotland' (V.ix.24). Macbeth had declared himself ready to applaud the doctor 'to the very echo, / That should applaud again' (V.iii.53–4) if he can cure Scotland. Malcolm's speech concluding the play is his first act as king, and the applause that follows it conveys, at least in part, the audience's response to the prospect, perhaps even the fact, that Scotland is now restored 'to a sound and pristine health' (V.iii.52).

Macbeth also doubles events. The play includes two banquets, each hosted by Macbeth and his wife. The stage direction '*Enter, and pass over the stage, a Sewer* [chief steward], *and divers servants with dishes and service*' signals the first, which takes place before the guest of honour (Duncan) is murdered and occurs offstage, perhaps beyond the same entrance through which Macbeth passes to commit the murder. The second occurs onstage, after the murder of Banquo, whom Macbeth designates as 'our chief guest' (III.i.11). The cauldron scene, at which Macbeth is a self-invited guest, doubles both banquets. On the one hand, it replaces the standard rituals of cooking, eating, and drinking with alternatives that are distasteful, if not fiendish. This can be especially pronounced in performance if Macbeth eats or drinks what the witches concoct. On the other, the cauldron scene, especially because of the overtones of cannibalism (among the witches' ingredients are human parts: a liver, a nose, lips, and a finger) harks back to the banquets hosted by the Macbeths, each a perversion of the ideal of an ordered, loving, and sharing human community of which the banquet is usually a symbol. The Macbeths prey upon their principal guests, in effect consuming those who partake of their food and hospitality.

Other events are also doubled. The cauldron scene is the second of Macbeth's two encounters with the witches, and their two appearances with him are doubled by the two they make without him, giving them four appearances in all during the play. Lady Macduff receives two warnings of imminent peril – from Rosse and an unnamed messenger – and the play has two doctors, one English, the other Scottish. The latter makes two appearances: in the first he observes Lady Macbeth sleepwalking, while in the second he warns Macbeth that her illness, more psychic than physical, exceeds the scope of his art. Twice someone is singled out as a future king. The witches salute Macbeth as one 'that shalt be King hereafter' (I.iii.50), and in the ensuing scene Duncan designates as his successor 'our eldest, Malcom; whom we name hereafter / The Prince of Cumberland' (I.iv.38–9). Before the play ends, each becomes king 'hereafter'. Alarm bells ring on two occasions in this play. The first sounds at

Macduff's command after the discovery of the murder that will make Macbeth king: 'Ring the alarum-bell' (II.iii.73). The second sounds at Macbeth's command ('Ring the alarum bell' – V.v.51) after he learns that Birnam wood is moving against Dunsinane as the powers arrayed against him advance under the cover of foliage – as if in alliance with nature itself – towards a battle that will end with him dead at Macduff's hands and with Malcolm hailed as king. As king, Malcolm is a successor in 'a double sense': to his father and to Macbeth.

The play's presentation of Duncan's murder is marked by two modes of doubleness at least. First, it doubles what audiences do not see. Well before he actually does it, Macbeth vividly imagines himself committing 'this terrible feat'. When the idea – the merest 'suggestion' – of killing Duncan enters his awareness, it stirs a 'horrid image' that prompts him to ask why, if the witches' 'supernatural soliciting' is 'good', that image

> doth unfix my hair,
> And make my seated heart knock at my ribs,
> Against the use of nature? Present fears
> Are less than horrible imaginings.
> My thought, whose murther yet is but fantastical,
> Shakes so my single state of man,
> That function is smother'd in surmise,
> And nothing is, but what is not.
>   (I.iii.130–1, 137–42)

That a 'murther' existing only as a fantasy produces such a reaction in a warrior of Macbeth's prowess, who does not agonise over shedding blood to defend Duncan, registers the intensity of the moral revulsion Macbeth must quell in order to perform the actual deed. Audiences do not see Macbeth's 'horrible imaginings' of what he has not yet done, nor do they see the murder when he actually performs it, since the play places it offstage. By doubling what is not seen, the play aligns the audience's mode of perception with Macbeth's imagination. Denied any sight of Duncan's killing, they know the murder only as Macbeth first experiences it – through the powers of imagination – and become in effect his accomplices.

The unseen 'fantastical' murder that 'shakes' Macbeth's 'single state of man', becomes, when doubled into actuality, the murder performed unseen that shatters his 'single state', the integrity of his being, by violating his reason and his deepest moral instincts. Unlike Othello, Macbeth does not kill out of ignorance or uncontrolled passion; unlike Hamlet, he does not find himself called upon to act in a morally ambiguous world, and the king he kills is not himself evil. Macbeth does what he fully knows and, in the depth of his being, *feels* is evil. His first words after murdering Duncan are 'I have done the deed' (II.ii.14). They hark back to his analysis of the deed's irrationality, futility, and immorality: 'If it were done, when 'tis done ...' He refuses to go back to Duncan's chamber to return the grooms' daggers: 'I am afraid to think what I have done; / Look on't again I dare not' (II.ii.50–1). What he has brought himself to do is, he understands, radically alien to the person – the distinctive human being – he knows himself to be. 'To know my deed, 'twere best not know myself,' he laments, then wishes, with his final words in the scene, that 'the deed' he has 'done' could be undone: 'Wake Duncan with thy knocking: I would thou couldst!' (II.ii.72–3).

The sleepwalking scene doubles Duncan's murder in a different way. It replays fragments of that night's events, thereby altering the perception of Lady Macbeth's participation in the deed. To function as Macbeth's partner in murder, Lady Macbeth must (try to) negate her own body and such stereotypical feminine virtues as pity, remorse, and compunction:

> Come, you Spirits
> That tend on mortal thoughts, unsex me here,
> And fill me, from the crown to the toe, top-full
> Of direst cruelty! make thick my blood,
> Stop up th'access and passage to remorse;
> That no compunctious visitings of Nature
> Shake my fell purpose, nor keep peace between
> Th'effect and it! Come to my woman's breasts
> And take my milk for gall ...
>
> (I.v.40–8)

'Top-full of direst cruelty', she will provide Macbeth with what he lacks: 'the illness [that] should attend' ambition (I.v.20). From her Macbeth will take the sustenance, the 'gall', needed to offset his 'nature', which is, she fears, 'too full o'th'milk of human kindness' (I.v.16–17).

The Elizabethan–Jacobean practice of casting boys to play female roles charged initial performances of the unsexing speech with a doubleness it does not have when an actress plays Lady Macbeth – in accord with the practice of casting women in female roles that has overwhelmingly dominated English-speaking theatre since becoming standard after. the reopening of the theatres in 1660. The female character whom the original audiences heard calling to be unsexed in order to perform evil with unwomanly ruthlessness was played by a boy who had to 'unsex' himself in order to perform the part of a woman. What the character wants to do – become less female – was the inverse of what the boy actor had to do – become less male. The sexual doubleness generated in such a situation called attention to the process of performing the role, both highlighting the challenge faced by the boy actor and easing it. The more male-like Lady Macbeth becomes, the less female the boy actor needed to seem to be.[3]

That sexual doubleness also enhanced the motif of ambiguous female sexual identity first made explicit when Banquo says to the witches: '. . . you should be women, / And yet your beards forbid me to interpret / That you are so' (I.iii.45–7). Audiences at performances of *Macbeth* before the theatres closed in 1642 faced a dilemma similar to Banquo's that made sexual ambiguity an integral element of how they experienced the play. They were aware that all female characters 'should be [regarded as] women', yet the fact that boy actors played those 'women' made it impossible to say unconditionally 'that you are so'. No such dilemma, no such sexual doubleness, exists for audiences who watch actresses playing the women. The witches that 'should be women' 'are so' in fact, and the Lady Macbeth whom audiences after 1660 behold unsexing herself remains physically female no matter how much she tries to put on a 'manly readiness' (II.iii.131) to act with unwomanly ruthlessness.

Lady Macbeth succeeds to a considerable degree in unsexing herself. She proves cruel enough to drug the grooms, remorseless enough to lay 'their daggers ready' (II.ii.11) for Macbeth to use on Duncan, and bold enough to return them when Macbeth refuses to re-enter the blood-stained chamber. However, during the sleepwalking scene, Lady Macbeth's final appearance in the play, the 'compunctious visitings of Nature' that she tries to purge from herself during her first appearance reassert themselves. Audiences behold her 'transformed from the pitiless instigator of murder to the guilt-ridden sleepwalker whose thoughts return to "the old man" who "had so much blood in him"' (Stallybrass, 1982, p. 198). Ultimately, she cannot escape those 'visitings' any more than (on the post-Restoration stage) she can negate her woman's body. An essential part of her cannot be – will not be – totally remorseless, absolutely unpitying.

One example of how the sleepwalking scene enables audiences to see Lady Macbeth's conduct during the murder 'double' – to place it in a different perspective – is the moment, seconds before Macbeth enters to announce Duncan's murder 'done', when she says, 'Had he not resembled / My father as he slept, I had done't' (II.ii.14, 12–13). Whether Lady Macbeth is exulting in her unwomanly ferocity as she speaks those words or is pondering (in surprise? dismay?) her own inability to kill Duncan will depend on how they are delivered. However spoken, they reveal the enduring pull of filial ties upon her and thus signal a residue of humanity, of 'human kindness', she has not managed to eradicate.[4] She is not 'top-full / Of direst cruelty'. Even if her reference to her father is merely a rationalisation of her inability to kill, the fact remains that, even as she participates in Duncan's murder, a part of her refuses to be inhuman and inhumanely pitiless. In the sleepwalking scene, that part of her, eluding her conscious control, wonders in horror at the smell of blood that cannot be washed from her hands.

The final mention of her in the play – Malcolm's reference to Macbeth's 'fiend-like Queen' (V.ix.35) – places her in a double perspective. His characterisation fits the being she labours to make herself into and, by virtue of her actions, becomes, but it does not fit the profoundly troubled, deeply self-injured, humanly vulnerable person whom audiences see and hear the final time she appears before them. In Roman Polanski's 1971 film, Francesca Annis heightened the audience's awareness of Lady Macbeth's womanhood and vulnerability by playing the sleepwalking scene nude. The difference between Malcolm's characterisation of Lady Macbeth and the audience's last sight of her corresponds to the gap between the person, the fundamentally *human* being, she could not fully stop being and the role of Macbeth's fiendishly unfeeling partner in murder and greatness to which she dedicates and subjugates herself. She is, and she is not, either and both of them.

The same gap opens, much more briefly, when the vengeful Macduff finally comes upon Macbeth and, addressing him by a term that denies him any humanity, calls, 'Turn, Hell-hound, turn' (V.viii.3). Macbeth's reply is unlooked for in one who has been labouring to extinguish the rationality and moral sense that makes one human: 'Of all men else I have avoided thee: / But get thee back, my soul is too much charg'd / With blood of thine already' (V.viii.4–6). That response, Howard Felperin comments,

> proceeds not out of his assigned and chosen role of stage-tyrant, but out of an unsuspected reserve of sympathetic and spontaneous humanity that exists beneath it, a self still fragile and unhardened in evil even at this point, against his own and Macduff's protestations and accusations to the contrary. (1977, p. 132).

A drop of 'the milk of human kindness' endures in Macbeth despite his increasingly frantic efforts to quell his own humanity.

The final moments of *Macbeth* extensively double earlier words and events. The play, which begins with the ending of a battle audiences do not see, ends with a battle that they do see. After that battle, first Macduff and then '*All*' 'hail' Malcolm as 'King of Scotland' (V.ix.25). Their use of 'hail' associates the moment when Malcolm is first acclaimed king with that earlier moment when the witches first greet Macbeth and 'hail' him three times – as thane of Glamis, as thane of Cawdor, and as 'King hereafter' (I.iii.50). Like his father after victory in the earlier battle, the newly-kinged Malcolm promises to punish foes and reward friends and pledges to carry out all appropriate actions: 'What's more to do, / Which would be planted newly with the time . . . / We will perform in measure, time, and place' (V.ix.30–9). Duncan used that planting metaphor when addressing Macbeth during the only moment audiences see them together: 'I have begun to plant thee, and will labour / To make thee full of growing' (I.iv.28–9).

Macbeth, who beheads the traitorous Macdonwald during the battle that is ending as the play opens, is himself beheaded – a point emphasised by a detail that registers far more vividly on theatre audiences than on readers: Macduff's entrance with 'th'usurper's cursed head'. The displaying of Macbeth's severed head, which can be the play's crowning visual effect,[5] illustrates how the doubleness that suffuses the final moments of *Macbeth* generates a double effect. On the one hand, doubleness signifies and reinforces restoration of the socio-political order Macbeth defiled. A royal son succeeds his royal father, taking that father's language and gestures as his own, and a legitimate and good king – hailed by his kinsmen and thanes – displaces the murderous, usurping tyrant whom witches hailed.

Macbeth's head functions, Felperin explains, as 'a totemic deterrent to tyranny, a public symbol of the inviolability of the social order and a glaring reminder of the inevitability of the moral law: the wages of ambition is, and always must be, death' (1977, p. 138).

On the other hand, that same doubleness registers the fragility and tenuousness of that order. The aligning of Macdonwald and Macbeth – emphasised in performance by the presence of Macbeth's severed head – suggests that Macbeth is not a unique case but an appallingly heinous instance of a pattern that sees traitorous ambition repeatedly flare up anew. Are there future traitors among those who, responding to Macduff's example, 'hail' their new king? Gold's production (1983) for BBC-TV conveyed that possibility by ending with Malcolm, the royal son who has become king, and Fleance, the son whose father will beget a line of kings, staring at one another as the others stared hard at both of them. Polanski's film made the possibility of future treason an actuality; its final shots show Donalbain, the newly hailed Malcolm's younger brother, approaching the hovel in which Macbeth had his last meeting with the witches. The pattern is not only beginning anew but spiralling into deeper horror. The king Macbeth murders is his guest and kinsman; Donalbain is preparing to murder the king who is his brother – to become a Scottish Claudius.

Macduff and Malcolm speak of Macbeth's defeat as the final, apocalyptic victory of good over evil and an absolute break with the blood-drenched past. 'The time is free,' Macduff proclaims, and Malcolm acts to emphasise the uniqueness of the order that has come into being by giving a new title to those who were previously his father's thanes – *and* Macbeth's: 'Henceforth be Earls; the first that ever Scotland / In such honour nam'd' (V.ix.29–30). The doubleness that marks the moments of which their words are part counterbalances the freedom and uniqueness they assert. What is happening is not utterly new, not totally free of previous events. Even the planting imagery Malcolm uses, as, addressing those he has just named earls, he speaks of 'what would be newly planted with the time', cuts across the singularity of the moment. In addition to echoing his father, that imagery invokes the cyclical process of the natural realm in which things and events recur as part of the ongoing seasonal flow. Does making thanes earls annul their ambition? It was, after all, the *Earl* of Gowrie who in 1600 tried to assassinate James while the king was his guest in his house at Perth. How 'free' is the time and for how long? Macbeth tries to bend time to his will, first by acting to make sure the witches' prophecy that he will be king comes true, then by acting to frustrate their prophecy that Banquo's issue will be kings. The play's first audiences lived under the rule of a descendant of Banquo's who had been the target of Gowrie and the Gunpowder Plot, and they were accustomed to seeing the heads of traitors displayed on London's battlements and bridges. Would they have concluded that, with the beheading of Macbeth, future times were 'free' of treason?

In time, through time, over time, Macbeth becomes the traitors against whom he first fights. He becomes the thane of Cawdor, in title and in treacherous deed, and his head, severed like Macdonwald's, becomes a display for all to learn from. Audiences (but not readers) see Macbeth's head, and the lesson it teaches is as double-edged as the swords and daggers audiences (but not readers) see during the play. Treason does not prosper; treason does recur. If *Macbeth* teaches a lesson, it, too, is double-edged. Good triumphs over evil; good can become evil. 'Fair is foul, and foul is fair' (I.i.11).

6

Coriolanus: 'Author of Himself'

Coriolanus, which takes its title from the name its protagonist Caius Martius wins for himself through his prowess in battle, is one in the series of six tragedies Shakespeare provided for the King's Men from 1604 through 1608. It is also one of a sub-group of four within that series in which the protagonist is a warrior. Like *Othello*, *Macbeth*, and *Antony and Cleopatra*, this play – by most estimates the last Shakespearean tragedy – directs attention to the warrior's relationship with a woman, but it is different in one vital respect. In them, the relationship between the warrior and the woman is sexual, involving the wives of Othello and Macbeth and Antony's lover Cleopatra, who, in her final moments, claims him as a spouse: 'Husband, I come' (V.ii.286). Coriolanus, too, has a wife, but primary emphasis does not fall on their relationship. The play stresses instead his relationship with his mother. The point of crisis for Coriolanus – and in the play – comes when his mother pleads with him to spare his native Rome, powerless to resist the army, composed of those he won fame by fighting against in the service of Rome, that he now leads against it. She implores him to change from warrior to peacemaker, to reconcile Romans and Volsci so that 'each in either side / Give the all-hail to thee, and cry, "Be bless'd / For making up this peace!" ' (V.iii.138–40).

That point of crisis is also a moment that demonstrates how the play takes thorough and repeated advantage of its nature as a work meant for collective performance by a company of actors before individuals assembled publicly to form a communal body called an audience. The fundamental theatricality of the moment, and of *Coriolanus* itself, comes into sharp focus when compared to the account in the play's primary source, Thomas North's translation, by way of an

130

earlier translation into French by James Amyot, of Plutarch's 'The Life of Caius Martius Coriolanus':

> *Martius* seeing that, could refraine no lenger, but went straight and lifte her up, crying out: Oh mother, what have you done to me? And holding her hard by the right hande, oh mother, sayed he, you have wonne a happy victorie for your countrie, but mortall and unhappy for your sonne: for I see my self vanquished by you alone. (Brockbank, 1976, p. 363)

The play's presentation of the same moment is significantly different. After Volumnia finishes speaking by vowing to keep silent 'until our city be afire, / And then I'll speak a little' (V.iii.181–2), the stage direction specifies that Coriolanus *'holds her by the hand silent'* before he speaks. The play is imprecise where Plutarch and North are not. It does not designate 'the right hande', and it does not specify that Coriolanus acts immediately ('straight'), thus leaving open the possibility that he hesitates before taking his mother's hand. However, the play does organise the moment so as to focus the attention of theatre audiences with precision. The North–Amyot – Plutarch account refers to three gestures: Coriolanus moves to his mother, then lifts her from her knees, and finally holds her by the right hand. The last two actions occur *as* he speaks to her. The play makes the single act of taking and holding Volumnia's hand the centre of attention, and the longer the actor playing Coriolanus waits before taking her hand, the more impact that gesture will have. Its implications will change as the timing varies. A Coriolanus who hesitates before taking his mother's hand is still struggling against her maternal claims upon him. A Coriolanus who – as in 'The Life' – immediately takes her hand has been overwhelmed by them.

The play further intensifies its focus on the single act of a fully grown son taking and holding his mother's hand by adding an element that has no counterpart in North–Plutarch: Coriolanus's silence as he holds his mother's hand. Accounts of three relatively recent productions suggest the impact that silence – over which a reader's eyes quickly pass – can have in performance. Roger Warren reports that in Peter Hall's 1984 production at the National Theatre, Coriolanus (Ian McKellen) 'suddenly grabbed her hand as she was about to storm away, and held her by force amid a prolonged, tense electric silence' (1986, p. 119). According to David Daniell, in Terry Hands's 1977 production for the Royal Shakespeare Company,

> Maxine Audley [Volumnnia] rose and moved forward to face Alan Howard [Coriolanus]. He, in an instant movement, with a military snap, clasped her hand to his breast and gazed on her. Howard held a long silence, sometimes of forty-four seconds, usually well over thirty, until, tears rolling down his cheeks, he broke. 'O, mother, mother, / What have you done?' (1980, pp. 39–40)

Alan Brien's description of the equivalent moment in the Royal Shakespeare Company's 1973 production, with Nicol Williamson as Coriolanus, emphasises both the length of Coriolanus's silence and the effect of its interplay with the words that end it:

> Only once does Mr Williamson pause, and what a pause, a single shot held longer than even Harold Pinter or John Ford would dream could grip an audience – when his mother begs him to spare Rome ... 'Mother ... what ... have ... you ... DONE?' the monster cries giving each word like a pint of blood. (quoted in Berry, 1981, p. 32)

The longer Coriolanus's silence lasts, the more an audience will sense his struggle to grasp and articulate the implications and consequences of what his mother is bringing him to do. Whatever its duration, the silence the play assigns to Coriolanus accentuates his act of holding his mother's hand by separating it from both the words (pledging herself to silence) Volumnia has just spoken and those that Coriolanus will subsequently speak.

When the silence mandated for Coriolanus as he holds his mother's hand ends, much of what the play then gives him to say closely follows 'The Life'. The question that it has Coriolanus ask – 'Oh mother, what have you done to me?' – corresponds to the one with which in the play Coriolanus breaks his silence: 'O mother, mother! / What have you done?' (V.iii.182–3). The play also draws upon what 'The Life' reports are Coriolanus's next words: 'oh, mother, sayd he, you have wonne a happy victorie for your countrie, but mortall and unhappy for your sonne'. However, it relocates its version of those words, placing them after a sentence that has no equivalent in 'The Life':

> Behold, the heavens do ope,
> The gods look down, and this unnatural scene
> They laugh at. O my mother, mother! O!
> You have won a happy victory to Rome;
> But for your son, believe it, O, believe it,
> Most dangerously you have with him prevail'd,
> If not most mortal to him. But let it come.
> (V.iii.183–9)

The 'scene' is 'unnatural' in at least two ways: a mother places her allegiance to her nation above her love for her son, and at the request of the mother who gave him life a son undertakes an act that he senses will cost him his life. The phrase 'This unnatural scene' is part of a sentence, unique to the play, that expresses Coriolanus's anguished sense of how his reconciliation with his mother looks from a divine perspective. That awareness is all the more shattering because his prowess in battle has given him standing in the eyes of other humans approaching that of the gods whom he now imagines are laughing. When Coriolanus returns in triumph to Rome, the tribune Brutus marvels at the people's reaction: it is 'As if that whatsoever god who leads him / Were slily crept into his human powers, / And gave him graceful posture' (II.i.217–19). Aufidius hails him as 'thou Mars' (IV.v.119) when welcoming him to Antium, and Cominius, the Roman general under whom Coriolanus fights at Corioli, describes his status among the Volscian soldiers he leads against Rome: 'He is their god' (IV.vi.91). Coriolanus is accused of treating the Roman people as if he 'were a god to punish, not / A man of their infirmity' (III.i.81–2), but when he takes his mother's hand, indicating his willingness to spare Rome, he acknowledges for all to see that, as he feared, he is 'not / Of stronger earth than others' (V.iii.28–9). Indeed, Coriolanus shows that, far from being god-like, he is not even 'Of stronger earth' than his son, young Martius, who enters, the playtext specifies, holding not, as one might expect, his mother Virgilia's hand but Volumnia's. 'My wife comes foremost', Coriolanus notes, 'then the honoured mold / Wherein this trunk was framed, and in her hand / The grandchild to her blood' (V.iii.22–4). The playtext does not specify when – or even if – young Martius stops holding Volumnia's hand, but it does specify that Coriolanus too takes her hand. Thus, audiences may see first young Martius and then Coriolanus holding Volumnia's hand, or they may

see both holding her hand simultaneously. In either case, what
audiences see confirms the equivalence of father and son, man and
boy.[1]

Coriolanus's reference to 'this unnatural scene' also invokes the
widespread Renaissance metaphor of the world as a stage, by means
of which the play draws attention to, and then takes further advantage of, its own nature as a theatrical work. The warrior-son who
envisages himself as an actor on the stage of the world is also a
dramatic character being portrayed by an actor on a stage in the
presence of a human audience – and the first stage on which an actor
played Coriolanus was in a theatre named, appropriately, the Globe.
Whenever members of an audience watching any actor playing Coriolanus in any theater do not join the gods in laughing at this moment
but instead behold what is happening in silence, their silence – like
Coriolanus's as he holds his mother's hand – affirms that they,
like him, are more human than god-like.

The silence that occurs as Coriolanus holds his mother's hand is
not his alone. She, too, says nothing. His silence ends when he speaks
to her, but hers does not. After declaring 'I am husht until our city
be afire, / And then I'll speak a little' (V.iii.181–2), she remains silent
for the rest of this scene and during her one subsequent appearance,
her return to the city, when she is hailed as 'our patroness, the life
of Rome' (V.v.1). The playtext gives us no clue as to how she
responds to winning 'a happy victory to Rome' that Coriolanus says,
speaking of himself in the third person as if already dead, will prove
'most mortal to him' (V.iii.186, 189). Does Volumnia weep? Do her
eyes, like Coriolanus's, 'sweat compassion' (V.iii.196)? Or is she
resolutely impervious, proving more implacably god-like in her
determination to save Rome than Coriolanus in his determination to
destroy it? Do audiences behold in the silent woman any sign of
conflict or strain at having placed her allegiance to Rome above her
maternal feelings in order to prevail 'most dangerously' (V.iii.188)
with her son?[2]

In Elijah Moshinsky's 1983 production for the BBC-TV series
'The Shakespeare Plays', with Alan Howard in the title role, Volumnia and Coriolanus both weep as he silently holds her hand and then
asks what she has done. The 1977 production for the Royal Shakespeare Company, also starring Howard, demonstrated a different,
but equally valid possibility. Daniell's account emphasises the 'tears
rolling down' (1980, p. 40) Howard's cheeks but says nothing at all

about Volumnia. Some sense of how she responded emerges from Daniell's description of what happened when she enters the city in a scene (V.v) that plays against her son's earlier return to Rome in military triumph *'crowned with an oaken garland'* (II.i.160):

> Large processional music brought on Cominius and Senators, Virgilia and Valeria, and then Volumnia with Young Martius, a cloak around him. . . . at the climax of the music she flung off Young Martius' cloak to show him, hands crossed over a sword, black leather armour and definant chin, the young image of his father. Clearly she is going to repeat the process of a special fanatical upbringing all over again. (Daniell, 1980, p. 40)

It is unlikely that tears rolled down the cheeks of this Volumnia.

Volumnia's appeal to Coriolanus to spare Rome is the second time she intervenes in an effort to change her son's mind. For her first intervention (III.ii), there is no precedent in the North–Plutarch 'Life', and that intervention, unique to *Coriolanus*, is part of a sequence that exploits the play's theatrical character – and does so in a way that stresses what might be called the theatricality of politics.

Puzzled at his mother's less-than-enthusiastic reaction to his denunciation of the plebeians whose approval he needs to become consul, Coriolanus asks her, 'Why do you wish me milder? Would you have me / False to my nature? Rather say I play / The man I am' (III.ii.14–16). She calls on him to solicit again the favour of the people, counselling that what he says and does in front of them need have no more relevance to his 'nature' – to what he truly thinks and feels – than what an actor does or says in front of a theatre audience. '[S]peak / To th' people' she advises, 'not by your own instruction',

> Nor by th'matter which your heart prompts you,
> But with such words that are but roted in
> Your tongue, though but bastards and syllables
> Of no allowance to your bosom's truth.
> (III.ii.52–7)

Like a director coaching an actor, she goes on to suggest, and even demonstrate, gestures he might employ to win their approval:

> Go to them, with this bonnet in thy hand,
> And thus far having stretch'd it, – here be with them –
> Thy knee bussing the stones – for in such business
> Action is eloquence, and the eyes of th' ignorant
> More learned than the ears . . . .

(III.ii.73–7)

She proposes that he tell the people 'thou art their soldier' (III.ii.81), even though he and she consider him *her* soldier. She directs that, above all else, Coriolanus accommodate himself to suit their wishes: '. . . thou wilt frame / Thyself, forsooth, hereafter theirs, so far / As thou hast power and person' (III.ii.84–6).

Coriolanus demurs at what he is being asked to do: 'You have put me now to such a part which never / I shall discharge to th' life' (III.ii.105–6). Those words closely echo his earlier reaction when Menenius tells him that all that remains for him to become consul is that he 'fit' himself 'to the custom' and 'speak to the people' as his 'predecessors have'; 'It is', Coriolanus says, 'a part / That I shall blush in acting, and might well / Be taken from the people' (II.ii.135, 141–5). Cominius, his old general, and Volumnia, also speak of what he must do to become consul as a 'part' he must play:

> COM.: Come, come, we'll prompt you:
> VOL.: I prithee, now sweet son, as thou hast said
> My praises made thee first a soldier, so,
> To have my praise for this, perform a part
> Thou hast not done before.

(III.ii.106–10)

The terminology they as well as Coriolanus use makes explicit the convergence of the political and theatrical.

Coriolanus agrees, reluctantly, to play the part his mother and the patricians have cast him in – 'Well, I must do't' (III.ii.110) – but the more he considers what such acting entails, the more he finds it repugnant. He sees it as tantamount to de-sexing himself:

> Away my disposition, and possess me
> Some harlot's spirit! My throat of war be turn'd
> Which choired with my drum, into a pipe
> Small as an eunuch, or the virgin voice
> That babies lulls asleep. . . .

(III.ii.111–15)

Such a change is all the more repugnant in his eyes because it will undo the full manhood he achieved in his first battle while still a boy. 'In that day's feats', Cominius says, in language that glances at the Jacobean practice of casting boys as women, 'When he might act the woman in the scene, / He prov'd best man i'th'field' (II.ii.95–7).

Committed to a notion of absolute integrity that refuses to tolerate any gap between his public gestures and what he regards as his essential being – between role and self – Coriolanus retracts his assent. 'I will not do't', he declares, 'Lest I surcease to honour mine own truth, / And by my body's action teach my mind /A most inherent baseness' (III.ii.120–4). He refuses to speak any words or perform any actions not totally compatible with whom and what he judges himself to be – with his conception of 'mine own truth'.

Coriolanus's heartfelt rejection of his 'part' is a powerfully authentic refusal to participate in a political process he finds corrupt and demeaning. On the other hand, a number of factors qualify the appeal of that refusal. After chiding him for being 'too absolute', Volumnia points out the inconsistency of his being willing to do on the battlefield what he is refusing to do in the political arena:

> If it be honour in your wars to seem
> The same you are not . . .
> . . . how is it less or worse
> That it shall hold companionship in peace
> With honour, as in war, since that to both
> It stands in like request?
>
> (III.ii.46–51)

There are additional inconsistencies. Audiences who hear Coriolanus declare that his 'arm'd knees . . . bowed but in my stirrup' will have already seen him kneel to Volumnia during his triumphal entry into Rome:

> COR.: You have, I know, petition'd all the gods
>   For my prosperity.   *Kneels.*
> VOL.: Nay, my good soldier, up.
>
> (II.i.169–70)

Further qualifying Coriolanus's refusal to act a 'part' is a fact that registers far more forcefully on members of a theatre audience than on readers: Coriolanus himself is a 'part' being played by an actor.

He is refusing to do what the actor playing him does throughout the performance. Playing a part is the very ground and condition of Coriolanus's theatrical being. Richard Burbage, the leading actor in the King's Men, almost certainly brought the role of Coriolanus to life before audiences at the Globe. Burbage was praised as 'a delightful Proteus, so wholly transforming himself into his part, and putting off himself with his Cloathes, as he never (not so much as in the Tyringhouse) assum'd himself again until the Play was done' (quoted in Montrose, 1980, p. 56). Burbage's ability to put off 'himself' while playing Coriolanus stands in telling contrast to Coriolanus's refusal to play a 'part' before the people, to be – as he puts it – 'false to my own nature' and to 'mine own truth'. What Coriolanus will not do is what every actor who plays him, from Burbage on, must do.

Coriolanus swiftly retracts his refusal and, armed 'to answer mildly', pledging to 'come home belov'd / Of all the trades in Rome', he leaves for 'the market-place' where the people and their tribunes wait (III.ii.139, 133–4, 131). Once there, however, he cannot successfully play his 'part', cannot 'discharge [it] to th'life'. His revulsion at what he is doing and at the people themselves breaks through as soon as he is called upon to answer the charge that he is 'a traitor to the people' (III.iii.66). Ultimately, then, his first assent to his mother's wishes proves nearly as disastrous as his second. The former brings banishment from Rome, the latter death.

* * *

The conception of himself that Coriolanus cannot and will not violate includes both a conviction of his own constancy and a sense of total self-sufficiency. 'I am constant', he declares when reminded of his promise to serve under Cominius in the impending campaign against the Volscians (I.i.238). That declaration is all the more pointed because it comes shortly after Coriolanus, making his first appearance in the play, denounces the citizens for being, among other things, mutable and inconstant:

> He that trusts to you,
> Where he should find you lions, finds you hares;
> Where foxes, geese. You are no surer, no,
> Than is the coal of fire upon the ice,
> Or hailstone in the sun. . . .
>
> (I.i.169–73)

'Trust ye!' he continues,

> With every minute you do change a mind,
> And call him noble that was now your hate,
> Him vile that was your garland.
>
> (I.i.180–3)

The timing sugggests that Coriolanus values constancy, at least in part, because it enables him to see himself as fundamentally different from the citizens he loathes.

The plebeians *are* inconstant. They are easily manipulated by the tribunes who supposedly speak for them as well as by Menenius, a patrician who, during the opening moments of the play, stops their participation in the uprising under way by telling them 'a pretty tale' (I.i.89), the fable of the belly. Later they give their voices to Coriolanus, then retract them, prompting him to ask, 'Must these have voices, that can yield them now / And straight disclaim their tongues' (III.i.33–4). The play's last mention of them is the report that they are pummelling one of the men they elected their tribune, 'all swearing . . . They'll give him death by inches' (V.iv.38–40). Nor is it just the Roman people who are fickle. The stage direction for Coriolanus's return to the Volsci after sparing Rome specifies that he enters '*Marching with Drum and Colours, the Commoners being with him*'. Within moments, those same people are demanding, 'Tear him to pieces! Do it presently!' (V.vi.70, 120).

However, by making it clear that Coriolanus himself changes, the play blurs what he regards as an essential difference between himself and the plebeians. During his mother's first appeal to him, he changes his mind several times, first vowing to continue to defy the people, then consenting to his mother's request that he appear again before them, then retracting his consent, then withdrawing that retraction and leaving for the marketplace. In banishment, Coriolanus changes from being Rome's defender to its attacker, and then, at the gates of Rome, he vows to withstand the instinctual pull of blood and affection he feels as his mother, wife, and son draw near to plead for Rome. 'Let the Volsces / Plough Rome and harrow Italy', he resolves, 'I'll never / Be such a gosling to obey instinct, but stand / As if a man were author of himself / And knew no other kin' (V.iii.33–7). He cannot so 'stand', and in response to his mother's second appeal, he changes from a warrior to a peacemaker. He becomes 'such a gosling', thereby erasing the distinction, central to his conception of his identity, between himself and the plebeians whom he denounces as 'geese' during his first speech in the play (I.i.171) and again when they flee in battle: 'You souls of geese, / That bear the shapes of men' (I.iv.34–5).

The play gives the mutability that Coriolanus resists acknowledging in himself a visual manifestation that can have far more impact on a theatre audience than on readers. The scene (IV.iv) in which audiences see him for the first time after his banishment opens with the stage direction '*Enter Coriolanus in mean apparel, disguised and muffled*'. Peter Hall's 1984 production of *Coriolanus* at the National Theatre linked the 'part' Coriolanus plays when entering Antium with the 'part' he was called upon to play before commoners of Rome by having his disguise include the broad-brimmed hat he wore with the gown of humility when asking for their voices. Wearing '*mean apparel*', he is visually indistinguishable from both the Roman plebeians whom he deems his inferiors and the Volscian servants who, in the next scene, treat him as their inferior. His appearance obliterates the differences in attire that are 'the readiest signs of social distinctions in a stratified and deferential society' (Montrose, 1980, p. 56). The Rome from which Coriolanus has been banished is, to his dismay, ceasing to be such a society. He denounces political arrangements that permit the people to share power he thinks should be exercised exclusively by the Senate. '[W]e nourish 'gainst our Senate', he warns, 'The cockle of rebellion, insolence, sedition, / Which we ourselves have plough'd for, sow'd and scatter'd / By mingling them with us, the honour'd number' (III.i.68–71).

The early Jacobean society within which *Coriolanus* came into being was, officially at least, a stratified culture in which distinctions in rank were both fixed and visible. It tried to regulate what people wore by 'sumptuary laws designed to enforce a congruity between the appearance and reality of status' (Montrose, 1980, p. 56). Coriolanus's '*mean attire*' undoes, or at least suspends, such congruity within the Roman world of the play, which is also what occurred when actors of the early modern era appeared on public stages attired in the cast-off clothing of noblemen and courtiers so that, while they played at being persons of such status, they might more convincingly 'seem / The same [they] are not'. 'Mingling' of the sort Coriolanus decries occurred with every performance in a Jacobean public theatre such as the Globe. Admission was open to anyone, regardless of social rank, who paid the price of a ticket. Composed of aristocrats and gentry as well as commoners and apprentices, the audiences who first heard Coriolanus's denunciations were themselves a body in which 'mingling' occurred.

The King's Men brought *Coriolanus* to the stage of the Globe several years after extensive rioting, triggered by food shortages in the Midlands of England during 1603–4, caused many to fear for the Jacobean social order. As if in response to that rioting, the play deviates from its source. The '*company of mutinous Citizens*' upon whom the play opens are incensed by the lack of food, not, as in the North–Plutarch 'Life', by usurious interest rates. The Midlands rioting and the hunger that sparked it were specific manifestations and consequences of enclosure – a process, under way since the reign of Elizabeth as part of the deeper, broader shift from a feudal to a pre-capitalist society, whereby landowners, in the interests of efficiency, clustered into larger groupings that would produce greater profit ancient strips of land long worked by individual tenant farmers. Those who resisted by tearing down the hedges that enclosed and demarcated those larger units were called 'levellers'. That term, Janet Adelman observes, suggests that such actions were seen as a challenge to the principle of hierarchy, the first steps in what would become 'a flattening of the whole society' (1978, p. 108). Cominius invokes the spectre of a levelled society devoid of ranks and differences when the tribune Brutus's call to seize and execute Coriolanus sets off a mêlée pitting Coriolanus and the patricians against the tribunes and the people:

> This is the way to lay the city flat,
> To bring the roof to the foundation,
> And bury all which yet distinctly ranges
> In heaps and piles of ruin.
>
> (III.i.201–5)

The Rome of *Coriolanus* is a nation undergoing a legitimation crisis, a state in which authority is for the taking – no longer exercised solely by the patricians but not yet possessed solely by the plebeians who cry, 'The people are the city' (III.i.198). England in the early seventeenth century was caught up in a similar struggle, which manifested itself in a variety of ways, including repeated clashes between James and Parliament over the issue of where ultimate authority lay.[3] That struggle led to the closing of all theatres in England in 1642, to a murderous civil war, and, in 1649, to what many then and since have regarded as an 'unnatural scene' played out on the stage of British history: the public beheading of James's son and successor on the throne of England, Charles I, by men claiming to act on behalf of the people.

The theatres of early Jacobean London were one site where the struggle for authority was played out, as the crown, the church, and civic officials, especially those in London, sought to control and regulate what was then a novel cultural practice: the almost daily performance of plays by professional actors in buildings erected specifically for that purpose and before people who paid to be part of the audience. Throughout Shakespeare's career, plays had to be approved by a censor (the Master of the Revels), and only players licensed to play were permitted to perform. In the 1590s, under Elizabeth, such licences went only to acting companies sponsored by great men of the realm, such as the Lord Chamberlain, and under James only to acting companies sponsored by members of the royal family – the King himself, Queen Anne, and Prince Henry. Royal patronage protected the acting companies from the hostility of the civic and ecclesiastical authorities, but it was also a means of royal control. That control was not absolute, however. Royal patronage allowed acting companies to play, but they were dependent for their livelihood on what they took in at the box office. Plays that people were not willing to pay to see were not performed; acting companies incapable of consistently attracting paying audiences did not survive. Thus, London audiences exercised a different form of authority over the theatres. The power to buy or not to buy a ticket – the power of the marketplace – gave the people a voice in deciding who played and what was played on the public stages of Jacobean London.

Constancy is one key element in Coriolanus's conception of his own 'truth', and his resolve to act as if he 'were author of himself' is his most explicit articulation of another: his sense of what might be variously called absolute autonomy, total self-sufficiency, full independence, or complete singularity. The play fosters that sense by re-working the North–Plutarch account of his conduct at the battle of Corioli. In 'The Life' he enters and is shut within its gates with 'very fewe men to helpe him' (Brockbank, 1976, p. 322), but in the play, when he rushes through the gates calling, 'Mark me, and do the like', no one follows, and 'he is himself alone / To answer all the city' (I.iv.45, 51–2).

The play further establishes Coriolanus's autonomy by presenting his disappearance into and emergence from the city of Corioli as a process like that of death and rebirth. When the gates of Corioli close upon him, he passes out of the Roman world he has known and, simultaneously, out of sight of audiences, who – in a manoeuvre that anticipates Hermione's 'death' in *The Winter's Tale* – are (mis)led briefly to believe he is dead. '*All*' the Romans who witness the event tell Titus Lartius that Coriolanus is 'Slain, sir, doubtless' (I.iv.48) and nothing audiences can see at this point prompts them to disagree. Lartius's response also signals that Coriolanus is dead. He eulogises Coriolanus as a fallen warrior, speaking of him in the past tense:

> Thou wast a soldier
> Even to Cato's wish, not fierce and terrible
> Only in strokes, but with thy grim looks and
> The thunder-like percussion of thy sounds
> Thou mad'st thine enemies shake, as if the world
> Were feverous and did tremble.
>
> (I.iv.56–61)

The play then contradicts the conclusion it has encouraged. The warrior who audiences think is 'slain, doubtless' re-enters alive and blood-smeared like a new-born baby: '*Enter MARTIUS, bleeding, assaulted by the enemy*' (I.iv.61). Later, again like a new-born baby, he receives a new name in recognition of that extraordinary feat of arms. '[F]rom this time', Cominius announces to the Roman army, 'For what he did before Corioles, call him, / With all th' applause and clamour of the host, / Martius Caius Coriolanus' (I.ix.61–4).

The man now named 'Coriolanus' is 'author of himself' to the extent that the life he now lives is no longer one he has simply received from his mother and from Rome but also one he has won for himself while 'alone' within Corioli. 'From this time', he moves through that life bearing, in addition to the names given him at birth, a name he has earned 'alone' – unaided, singlehandedly – by virtue of his extraordinary valour. His mother's greeting when he triumphantly returns to Rome registers the implications of that name: 'My gentle Martius, worthy Caius, and / By deed-achieving honour newly nam'd – / What is it? – Coriolanus, must I call thee?' (II.i.171). The son whose new name she stumbles over is now, in ways he was not before, the offspring of his own prodigious powers as a warrior.

The power to act 'alone' as an autonomous individual helps to differentiate Coriolanus from the tribunes and plebeians, whose 'infant-like' reliance on collective action Menenius mocks:

I know you can do very little alone, for your helps are many, or else your actions would grow wondrous single: your abilities are too infant-like for doing much alone. (II.i.34–7)

For Coriolanus, the differences between himself and the plebeians are absolute, and he resists acknowledging any dependence upon them, any need or want of his that they can satisfy. His distaste for what Roman custom entitles them to demand that he do in order to be consul is not simply patrician disdain. Coriolanus will not accept what the civic rituals of displaying his wounds to them, wearing humble garments before them, and asking for their voices (votes) affirm: that they as well as he are parts of Rome, members of the same civic body. Early in the final scene, Aufidius, Coriolanus's great rival, cautions those who tell him they are ready to kill Coriolanus: 'We must proceed as we do find the people' (V.vi.16). His words convey recognition of a fact of political life that Coriolanus refuses to acknowledge while in Rome: public actions must take into account the feelings of the common people. They have a 'part' in the political process that must be accommodated, even manipulated. Theirs is not, as Coriolanus insists, a 'part' that 'might well / Be taken from the people' (II.ii.144–6).

Coriolanus juxtaposes two modes of social existence: one, voiced by Coriolanus, stressing the singularity and autonomy of the individual, the other, voiced by the tribunes and the people, stressing every citizen's membership in a corporate and collective entity. The two clash most nakedly at the moment when the people '*All*' affirm the sentence of banishment upon Coriolanus – 'It shall be so! It shall be so!' – and he in turn responds, 'I banish you' (III.iii.119, 123).

Coriolanus's banishment from Rome is the inverse of his isolation within Corioli. Then he was shut within an alien city; now he is cast out of his native city. In each instance, Coriolanus finds himself cut off from his fellow Romans, and, as it did with the battle at Corioli, the play re-works the North–Plutarch account to emphasise his isolation. In 'The Life', he went into exile 'with three or foure of his friendes only' (Brockbank, 1976, p. 343), but in the play he declines Cominius's offer to accompany him, choosing instead to 'go alone, / Like to a lonely dragon' (IV.i.29–30).

The play explores the paradox and limitations of the 'aloneness' Coriolanus prizes. Shakespeare's Coriolanus goes into exile alone, but the first view of him in exile that the play gives shows him in Antium seeking human company even if it means his death: 'Direct me . . . Where great Aufidius lies' (IV.iv.7–8). Early in the play the First Citizen explains how the 'misery' of the commoners is a 'gain' to the patricians because without it they cannot 'particularise' – cannot measure and savour – their own 'abundance' (I.i.19–20). Just as the wealth of the patricians becomes meaningful only in relation to the misery of the plebeians, the power to be and to act 'alone' becomes significant only in relationship to others who do not or cannot. Just as Coriolanus needs the voices of the people to be consul, so he needs their multitudinous and many-headed variety as a ground or backdrop against which to define his own self-sufficiency and autonomy. If he is to see himself as a man, they must be 'infant-like'.

To be a warrior, Coriolanus must have enemies, be they the Volsci and Aufidius or, later, the Romans. When the gates of Corioli close upon him, he is 'alone' only in the sense that no Roman is with him, but he needs the Volsci he fights against there in order to display his remarkable valour, which is 'the chiefest virtue' (II.ii.84). The name he wins in that battle sets him apart to some degree from his mother, but it also binds him inextricably to the Volsci, whose humiliation is the basis for his glory – which is why, calling him Martius, Aufidius refuses to address him as 'Coriolanus' in the final scene: 'Dost thou think / I'll grace thee with that robbery, thy stol'n name / Coriolanus, in Corioles?' (V.vi.88–90). Won 'alone' and 'aidless' (II.ii.110, 112), the name 'Coriolanus' announces its bearer's self-sufficiency, yet at the same time it also signals his inescapable involvement with others. A name 'stol'n' from the Volsci, it is conferred in a public Roman ceremony, and 'Coriolanus' functions as a name only if others, including Volumnia and Aufidius, use it. The name 'Coriolanus' belongs not only to its bearer but also to the people and the societies that agree to call him that.

The play also qualifies the degree to which Coriolanus's martial actions are exclusively his. Twice Volumnia insists that she shares in his accomplishments as a soldier: 'Thy valiantness was mine, thou suck'st it from me' (III.ii.129) and 'Thou art my warrior: / I holp to frame thee' (V.iii.62–3). Even before audiences behold Coriolanus in battle, they hear Volumnia describe how he will 'pluck Aufidius down by th' hair' and wipe 'his bloody brow / with his mail'd hand'

(I.iii.30, 34–5). She also performs actions and speaks words that correspond to what he later does and says on the battlefield: 'Methinks I see him stamp thus, and call thus / "Come on you cowards . . . ." ' (I.iii.32–3). Volumnia's power to anticipate accurately the acts and words of her warrior son gives weight to her claim that his martial prowess is hers as well as his.

Coriolanus is never simply his own warrior, never simply his own creation. He is his mother's, and he is Rome's, too, since she identifies herself with the city. '[T]hou shalt no sooner / March to assault thy country', she warns during her second appeal to him, 'than to tread . . . on thy mother's womb / That brought thee to this world' (V.iii.122–5). He is also the patricians' soldier. The First Senator's observation that 'He cannot but with measure fit the honours / Which we devise him' (II.ii.121–2) implies that the patricians also participate in shaping him. The words can and do mean that Coriolanus deserves the honours he is to receive, but at the same time they can and do mean that Coriolanus will conform to whatever form they 'devise' for him. Coriolanus is also the warrior of those who are Rome's enemies. His first words when he returns to Corioli after sparing Rome extends Volumnia's claim that he is her warrior to '*the Lords of the City*', who are the Volscian equivalent of Roman senators, 'Hail lords, I am return'd your soldier' (V.vi.60,71). Coriolanus does not exist autonomously but within and with respect to a network of relationships, among them those between his mother and himself, Aufidius and himself, and the commoners and himself as well as those between patricians and plebeians and between Volscians and Romans.

Coriolanus's first appearance in the play is timed to encourage audiences to view him in relation to others. He enters directly after Menenius completes his fable of the belly, which articulates the conviction that the state, like a heathy human body, is, or ought to be, an organic unity, each member contributing to the welfare of the whole by carrying out its distinctive function: 'The kingly crown'd head, the vigilant eye, / The counsellor heart, the arm our soldier, / Our steed the leg, the tongue our trumpeter' (I.i.114–16). There is no trace of the fable in the North–Plutarch 'Life', and its placement at this point frames the audience's initial perception of Coriolanus, disposing them to ask whether he is a part of the corporate whole of Rome, and if so, what is the relationship between this uniquely skilled warrior and the city that needs him for its defence? Is he, as

Sicinius the tribune later argues, 'a disease that must be cut away', or is he, as Menenius replies, 'a limb that has but a disease: / Mortal, to cut it off; to cure it, easy' (III.i.292–4).

The most succinct expession of Coriolanus's ambiguous place within the Roman body politic occurs when Titus Lartius, thinking him slain within Corioli's walls, likens him to a carbuncle: 'Thou art left, Martius: / A carbuncle entire, as big as thou art, / Were not so rich a jewel' (I.iv.54–6). In Shakespeare's time, 'carbuncle' could refer to a precious stone deep-red in colour (e.g., a garnet), which is the meaning Lartius intends. However, that meaning co-existed with another still widely used today: a 'carbuncle' is also a pus-bearing inflammation of the tissue beneath the skin. Coriolanus is both forms of 'carbuncle', simultaneously a person of extraordinary value to a Rome that needs defending from external enemies and a site of infection in the Roman body politic.

What proves to be Coriolanus's supreme moment also reveals the paradox and limits of autonomy. It comes when Coriolanus calls a second time for the Roman troops battling the Volsci to follow him:

> If any think brave death outweighs bad life,
> And that his country's dearer than himself;
> Let him alone, or so many so minded,
> Wave thus to express his disposition,
> And follow Martius.
>
> (I.vi.71–5)

Earlier, he had called for men to follow him through the gates of Corioli – 'Mark me, and do the like' – but none did, leaving him 'alone, / To answer all the city' (I.iv.45, 51–2). Now, '*They all shout and wave their swords. . . . They take him up in their arms, and cast up their caps*' (I.vi.75). Those who cheer and lift Coriolanus here are common men like those he scorns and dismisses at every other point in the play, but his reaction to them now is radically different. Delighting in their acclaim and in the physical contact their lifting arms provide, he exclaims, 'O me alone! Make you a sword of me!' (I.vi.76). The moment works against the sense of isolation and autonomy associated elsewhere with the word 'alone'. In this context, Michael Goldman points out, 'alone' means 'singled out by others, uniquely valued by people with whom he feels a bond' (1985, p. 155). Coriolanus here accepts, as he does nowhere else in the play, the ties that bind him to the commoners as his fellow Romans. He accepts, even revels in, their touch. Later he will assert his absolute autonomy and refuse to participate in public rituals that acknowledge the commoners' power to participate in making him consul. Now, however, he testifies to the capacity of common soldiers to make him into what he longs to be, the heroic sword of the community: 'Make you a sword of me'.

That acceptance does not endure, but while it lasts, it contributes to a moment of heartfelt *communitas*, a sense of oneness and equality. Suspended for the instant are the distinctions in social rank, the hierarchical ordering of individuals and classes that elsewhere Coriolanus insists upon and prizes as the principle that makes Rome Rome. Paradoxically, the feeling of *communitas* produces a stage picture that at first glance seems to confirm that hierarchy, for the commoners' arms lift and hold Coriolanus above them – a position that testifies to his superiority. The difference is that the social organisation pictured briefly when they take Coriolanus up in their arms is one that they help to create and maintain, not the one to which, he elsewhere insists, they must submit.

The sense of *communitas* also manifests itself in how Coriolanus addresses the commoners in whose hands he finds himself lifted and held willingly, even jubilantly above them. For the only time in the play he ungrudgingly uses words like 'please' and 'thanks' that convey respect as he speaks to them: 'A certain number, / (Though thanks to all) must I select ... Please you to march' (I.vi.80–3). Soldiers whom he before denounced as having 'souls of geese' when they fled from the Volscians he now proclaims to be the equal of Aufidius: 'None of you but is / Able to bear against the great Aufidius / A shield as hard as his' (I.vi.78–80). With those words, he makes each of those who make 'a sword' of him virtually his own equal, since Aufidius is the one man Coriolanus regards as possibly his equal: 'And were I anything but what I am, / I would wish me only he' (I.i.230–1). While their arms hold him aloft, Coriolanus experiences himself not as a distinct, autonomous, utterly self-sufficient human being but as one singularly prized member of a corporate whole, as the cherished limb – the soldierly arm and sword – of a healthy social organism engaged in (what he regards as) the most vital of communal enterprises, war.

The play further defines the limits of Coriolanus's self-sufficiency by controlling both how audiences see during a performance and what they do (and do not) see. It denies them any sight of the combat within the walls of Corioli that is the most compelling proof of the superior valour that sustains Coriolanus's sense of autonomy. On the other hand, it does ensure that they see Coriolanus die as he earlier fought in Corioli – 'alone' among the Volsci.[4] The death they watch him die is nothing like the heroically valorous death his fellow Romans and audiences (momentarily) think he dies the first time 'he is himself alone / To answer all the city'. He dies at the hands of assassins acting on behalf of Aufidius, the only man with whom he engages in one-to-one combat and whom he described earlier as 'a lion / That I am proud to hunt' (I.i.234–5). Aufidius offers, as one possible explanation of Coriolanus's banishment, his inability to change, 'to be other than one thing', and to shift from war to peace, 'from th'casque to th'cushion' (IV.vii.42–3). The Coriolanus whom the conspirators slay has changed, however. Coriolanus dies as a peacemaker – as he presents to the Volsci the treaty he has compelled the Romans to sign.

During the battle of Corioli, audiences see Coriolanus use his sword effectively in single combat against Aufidius. When other Volsci join the fight '*in the aid of Aufidius*', the stage direction makes clear Coriolanus is not daunted: '*Martius fights till they be driven in breathless*' (I.viii.13). Audiences also see him draw his sword in defiant resistance when the tribune Brutus calls for the citizens to seize and execute him:

> BRU.: Lay hands upon him,
>   And bear him to the rock.
>   *Coriolanus draws his sword.*
> COR.: No, I'll die here.
>   There's some among you have beheld me fighting:
>   Come, try upon yourselves what you have seen me!
>   (III.i.220–3)

What audiences see on those two occasions makes all the more significant what they do not see when Coriolanus dies. With his last words, Coriolanus proclaims his desire to 'use my lawful sword' against one Aufidius, 'six Aufidiuses, or more, his tribe' (V.vi.128–9), but the playtext offers no evidence that he uses that sword against the conspirators. No stage direction and no signal in the dialogue establishes that audiences see him kill or wound or even resist any of those who slay him. That omission establishes a telling contrast not only with the Coriolanus seen earlier on the battlefield and in Rome but also with Shakespeare's other warrior protagonists. Othello and Antony turn their weapons on themselves and die at their own hands, and Macbeth, whose valour and skill in defence of Duncan's crown audiences never see, dies engaged in a single combat he knows he cannot win against Macduff, a man 'of no woman born' (V.viii.31). Audiences watching *Coriolanus* see this most gifted of warriors die without exercising the prowess that makes him extraordinary, either because the conspirators' attack catches him totally offguard or because he does not resist. The Coriolanus (Laurence Olivier) of Peter Hall's 1959 production at Stratford-upon-Avon clearly chose not to resist, according to Kenneth Tynan:

> Olivier is roused to suicidal frenzy by Aufidius' gibe – 'thou boy of tears'. '*Boy!*' shrieks the overmothered general . . . and leaps up a flight of precipitous steps to vent his rage. Arrived at the top, he relents and throws his sword away . . . [and] allows a dozen spears to impale him. He is poised, now, on a promontory some twelve feet above the stage, from which he topples, to be caught by the ankles so that he dangles, inverted, like the slaughtered Mussolini. (quoted in Berry, 1981, p. 29)

Audiences see Coriolanus slain by '*Conspirators of Aufidius's faction*' (V.vi.8), but who, exactly, are those conspirators? The playtext makes it clear that they are neither '*the Commoners*' who enter with Coriolanus and are then provoked into calling for his death, nor the '*Lords of the city*', who first try to prevent the slaying and then resolve to 'make the best of it' (V.vi.59, 146). Beyond that, however, the playtext does not specify the identity and social rank of the conspirators. It is as if the act they perform is, on the one hand, so heinous that it defies the social classifications recognised within early Jacobean culture and, on the other, the expression of feelings either so widely or so secretly held that the deed cannot be assigned to any one group in that culture. Are the conspirators civilians or soldiers? plebeians or patricians? The playtext does not answer such questions, but each production, in determining what its audiences will see, must. In the Hall production, the conspirators are military men; audiences saw Coriolanus allow 'a dozen spears to impale him'. In the Royal Shakespeare Company's 1990 production, directed by

Terry Hands with John Barton, those who cut down Coriolanus are Volscian women. Audiences saw their knives complete the deadly process that Volumnia, the woman who gave Coriolanus life, set in motion when she prevails upon her son – 'most dangerously . . . If not most mortal to him' – to spare Rome.

After Coriolanus falls, the stage direction specifies that *'Aufidius stands on him'*, and that detail, along with the cry 'Tread not upon him', guarantees that the contrast between Coriolanus's status as a warrior and the manner of his dying registers vividly on audiences (V.vi.130, 134). What they see inverts Volumnia's prediction, awaiting news of the battle of Corioli, that Coriolanus will 'beat Aufidius's head below his knee / And tread upon his neck' (I.iii.46–7). That sight also reverses what audiences see during that moment of *communitas* as Coriolanus exults in being borne aloft in the hands of those he hails as the equals of Aufidius. The overall effect of the play's presentation of Coriolanus's death is to ensure that audiences see him die in a way at odds with his stature as a warrior, which is at the core of his conception of his unique identity and his sense of autonomous self-sufficiency.

Coriolanus also take advantage of other aspects of what and how its audiences see during a performance. For example, although it re-works 'The Life' so that Coriolanus enters the gates of Corioli 'alone' and goes into exile 'alone', it rarely allows audiences to *see* him alone onstage. He is briefly alone as many as three times during the scene (II.iii) in which he solicits the citizens' votes, while he waits for one cluster of citizens to arrive after another has departed, and he has only two soliloquies (II.iii.111–23; IV.iv.1–6, 12–26), neither as sustained nor as intensely personal as any of those Hamlet speaks. *Coriolanus* never gives audiences the sense, so pronounced in *Hamlet*, that they are privy to the protagonist's innermosts thoughts and feelings. Far from fostering intimacy between Coriolanus and the audience, the play denies it. It gives audiences no opportunity to see and hear Coriolanus struggling to decide whether to betray Rome and offer his services to the Volsci. Instead of providing a soliloquy like the one in which Macbeth weighs whether or not to kill Duncan, the play has Coriolanus simply announce – as one more example of the world's 'slippery turns' – his change of heart: 'My birthplace hate I, and my love's upon / This enemy town' (IV.iv.12, 23–4).

Even during the infrequent moments when Coriolanus is alone on stage, audiences see him (and the actor playing him) in a way that is

radically public and communal, inescapably different from the autonomy he asserts. Because each member of the audiences is in the
presence of other members, each sees Coriolanus much as the citizens
of Rome see him – as members of a collective entity, of a corporate
body. In contrast, those who read the playtext of *Coriolanus* read
alone, in isolation, experiencing the playtext and its protagonist in a
way that is inherently individualistic and solitary and thus fundamentally different from how audiences do. The process of reading – as
distinct from the judgements and attitudes individual readers might
form – is compatible with the autonomy Coriolanus claims, but the
processes of seeing and hearing in which theatre audiences engage
during a performance work to qualify and question, if not undercut,
that claim.

7

The Winter's Tale: 'Awake Your Faith'

As it enacts the consequences, destructive yet ultimately joyous, of a king's loss of faith in his queen, *The Winter's Tale* tests, more audaciously than any other play called 'Shakespeare's', the fidelity of its audiences – their capacity and willingness to participate, with players and playwright, in the processes of creating and sustaining theatrical life. Composed sometime between 1609 and 15 May 1611 (the date of the earliest performance on record), the play also illustrates two developments – described in Chapter 1 – central to what proved to be the final phase of Shakespeare's career. One is a distinct shift, away from tragedy, in the kind of plays he provided for the King's Men to perform after 1608. The second is a radical change, also after 1608, in the immediate circumstances under which he and they carried out the theatrical work by which they earned their livings.

The Winter's Tale demonstrates the lengths to which Shakespeare went after 1608 to avoid writing tragedy. With *King Lear* a few years earlier, he had fashioned a tragedy by inverting the sources on which he drew. In all of them, Lear and Cordelia emerge alive and victorious, but the Shakespearean play ends with the aged king and the daughter who loves him most defeated and dead. With *The Winter's Tale*, Shakespeare inverts the potentially tragic material of his major source, Robert Greene's prose romance *Pandosto: The Triumph of Time*, in precisely the opposite way. In *Pandosto*, Hermione's prototype dies, and Leontes's prototype commits suicide upon discovering that the young woman to whom he is sexually attracted is the child whom he had rejected at birth as a bastard and had ordered to be cast adrift on the sea. In *The Winter's Tale* the desire that the sight of Perdita awakes in Leontes leads not to his suicide but to his renewed

153

involvement in 'Dear life' (V.iii.103). Paulina's announcement of Hermione's death makes her, like her counterpart in *Pandosto*, a victim of her husband's erroneous but lethal jealousy. However, in a defiance of his source at least as bold as that he carried out with *King Lear*, Shakespeare then goes on, during the play's final moments, to undo the death to which he and *Pandosto* had consigned Hermione. He stages the theatrical equivalent of a resurrection by having what is supposed to be a statue of the dead queen turn out to be Hermione herself – not dead, but alive, warm to her husband's touch and moved to speech by the presence of the daughter taken from her at birth.

In the summer of 1608, the same year that Shakespeare wrote what proved to be his last tragedy, the King's Men took a step that profoundly altered the company's professional and commercial circumstances. They signed a lease giving them playing rights at the 'private'[1] theatre located in what had been a monastery for Black-friars (Dominicans) within the boundaries of the city of London. Displacing the previous occupants, a company of boy actors, the Children of the Queen's Revels, they began performing there some-time in 1609. They made it their winter playhouse while continuing to perform during the summer months at the Globe, the open-air 'public' theatre, located beyond the city limits, that had been their principal playing site since 1599.

The move to Blackfriars marked the triumph of the King's Men over one of the boys' companies, but it also posed specifically theatrical challenges different from any they and their principal playwright had faced since the company's founding in 1594 as the Lord Chamberlain's Men. For the first time, the King's Men found themselves in need of, and Shakespeare found himself called upon to provide, plays that could be performed effectively in two playhouses where the circumstances of performances and the composition and expectations of the audiences were sharply different.[2]

The Winter's Tale is one such play, and it makes clear how, in turning away after 1608 from tragedy, the genre upon which his creative energies had been intensely, if not exclusively, concentrated for the previous five years, Shakespeare also turned towards plays that, in a variety of ways, especially their dramaturgy, resemble the romances and tragicomedies the boys' companies had taken to per-forming as part of their effort to establish an identity different from that of the adult companies. The success of the boys' companies had helped to create a demand for such plays, to which the King's Men had to be responsive if they were to hold the audiences they gained after taking over Blackfriars. One sign of the extent of that resemblance is that most editions of Shakespeare's complete plays widely used today present *The Winter's Tale* and the other 'late' plays as a generically distinct group – variously labelled 'tragicomedies' or 'romances' – separate from his tragedies, comedies, and histories.[3]

The Winter's Tale, David Bevington notes, 'illustrates perhaps more clearly than any other Shakespearean play the genre of tragicomedy' (1992, p. 1484). It combines features associated with both tragedy and comedy in the manner of such plays as John Marston's *The Malcontent* (1603–4) and John Fletcher's *The Faithful Shepherdess* (1608), both written for performance by the boys' company the King's Men displaced from Blackfriars. It deals – as Shakespearean tragedies typically do – with events that directly involve the fate of nations, the kingdoms of Sicilia and Bohemia. It includes the deaths of two characters who appear onstage and with whom therefore audiences have some degree of involvement: the courtier Antigonus and the young prince Mamillius. No such deaths, which are staple elements of Shakespeare's tragedies, occur in any of the comedies he wrote while Elizabeth reigned or in the comedy that was his first Jacobean play, *Measure for Measure*.[4] Such features co-exist, however, with others that are comedic. Polixenes's command that Florizel break off his relationship with Perdita sets in motion a typically comedic conflict arising from a father's opposition to his child's choice of a spouse. Florizel's defiance is equally typical of comedy. Valuing his love for Perdita more than his status as his father's son and his successor as king, he declares, 'I / Am heir to my affection' (IV.iv.481–2). Seeking fulfilment of their love, Florizel and Perdita then flee Bohemia just as the lovers Lysander and Hermia in *A Midsummer Night's Dream* flee Athens, seeking a place beyond the forest where 'the sharp Athenian law' (I.i.162) cannot pursue them. *The Winter's Tale* also ends like most of the comedies Shakespeare wrote during Elizabeth's reign: with prospective marriages and the reunion of family members long separated.

By mixing features specific to different genres, *The Winter's Tale* affiliates itself with the kind of play that Sir Philip Sidney scorned as 'mongrel tragi-comedy' in his *Defence of Poesy* (1965, p. 135), written in the early 1580s and first published in 1595. The existence of plays in such a 'mongrel' form challenged the very idea of absolute distinctions between genres, which in turn was the basis for the concept of a hierarchy of genres ranging from high (tragedy) to low (comedy).

In the cultural conditions of the early Jacobean era, which emphasised social hierarchy and fixed distinctions between classes, the
ramifications of that challenge were more than simply literary and
theatrical. Polixenes, stepping out of the disguise that conceals his
distinctive identity as king, prohibits the marriage between Florizel
and Perdita because – like tragicomedy – it would violate the
distinction between high and low by uniting the base-born daughter
of a lowly shepherd and a prince, 'a sceptre's heir' (IV.iv.420). The
discovery of Perdita's full identity as a princess of royal blood allows
the marriage to go forward in a way that reconciles the conflict
between erotic desire and fixed social hierarchy.

At the same time, however, the moment of that discovery also
begets a social mobility that eludes and transgresses the distinctions
of blood and birth that Polixenes is determined to uphold. After
Perdita's identity becomes known, the Clown appears, now wearing
garb appropriate for a gentleman, and recounts how he and his
father have risen to the rank of gentlemen and acquired as 'our
kindred' the members of two royal families:

> . . . for the king's son took me by the hand, and called me
> brother; and then the two kings called my father brother; and
> then the prince, my brother, and the princess, my sister, called
> my father father; and so we wept; and there was the first
> gentleman-like tears that ever we shed. (V.ii.173, 140–5)

The Clown's insistence that he is 'now' not only 'a gentleman born'
but also 'a gentleman born before my father' (V.ii.134–5, 139–40)
draws attention to the gap that has opened between social station
and birth, straining, if not severing, a linkage that was a linchpin of
the official Jacobean conception of social hierarchy and stability.

A similar gap between theory and practice existed in Jacobean
society. In 1611, the same year as the first recorded performance of
The Winter's Tale, King James, needing revenue, established a new
aristocratic rank – the baronetcy – and began conferring the titles of
baron and baroness on those wealthy enough to purchase them. The
sale of baronetcies is but one particularly glaring example of how, in
contravention of official social theory and ideology, marriage and
wealth enabled people to move into social ranks into which they had
not been born. In fact, Shakespeare himself was one who rose socially
as a result of wealth he accumulated, primarily through his theatrical

activities. In 1596, 'Shakespeare the player' was granted a coat of arms, indicative of the rank of gentleman, and in 1599, the grant was extended to his father John. Shakespeare was not 'a gentleman born' before his father but he was a gentleman made before him.

In a manner typical of tragicomedy, *The Winter's Tale* first moves towards tragedy, then, abruptly reversing its trajectory, moves to a comedic conclusion. By the end of Act III, Scene ii, Leontes's jealousy has cost him his wife, his son, and his infant daughter. Those losses strip him of his capacity to resist Time and his own mortality by participating, through offspring, in the broad natural cycle of birth, growth, death, and renewal. They also jeopardise the well-being of the kingdom by breaking the line of royal succession, leaving Bohemia without an heir to the throne and facing a dangerously uncertain future (much as England did during the final decade of the childless Elizabeth's reign).

The reversal begins in the next scene, which shifts the play's locale from Leontes's court in Sicily to an isolated place somewhere along the coast of Bohemia. There, Antigonus, obeying Leontes's orders, abandons the infant Perdita as a storm descends and then, *'pursued by a bear'* (III.iii.58), flees for his life. Directly after that exit, the Old Shepherd enters and takes the helpless infant into his care. Perdita's rescue is timed to coincide with the (offstage) destruction of those who carried her to Bohemia; the Clown enters and tells of seeing Antigonus being torn apart and devoured by the bear and the ship that carried him breaking up in the storm with the loss of all aboard. The Old Shepherd's response includes a sentence that brings into concentrated focus both the play's shift in direction and its characteristic merging of opposites: 'thou met'st with things dying, I with things new-born' (III.iii.112-3).

The shift from tragedy to comedy overlaps with other broad movements that, cumulatively, give *The Winter's Tale* compelling mythic and even religious resonances. The song that Autolycus sings at his first entrance announces one of them, the movement from winter to spring:

> *When daffodils begin to peer,*
> *With heigh! the doxy over the dale,*
> *Why then comes in the sweet o' the year,*
> *For the red blood reigns in the winter's pale.*
> (IV.iii.1-4)

The most striking verbal reference to the movement of the seasons occurs when, greeting Florizel and Perdita, newly come to his court, Leontes links their arrival and the return of spring. 'Welcome hither', he tells them, 'As is the spring to th' earth' (V.i.150–1).

Productions of *The Winter's Tale* frequently use the process of performance to convey the movement from winter to spring. The Royal Shakespeare Company's 1976 production, directed by John Barton with Trevor Nunn, used Autolycus's entrance as a visual metaphor for that seasonal movement. He emerged from under white sheets suggestive of winter snow. Peter Brook's 1961 production at the Phoenix Theatre (London) employed a different strategy. Snow began falling heavily after the bear chased Antigonus offstage, and Time emerged, shivering, to speak the chorus. As Time spoke, the storm eased and warm sunlight gradually filled the stage. In the 1981 BBC-TV production, directed by Jane Howell, a tree that is utterly bare during the first three acts is in leaf during the fourth and fifth.

The movement from winter to spring coincides with another, from death to rebirth. Perdita's invocation of Proserpina (IV.iv.116–8) enables *The Winter's Tale* to invoke one of the chief myths by which classical Greece and Rome had come to terms with the process of death and rebirth that accompanies the passing of the seasons. Proserpina, the daughter of the goddess Ceres, spends six months of each year above ground with her mother and then six months out of her mother's sight and beneath the ground with the god of the underworld who had raped and kidnapped her. *The Winter's Tale* gives that myth a specifically theatrical inflection by keeping Hermione out of the audience's sight for nearly half the play – from the moment in Act III, Scene ii when she is carried off in a faint that Paulina subsequently announces is mortal until after her daughter has returned to Sicily like 'spring to th'earth' and has gained her rightful place in her father's court. Then, during the final scene, as what is supposed to be her statue becomes Hermione herself, audiences see her re-enter the world to which she has been effectively, if not actually, dead for sixteen years. They also see, for the first and only time in the play, mother and daughter together.

Hermione's return from death endows *The Winter's Tale* with what, for many, are profound religious resonances. The process by which she comes to life takes on not just a magical but also a liturgical, even sacramental character. Presiding over that process, Paulina urges any who 'think it is unlawful business / I am about' to withdraw – 'let them depart' – and she summons all those who are present, including the theatre audience, to form a community of believers: 'It is requir'd', she tells them, 'you do awake your faith' (V.iii.94–7). When Leontes embraces the wife taken from him because he lost faith in her fidelity, he completes a passage from sin through contrition and expiation to a new life of grace. Repeatedly, *The Winter's Tale* associates the word 'grace' with Hermione, most conspicuously during its final moments, when, with the first words she speaks after rejoining the living, she prays, 'You gods, look down, / And from your sacred vials pour your graces / Upon my daughter's head!' (V.iii.121–3). In Shakespearean comedies, as Alfred Harbage noted, 'the perpetuation of life seems a merry business' (1969, p. 1257), but in *The Winter's Tale* it verges on the mystical and the sacred.

Conceptions of the sacred change over time, yet even today, during what many regard as a post-Christian era, *The Winter's Tale* remains capable of profoundly moving its audiences, many of whom do not believe in resurrection after death. The play has such power because the passage Leontes undergoes corresponds to one of the most basic and compelling patterns in human experience. As winter gives way to spring, Leontes passes through the different seasons and climates of the human heart. His is also a journey from error through suffering to fuller knowledge and new happiness, as well as a psychological passage from solopsistic neurosis and sustained isolation into a new, deeper engagement with loved ones from whom he had severed himself. Leontes's journey appeals to and sustains one of the most persistent of human hopes – the possibility that the forces shaping human lives are fundamentally benevolent and will provide a second chance all the more welcome because it is undeserved and unexpected.

Much of what happens in *The Winter's Tale* is, for characters and audiences alike, outside, beyond, at odds with what ordinary experience says is probable, credible, likely, plausible. That is consistent with Frank Kermode's definition of romance as 'a mode of exhibiting the action of magical and moral laws in a version of human life so selective as to obscure, for the special purpose of concentrating attention on those laws, the fact that in reality their force is intermittent and only fitfully glimpsed' (1954, p. liv). Paulina declares that the possibility that Leontes's 'lost child will be found . . . Is all as monstrous to our human reason / As my Antigonus to break his grave / And come again to me' (V.i.40–3). What is 'monstrous' comes to pass. The 'lost child' is found, and although Antigonus does not 'break his grave' and return, Hermione does. The implausibility of those and other events is, for some commentators, a serious, even crippling, deficiency in the play, but it is also the quality that most forcefully establishes the play's character as a romance, the essence of which, according to Brian Gibbons, is 'an encounter with events so strange that the hero is challenged to the limits, yielding an experience so radical that it produces a transformation' (1990, p. 234).

The Winter's Tale includes many elements associated with romances that earlier generations had enjoyed both as plays and in story form: prolonged separations, unexpected reunions, abandoned infants, royal offspring raised in ignorance of their true identities and recognised by tokens or birthmarks, the seemingly miraculous return of persons thought dead. Its major source, Greene's *Pandosto* (1588), is a narrative romance, and *The Winter's Tale* has specific affiliations with the anonymous *Mucedorus* (*c*.1590), which the King's Men revived in 1610, and with George Peele's *The Old Wives Tale* (*c*.1593) that reveal how it draws upon and re-casts elements of earlier romance plays, fashioning 'something fresh out of the fragments of a ridiculed past' (Bliss, 1990, p. 237).[5]

The Winter's Tale repeatedly draws attention to its own implausibility. For example, it violates geographical fact by having Antigonus abandon the infant Perdita on the seacoast of Bohemia, a land-locked country, and not, as in *Pandosto*, on the coast of Sicily, an island. Characters in *The Winter's Tale* repeatedly compare the surprising events they are part of to the plot twists of ancient stories that challenge credulity. When Rogero reports that 'the Oracle is fulfilled; the king's daughter is found', he compares what has come to pass to the highly improbable events associated with 'an old tale:' 'This news, which is called true, is so like an old tale that the verity of it is in strong suspicion' (V.ii.22–3, 27–9). Explaining what has befallen Paulina's husband Antigonus, her steward makes the same comparison: 'Like an old tale still . . . He was torn to pieces with a bear' (V.ii.62–4). Paulina herself uses the comparison during the most conspicuously improbable turn of events in this or any other Shakespearean play. As Hermione, 'stone no more', embraces the husband who has mourned her death for sixteen years, Paulina comments, 'That she is living, / Were it but told you, should be hooted at / Like an old tale' (V.ii.99, 115–17).

The play's flamboyant implausibility is one facet of a dramaturgy that is defiantly experimental and risky, even provocative, in the demands it makes on its audiences. In places, the play's stagecraft is self-consciously old-fashioned and inexpert to the point of being crude – proof, it has occasionally been argued, that Shakespeare's powers were waning after peaking some years earlier in the tragedies. The Old Shepherd's discovery of the infant Perdita immediately after Antigonus abandons her is one of several wild coincidences in the play. The stage direction *'exit pursued by a bear'* allows for stage business that can verge on slapstick. The use of Time as a chorus draws attention to how the play splits abruptly into two parts, leaping from one point in time at the end of Act III to another point sixteen years later at the start of Act IV. In contrast to the Chorus in *Henry V*, Time does not call upon the audience to assist in remedying the shortcomings of the performance process, does not appeal to them to 'Piece out our imperfections with your thoughts' (Prologue 23). Instead, in *The Winter's Tale* Time urges them to accept the decision to 'slide / O'er sixteen years' by emphasising that the dramatic rules and conventions such a 'wide gap' violates are themselves the products of time and thus subject to his arbitrary authority: 'it is in my power / To o'erthrow law, and in one self-born hour / To plant and o'erwhelm custom' (IV.i.5–9). Autolycus, a character essential to the play's resolution, does not appear until the fourth act, and the sequence of events by which he, Perdita, Florizel, Perdita, the Old Shepherd, and the Clown all find themselves aboard the same ship bound for Leontes's court is blatantly contrived.

* * *

Such stagecraft is part of the process by which *The Winter's Tale* makes extraordinary demands on its audiences, testing their willingness to accept as theatrically engaging the characters and events they are hearing and seeing. That testing is most audacious and most risky during the play's first two scenes and its last two scenes. With its opening dialogue, *The Winter's Tale* calls upon its audience to accept the existence of a lifelong friendship between two kings so deep it can withstand the effects of time and distance. '[T]rained together in their childhoods', Camillo says, Leontes and Polixenes have 'seemed to be together, though absent; shook hands, as over a vast; and embraced, as it were, from the ends of opposed winds' (I.i.22–31). Archidamus's reply declares his faith in the kings' friendship: 'I think there is not in the world either malice or matter to alter it' (I.i.33–4).

In its next scene, the play challenges its audiences to witness and accept the virtually instantaneous destruction of that friendship as Leontes convinces himself that the father of the child to whom his wife will soon give birth is not he but Polixenes. That jealous conviction does more than 'alter' Leontes's feelings of friendship for Polixenes. It transforms them into murderous malice.

In *Othello*, Shakespeare's first Jacobean tragedy, another husband becomes unshakably and murderously certain of his wife's infidelity, and comparing that play with *The Winter's Tale* reveals how Leontes's jealousy is presented in a manner that makes it more rather than less difficult for audiences to credit. *Othello* traces the progressive development of Othello's jealousy – from the moment when Iago plants the seed of suspicion to the instant when Othello concludes that Desdemona has been unfaithful: 'Now do I see 'tis true' (III.iii.451). Audiences see clearly how Othello comes to be possessed by 'a jealousy so strong / That judgement cannot cure' (II.i.296–7). *The Winter's Tale* provides no such clarity. No malevolent external agent equivalent to Iago provokes Leontes's jealousy. He, unlike Othello, is not 'abus'd . . . by some putter-on / That will be damn'd for 't' (*WT*. II.i.141–2). His jealousy is self-generated, the offspring of his own imaginings, insecurities, and fears. 'My life stands', Leontes's wife Hermione tells him at her trial, 'in the level of your dreams', to which he replies, 'Your actions are my dreams' (III.ii.81–2). What Emilia says of Othello's jealousy proves far more true of Leontes's: ' '[T]is a monster, / Begot upon itself, born upon itself' (*Oth*. III.iv.159–60).

Greene's *Pandosto* leaves no doubt that Hermione's prototype is innocent of adultery, yet it also provides a plausible explanation for her husband's conviction that she has been unfaithful with his closest friend: 'oftentimes' she came 'herself into his bed chamber to see that nothing should be amiss to mislike him' and 'there grew such a secret uniting of their affections, that the one could not well be without the company of the other . . .' (Pafford, 1963, pp. 185–6). *The Winter's Tale*, in contrast, conveys no comparable information to its audiences, even though the opening dialogue between Archidamus and Camillo provides an ideal opportunity to do so. The first words audiences hear Polixenes speak – 'Nine changes of the watery star' (I.ii.1) – establish that his visit to Leontes's court has lasted long enough for it to be biologically possible for him to have fathered Hermione's unborn child. Beyond that, however, the play avoids providing a basis for Leontes's jealousy that would make it less 'monstrous to our human reason'. In so doing, it violates conceptions of what makes a novel or a play worthy of sustained attention that have been dominant since at least the Romantic era: the exploration of the inner depths of three-dimensional, believable characters with whom one can empathise, if not identify, because their deeds, thoughts, and feelings correspond to what reason and the patterns of daily living say are the facts of the human situation. *The Winter's Tale*, through its commitment to non-realistic modes, tries to engage its audiences with what lies beyond, behind such facts.

Othello, during his final moments, tries to learn 'why' Iago 'hath thus ensnar'd my soul and body' (V.ii.303), but the play denies him and its audience any answer by having Iago refuse to provide one. With that refusal, *Othello*, as it closes, takes the risk of making its audiences face the limits of powers of rational cognition, of humanity's capacity to fathom defiantly inscrutable evil. *The Winter's Tale* takes much the same risk but at a far more precarious point: very early in the play, when the bond with the audience is still being formed. It presents Leontes's jealousy as an arbitrary, ungovernable element of human experience with which audiences (as well as characters) must come to terms even if, and precisely because, it defies rational comprehension and analysis. The focus is not on the genesis and growth of Leontes's jealousy but on its effects and repercussions. It sets in motion events that first rupture and then restore, across a 'wide gap of time' (V.iii.154) – some sixteen years – a matrix of interlocking personal relationships that affect the well-being not just of individuals and families but also of courts and kingdoms: between lifelong friends, between royalty and those who serve them, between husband and wife, and, reaching vertically through time across generations, between father and child, mother and child, aged subjects and the young prince in whom they see the kingdom's future and whose very existence makes their 'old hearts' fresh (I.i.39).

The stage history of *The Winter's Tale* offers many examples of steps taken to blunt the challenge posed by the presentation of Leontes's jealousy. Perhaps the most common is to prepare audiences for the outburst of jealousy that comes with 'Too hot, too hot' (I.ii.108) by playing Leontes as jealous from his first moment onstage – as Charles Kean did in 1856 and Patrick Stewart did in Ronald Eyre's 1981 production for the Royal Shakespeare Company. That strategy makes Leontes's jealousy less 'monstrous' by having it originate in events before the play begins. Audiences can more easily credit it

because 'Too hot, too hot' becomes the moment when Leontes at
last declares and begins to act upon a jealousy he has long felt and
can no longer restrain – not a moment when something that did not
previously exist bursts into being without warning. The Royal
Shakespeare Company's 1976 production, directed by John Barton
with Trevor Nunn, used Eskimo-like attire and furnishings to establish
a Scandanavian, if not Arctic, location, thereby setting the play in an
Ice Age, a time so far in the past that Sicily was a wintry place. The
suggestion was that Leontes's jealousy arose from primitive, almost
primeval impulses that the still-forming protocols and constraints of
early civilisation could not check. On the other hand, Robin Phillips
and Peter Moss set the 1978 Stratford (Ontario) Festival production
in the late nineteenth century, thus encouraging audiences to see
Leontes's jealous outburst as the result of sexual repression intensified
by the rigid codes associated with the Victorian era.

The Phillips–Moss production also used a dazzling *coup de théâtre* to
prepare audiences for the sudden appearance of Leontes's jealousy.
Instead of following the customary practice of signalling the start of
a performance by gradually dimming the house lights while bringing
up the stage lights, the production abruptly plunged the entire
theatre into total darkness. Then, after a pause, brilliant light burst
over the stage, which, empty moments before, was now teeming with
couples dancing at a formal court ball. The process made the
audience experience (in a way that no reader can) how something of
which there was no visible sign just seconds earlier can have an
intense, vivid impact.

In its penultimate scene, *The Winter's Tale* tests its audiences in a
different fashion – by denying them any sight of what the play leads
them to believe will be its climax: the moments when Perdita's
identity is discovered, father and daughter are reunited, and Leontes
and Polixenes are reconciled. Such scenes exist in earlier Shakespearean plays. At the end of *The Comedy of Errors*, for example, one
of Shakespeare's earliest plays, audiences witness a series of reunions
between family members who have been separated for an unspecified
period of time that could well be longer than sixteen years: between
a husband and wife, between them and their twin sons, between
those twin brothers, and between their servants, who are also twins.
In *Pericles*, closer in time to *The Winter's Tale*, audiences look on as a
king, whose grief at the reported death of his daughter has plunged
him into a state of mute withdrawal from human contact, emerges

from that condition in response to the appeals of a young woman who is, he learns, the daughter he thought he had lost to death.

When Leontes agrees to intercede on behalf of Florizel and Perdita, audiences anticipate, justifiably, that they are about to see a scene of discovery, reunion, and reconciliation. Calling 'mark what way I make' (V.i.232), he leads the lovers off to greet Polixenes, newly landed in Sicily. Having watched Autolycus manoeuvre the Old Shepherd and the Clown aboard the ship that will carry Florizel and Perdita to Sicily, audiences know that the identifying tokens Antigonus left with the infant Perdita have reached Sicily, providing the means by which Leontes will be able to recognise her as his daughter. In the scene directly after Perdita and Florizel flee Bohemia for Sicily, Leontes agrees not to marry again unless Paulina bids him to, and she states the only condition under which she would give her assent: 'That / Shall be when your first queen's again in breath: / Never till then' (V.i.82–4). That statement comes immediately before a servant enters to announce that Florizel 'with his princess . . . desires access / To your high presence' (V.i.86–8). Leontes's first words to Florizel stress his resemblance to his father:

> Your mother was most true to wedlock, prince;
> For she did print your royal father off,
> Conceiving you. Were I but twenty-one,
> Your father's image is so hit in you,
> His very air, that I should call you brother,
> As I did him, and speak of something wildly
> By us perform'd before.
>
> (V.i.123–9)

That greeting returns to the motif of the child as a 'copy' or 'image' or 'print' of its parents emphasised in the play's second scene, most conspicuously when, gazing on his son Mamillius, Leontes says,

> Looking on the lines
> Of my boy's face, methoughts I did recoil
> Twenty-three years, and saw myself unbreech'd,
> In my green velvet coat; my dagger muzzl'd
> • • •
> How like, methought, I then was to this kernel,
> This squash, this gentleman.
>
> (I.ii.153–60)

With Leontes's greeting of Florizel, the play directs the audience's attention to how Paulina's seemingly impossible condition will be met. Just as Florizel is the 'image' of his father, so Perdita is the 'image' of her mother. In her, Hermione is 'again in breath'.

What *The Winter's Tale* proceeds to give its audiences, however, is not the scene for which it has prepared them. Instead of seeing the the 'meeting of the two kings' (V.ii.41), the discovery of Perdita's identity, and her reunion with the father who had denied her, they merely hear those moments described. By denying its audiences any sight of those events, the play takes the risk of frustrating expectations it has fostered. Then, further testing the fidelity of its audiences, it intensifies that already very substantial risk by insisting that they be satisfied with accounts that announce their own inadequacy:

> Then have you lost a sight which was to be seen, cannot be spoken of. . . . I never heard of such another encounter, which lames report to follow it and undoes description to do it. (V.ii.43–59)

* * *

The most audacious and risky testing comes during the final scene when *The Winter's Tale* violates a principle fundamental to the relationship between audience, players, and playwright: never trick the audience. After denying audiences any sight of the conclusion it has prepared them to see, the play then moves to a climax that is all the more surprising because it contradicts what they had accepted as true: that Hermione dies upon learning of her son Mamillius's death. As they look on, what they have been told is an amazingly lifelike statue of Hermione shows itself to be the living Hermione, 'wrinkled' and 'aged' by the sixteen years that have passed. Having asked its audiences to witness, and accept, the transformation of cold stone into warm flesh, the play then undercuts that seeming miracle by revealing that Hermione was never dead but secretly 'preserv'd / Myself to see the issue' (V.iii.127–8).

Shakespearean plays typically privilege their audiences by giving them information that is withheld from most, if not all, characters, and where Perdita is concerned, *The Winter's Tale* allows its audiences that advantage. They know when no one in Sicily does that she is alive in Bohemia, and they know before anyone in the play does (including Perdita) her royal identity. In the case of Hermione, however, the play withholds from audiences such privileged information. It also takes the even greater risk of actively misleading them about Hermione's supposed death in a fashion that makes *The Winter's Tale* unique among Shakespearean plays. The play gives its audiences no reason to question the veracity of Paulina's report that 'the queen, the queen, / The sweet'st dear'st creature's dead . . .' (III.ii.200–1). 'I'll swear't', she declares, adding 'If word nor oath / Prevail not, go and see' (III.ii.203–4). The scene ends with Leontes, now convinced of his error and deeply contrite, leaving to look upon 'the dead bodies of my queen and son': 'Come, and lead me / To these sorrows' (III.ii.235, 242–3). In the next scene, Antigonus, as he sets about abandoning Leontes's infant daughter, reports that Hermione has visited him in a dream, which he takes as proof of what audiences are asked to believe: 'Hermione hath suffer'd death' (III.iii.42). Not until the play's final moments do audiences learn that Paulina's report was false, the beginning of a deception sustained over sixteen years (and two acts) until, with Perdita's return, the condition set by the oracle is met: 'the king shall live without an heir, if that which is lost be not found' (III.ii.134–6).

Such sustained deception of the audience is a sharp break with Shakespeare's previous practice. *Much Ado about Nothing*, one of his Elizabethan comedies, forgoes a comparable opportunity to deceive its audiences. The moment when Hermione faints at the news of Mamillius's death resembles the moment in *Much Ado* when Hero swoons after Claudio, convinced she is not a 'maid' but 'knows the heat of a luxurious bed' (IV.i.38, 40), stops their marriage ceremony and rejects her as his bride. *Much Ado*, however, ensures that its audiences know that Hero's swoon is not fatal. She is not carried off as Hermione is, and audiences see her revive. They also hear the Friar presiding at the disrupted marriage ceremony propose a deception: 'Let her awhile be secretly kept in, / And publish it that she is dead indeed' (IV.i.203–4). Audiences of *The Winter's Tale*, on the other hand, do not see Hermione revive and are not privy to Paulina's deception. Instead, they, like every character in the play except Hermione, are subject to it. What Paulina does to Leontes and all his court, Shakespeare and those who, beginning with the King's Men, perform the play do to their audiences.

In *Pericles*, generally considered the first of Shakespeare's 'late' plays, a woman who, like Hermione, is a new mother, dies and then returns to life. Audiences learn of Thasia's death in childbirth on board a ship caught in a raging storm and hear Pericles order that she be buried at sea, lamenting that he has no time 'To give thee hallowed to thy grave' (III.i.59). *Pericles*, however, in contrast to *The Winter's Tale*, keeps its audiences fully and accurately informed of the processes by which that 'dead queen' (III.i.18) regains life. In the next scene, they see Thasia's coffin, which has washed ashore, opened before Cerimon, a physician deeply learned in 'the disturbances / That nature works, and of her cures' (III.ii.39–40). Audiences witness the resurrection that then occurs as Cerimon, by 'good appliance' of his expertise, using what is in 'boxes' brought from his closet as well as napkins, fire, and music, recovers Thasia from death: 'See how she 'gins / To blow into life's flower again' (III.ii.88, 89, 96–7). As they look on, what had been Thasia's corpse first moves and then speaks.

In *The Winter's Tale* Hermione's return to life also registers initially, on audiences and characters alike, as a resurrection, brought about not by a physician's skills but by Paulina's exercise of powers that are magical, even miraculous. Like Cerimon she calls for music, but there are no boxes, no napkins, no fire. As those she has called upon to 'awake your faith' look on, the statue seems to come to life in response to the words she speaks:

> 'Tis time, descend; be stone no more; approach;
> Strike all that look upon with marvel. Come!
> I'll fill your grave up: stir, nay, come away:
> Bequeath to death your numbness; for from him
> Dear life redeems you. You perceive she stirs.
>
> (V.iii.99–103)

The moment when the statue stirs is the most compelling example in all of Shakespeare's plays of what David Daniell calls 'the power of theatre to make miracles happen' (1986, p. 118). After allowing audiences to experience and enjoy that power, however, the play then undercuts it by having Hermione reveal that she was never dead. Nothing compels that revelation, and by having Hermione make it, *The Winter's Tale* converts what is initially presented as – and what could have remained – the miraculous transformation of sculpted stone to a living person into a theatrically contrived surprise that completes a process of deception that began sixteen years (and two acts) earlier.

The kind of audience deception in which *The Winter's Tale* engages is not unique to it or to Shakespeare. Two plays by rival playwrights that are approximately contemporaneous with it also trick their audiences: Ben Jonson's *Epicoene or The Silent Woman*, performed in 1609 by the boys' company at Whitefriars, and *Philaster*, co-written for the King's Men by Francis Beaumont and John Fletcher (Shakespeare's eventual successor as the company's principal playwright) sometime between 1609 and early 1610. *Epicoene*'s audiences learn during its final moments that the 'silent woman' of the title – whom one character has wed and with whom others claim to have had sexual relations – is in fact a boy disguised as a woman. As *Philaster* ends, a page accused of having sexual intercourse with a princess proves his innocence and hers by revealing a fact unknown to members of the audience: 'he' is a woman who – like such Shakespearean heroines as Rosalind of *As You Like It*, Viola of *Twelfth Night*, and Imogen of *Pericles* – has disguised herself as a boy.

Epicoence and *Philaster* take advantage of the blurring of gender distinctions that the Elizabethan–Jacobean practice of casting boys in women's roles facilitated. *The Winter's Tale*, on the other hand, adapts for use on the commercial stages of the Globe and Blackfriars, the practice in Jacobean court masques of having aristocratic women pose as statues.[6] It tricks its audiences by exploiting the fact that drama is an incarnational art, one that works through and with the living bodies of actors (and after 1660 actresses), who move and speak as audiences look and listen, caught up in a double consciousness that allows them to respond to both the performers and the characters they portray. As Hermione, 'stone no more', embraces Leontes, a comment by Paulina emphasises the presence of living bodies that distinguishes a play in performance from a tale, a narrative that is heard or read: 'That she is living, / Were it but told you, should be hooted at / Like an old tale'. Audiences actually see what they take to be a statue come to life; readers do not. Julio Romano, 'that rare Italian master' who has supposedly 'newly performed' the statue of Hermione, is immensely gifted, but he cannot 'put breath into his work' (V.ii.95–8). Gazing on the statue, Leontes asks in wonderment a question that defines the limits of the sculptor's art: 'What fine chisel / Could ever yet cut breath?' (V.iii.78–9). Romano works in lifeless stone, but the playwright Shakespeare works with and through living players. Their bodies carry out the actions he calls upon characters to perform; their breath gives voice to the words he gives characters to speak.

By (mis)leading its audiences to believe that Hermione is dead, *The Winter's Tale* creates a situation in which, as they look upon what they take to be Hermione's statue, they will be conscious of how lifeless the performer posing as the statue seems while, at the same time, the characters themselves are struck speechless by how lifelike the statue is. 'I like your silence', Paulina says after revealing the statue, 'it the more shows off / Your wonder' (V.iii.21–2). Their silent wonder is a response to the artistry of Julio Romano; theatre audiences, also silent, are responding to the artistry of the performer. That artistry cannot negate the fact that no living person can be absolutely motionless, as still as stone, for any sustained length of time. Audiences, however, will disregard any sign of life – the blink of an eye, the twitch of a muscle, the movement of breathing – they see in the 'statue' because they are (at that point) persuaded that the performer represents a statue, not a living character. In fact, the play puts them in a position where they must discount the testimony of their eyes if they are to accept what the play to this point has insisted is its truth: Hermione is dead, and the object they gaze upon is her statue.

Such discounting is typical of the specifically theatrical mode of seeing in which audiences engage during any performance of any play, but *The Winter's Tale* complicates and ultimately undercuts that mode. By having characters, once their silence ends, comment repeatedly on how lifelike the statue is, the play calls attention to the signs of vitality in the performer that its audiences are trying to disregard. Leontes, for example, is convinced that the statue's eyes move: 'The fixure of her eye hath motion in't' (V.iii.67). Twice he comments on how the statue seems to breathe. 'Would you not deem it breath'd?' he asks, and moments later he rephrases that question: 'Still methinks / There is an air comes from her. What fine chisel / Could ever yet cut breath?' (V.iii.64, 77–9).

The situation is comparable to the final moments of *King Lear* when, grieving over Cordelia's corpse, Lear looks for breath from her that will mist a mirror or move a feather. That 'corpse' is actually the living body of the person playing Cordelia, and at least some in the audience will see the life-signifying breath that Lear in his anguish hopes to find. *King Lear* places its audiences in a position where, if they are to accept the truth that Cordelia is dead, they must deny any sign of life they see in the performer, and they must do that as they see and hear Lear struggle to deny the death he sees in his most beloved daughter. There is, however, a crucial difference between *Lear* and *The Winter's Tale*. What Lear so desperately wants does not come to pass. Cordelia does not, miraculously, return to life; she remains, in Lear's heartbreaking words, 'dead as earth' (V.iii.260). What Leontes and Perdita want and what audiences want for them – a chance to be with Hermione, to touch her flesh and hear her voice – does come to pass: she returns to life and to them. With her return the vital signs the play has been asking the audience to disregard – signs that no one sees while reading the words of the play – prove to be signs of a deeper truth: Hermione is, and has been, alive.

At first, audiences and characters see a living Hermione who moves but does not speak. She stirs, goes to Leontes, presents her hand to him, and then embraces him – all the while saying nothing. As they embrace, Camillo comments, 'If she pertain to life, let her speak too' (V.iii.113). His comment directs attention to Hermione's muteness, raising the possibility that her return to life is less than complete. That muteness persists until, at Paulina's invitation, she turns and looks upon Perdita. Only then does Hermione speak, calling for the gods to 'pour your graces / Upon my daughter's head'. She finds her voice at the very moment she finds her daughter. In contrast to Leontes, who must find and accept the daughter he denied before he can regain the wife he lost, Hermione must share an embrace with the husband who rejected her before she can turn to her daughter and speak. Hermione's ability to speak as well as move coincides with and affirms her full participation, as a wife and as a mother, in the world she rejoins after an absence of sixteen years.

Hermione's unexpected return from a death that never claimed her is the most audacious of the suprises by which *The Winter's Tale* tests its audiences, but it is not the last of them. Another unfolds immediately after Paulina, with the final words she speaks, voices her resolve to spend the rest of her life mourning the loss of her husband Antigonus:

> Go together,
> You precious winners all; your exultation
> Partake to every one. I, an old turtle,
> Will wing me to some wither'd bough, and there
> My mate (that's never to be found again)
> Lament, till I am lost.

> (V.iii.130–5)

Leontes responds by calling for her to be silent – 'O, peace, Paulina!' – and then proposing that she marry Camillo: 'Thou shouldst a husband take by my consent / As I by thine a wife. . . . Come, Camillo, / And take her by the hand' (V.iii.135–44). With that call for a marriage between Camillo and Paulina, the play once again asks its audiences to subordinate their sense of plausible behaviour to other concerns. Camillo and Paulina have not seen each other for at least sixteen years and have not even been onstage together before this scene. At no time do they voice any sense of mutual love.

While marriage between Camillo and Paulina is highly implausible – unprepared for to the point of being undeniably arbitrary – it is, at the same time, fully consistent with the generic affiliations that link *The Winter's Tale* to 'tragi-comedy', to 'romance', and even to 'comedy'. Each of those genres requires a happy ending, and the marriage Leontes calls for would deepen the happiness of the play's ending by making 'precious winners' of 'all', including Paulina, who have survived the events of the past sixteen years. Earlier, she had said that the possibililily that Antigonus would 'break his grave / And come again to me' was 'monstrous to our human reason'. Now, Leontes offers her, in the person of Camillo, a husband to replace her 'mate' who is 'never to be found again'.[7] The prospect of Paulina's marriage to Camillo demonstrates, again, how, working in implausible ways 'monstrous to our human reason', 'great creating nature', 'Dear life' recoups and compensates for the deaths arising from Leontes's jealousy. Hermione's seeming tranformation from statue to warm flesh is the most breathtaking manifestation of those processes, which also provide in Florizel a son (by marriage) to offset the loss of Mamillius. Leontes's call for marriage between Camillo and Paulina is the final one.

Neither Camillo nor Paulina speaks in response to Leontes's proposal, and each remains silent for the rest of the play. No stage direction specifies what either does, and no other character says anything indicating how either acts. The situation is akin to that at the end of *Measure for Measure*, where Angelo never speaks after the Duke orders his marriage to Mariana and Isabella says nothing when the Duke twice proposes to her. The silences that Camillo and Paulina maintain, speaking neither to one another nor to anyone else, do not, in and of themselves, establish that the marriage is refused, but it is equally true that their silences do not establish their acceptance of Leontes's proposal. Camillo may or may not act to 'take her by the hand', and if he does, three broad alternatives present themselves: Paulina may willingly offer her hand in response to his, or she may, passively, perhaps even reluctantly allow him to 'take' her hand, or she may refuse to give him the hand he reaches out to 'take'.

Although the silences of Camillo and Paulina allow for a range of possible responses, there is no record of a production of *The Winter's Tale* in which they do not assent to the marriage once it is proposed.[8] The unanimity evident in the play's performance history extends to its critical history. The few critics who take note of Leontes's proposal assume that Paulina and Camillo obey his wishes. Peter Erickson, for example, comments that Paulina resumes 'her normal place when she accepts a second marriage, which Leontes arranges for her' (1982, p. 826). The assumption that Camillo and Paulina agree to marry has hardened, over an expanse of time far wider than sixteen years, into a stage tradition and an unexamined tenet of the critical consensus.

The failure to acknowledge even the *possibility* that the marriage Leontes calls for does not happen demonstrates the gap between what the playtext allows and what theatrical and critical practice have long authorised. That narrowing of a range of options to a single authorised alternative is proof of the power of the ideology of the 'happy' ending, the often unarticulated values and assumptions that define what such an ending is. In this instance, one aspect of a 'happy' ending is its revalidation of kingly authority. Earlier, Leontes used his regal authority to sunder his own marriage by proclaiming his wife an adulteress, and his brother king, Polixenes, subsequently used his authority to forbid Florizel's betrothal to Perdita. If Camillo and Paulina agree to marry, their betrothal is an obedient response to the authority of 'a pair of kings' (V.iii.146), not – as in the case of Perdita and Florizel – an act, arising from erotic desire, that defies kingly authority. The counsellors' betrothal, if it occurs, redeems kingly authority by making it, like sexual desire, an instrument through which 'great creating nature' works.

Also embedded in the 'happy' ending are assumptions about gender relations. Earlier, Paulina, defying both her husband and her king, had insisted on speaking out on behalf of Hermione and her newborn daughter. Her refusal to stop talking, which prompts Leontes to denounce her as 'a man-kind witch' and 'a callat / Of boundless tongue' (II.iii.67,90–1), violates conceptions of appropriate womanly

behaviour that were dominant in the Jacobean era and have force to
this day. During the play's final moments, Leontes again calls upon
her to stop speaking: 'O, peace, Paulina!'. This time, she falls silent.
If she then wordlessly accepts Camillo as her husband, she conforms
to and thus confirms the code of womanly behaviour she had earlier
transgressed. That silent acceptance, if it occurs, also signals her
submission to specifically male authority. She lost her first husband
because he obeyed Leontes; she gains a second husband because she
obeys Leontes. Each time during a performance of *The Winter's Tale*
that Paulina and Camillo silently agree to marry, that agreement is
part of an ending that is 'happy'. It is 'happy' because it includes
Paulina among the 'precious winners'. It is also 'happy', however,
because it redeems and locks into place a social order resting upon
specific conceptions of authority and gender relationships that performance and criticism, cooperating with generic expectations, continue to reinforce. Perhaps the final surprise that *The Winter's Tale*
offer is one that is only now – after a 'wide gap of time' – coming into
perspective: the play's potential to expose, and in exposing to challenge, the ideology of the 'happy ending' that it offers and its
audiences desire.

8

The Tempest:
'Something Rich and Strange'

No Shakespearean play uses music more extensively than *The Tempest*, widely regarded for more than one hundred and fifty years now as the final play Shakespeare wrote singlehandedly even though, as Stephen Orgel notes, there is no way to determine 'chronological priority' between it and *The Winter's Tale* (1987, p. 63). The second of nine songs in *The Tempest* tells of changes being worked upon the body of Ferdinand's father, drowned, he is certain, in the shipwreck he himself has just survived:

> *Full fadom five thy father lies;*
> *Of his bones are coral made;*
> *Those are pearls that were his eyes:*
> *Nothing of him that doth fade,*
> *But doth suffer a sea-change*
> *Into something rich and strange.*
> (I.ii.399–404)

The song itself – sung by Ariel – is 'something rich and strange'. On the one hand, it is a lie; Ariel knows that Ferdinand's father is not dead. On the other, it is the play's most compelling articulation of the profoundly transformative process – equivalent to a 'sea-change' – through which characters pass as their sense of the past, their visions of others and of themselves, and their personal and political relationships are radically reshaped.

The song is part of a play that is itself not only 'rich' but also 'strange' in the sense of being different from the other plays called Shakespeare's. That strangeness makes itself felt in various ways,

175

including a decidedly atypical opening moment. Unlike the vast majority of Shakespearean plays, *The Tempest* begins (like *Macbeth*) with a stage effect: '*A tempestuous noise of thunder and lightning heard*'. Audiences take that '*noise*' as evidence of a ferocious storm raging within the fictional realm of the play. That they do is fully consistent with perhaps the most basic of the conventions – the network of assumptions, habits, and practices agreed upon by audience, players, and playwright – without which no theatrical performance can occur: that audiences accept what they know full well to be theatrical illusions as actual events within the world of the play. As audiences continue to look and listen, they behold a ship caught in that storm break apart, exposing all on board to watery deaths.

In the next scene *The Tempest*, taking the kind of risk that *The Winter's Tale*, the Shakespearean play written closest in time to it, delays until the final moments, makes its audiences aware that they have been deceived. That awareness does not come in a manner – via a soliloquy by Prospero, for example, or a chorus – that preserves their customary privileged position by giving them knowledge withheld from other characters. As they see and hear Prospero comforting Miranda, distraught at the shipwreck she, too, has witnessed, her perspective as a character within the theatrical fiction and theirs as spectators of that fiction converge. Deceived like Miranda by what they have just seen and heard, they become, in effect, Prospero's daughters, learning in tandem with her, as virtual equals, that the tempest has harmed no one. 'The direful spectacle of the wrack,' Prospero says,

> I have with such provision in mine Art
> So safely ordered that there is no soul –
> No not so much perdition as an hair
> Betid to any creature in the vessel
> Which thou heard'st cry, which thou saw'st sink.
>
> (I.ii.26–32)

Even the ship that broke apart, audiences soon hear Ariel report, is intact, 'safely in harbour', the mariners themselves out of peril and asleep, 'all under hatches stow'd' (I.ii.226, 230).

The storm with which *The Tempest* opens is not the only one in a Shakespearean play. There are storms in *Othello*, *King Lear*, and *Macbeth*, to name but three. What makes the storm in *The Tempest* 'strange' is that it is the only one controlled by a character within the play. Nor is the shipwreck that the storm (seemingly) causes the only one in a Shakespearean play. Storms destroy ships in *Twelfth Night*, one of Shakespeare's Elizabethan comedies, and in *Pericles* and *The Winter's Tale*, both written closer in time to *The Tempest*. None of those shipwrecks is enacted onstage, however. The (seeming) shipwreck in *The Tempest* is, strangely, the only one that Shakespeare ever calls upon the King's Men to take the theatrical risk of actually staging. Even more strangely, it is also the only one that proves to be an illusion *within* the fictional world of the play.

During the opening two scenes, the illusions of storm and shipwreck generated by playwright and players while performing *The Tempest* merge with those generated by Prospero. Although deprived twelve years earlier of his office as Duke of Milan by his younger brother Antonio and Alonso, the King of Naples, Prospero possesses magical powers that give him control and thus *de facto* authority over all who are on or even near the island, including Antonio and Alonso, that is far greater than that exercised by any other Shakespearean character. Working with and through Ariel, Prospero not only raises a storm but also induces sleep, inflicts pain, compels manual labour, imposes paralysis, and conjures visions that confound as well as enchant. What is most extraordinary about Prospero is the degree to which he exercises authority over not only his fellow characters but also the audiences of *The Tempest*. To an extent unmatched by any other Shakespearean character, he has the power to determine what audiences see and hear, and he is frequently taken as Shakespeare's self-portrait, the character through whom he most directly expresses his own feelings.[1]

The characters who survive what they think is a shipwreck find themselves on an unfamiliar island, in a landscape all the stranger because Prospero's 'art' enables him to determine what they hear and see. *The Tempest* places its audiences in an theatrical situation that is analogously unfamiliar, strange – one in which the convention that enables what audiences know are theatrical illusions to function as signs of actualities within the dramatic fiction is no longer a reliable frame of reference. One measure of the deception generated by the merging of theatrical illusion and Prosperian magic is that were 'the direful spectacle' of the opening scene an actual shipwreck within the dramatic fiction, nothing in the opening scene would be different.

The Tempest is also 'strange' by virtue of being the only Shakespearean play set in a place associated with the New World. The island over which Prospero rules and on which the survivors of what they think is the destruction of the ship carrying them from Tunis to Naples find themselves is situated somewhere in the Mediterranean, yet it is endowed with New World qualities. In fashioning *The Tempest*, Shakespeare drew upon accounts of what happened in 1609 to the *Sea-Adventure*, a ship bearing the governor of Virginia to Jamestown as part of a fleet carrying several hundred colonists. In late July a hurricane off the coast of Virginia separated the *Sea-Adventure* from the rest of the fleet, eventually driving it aground in what Ariel refers to as 'the still-vexed Bermoothes' (I.ii.229). Those on board spent the winter there, then set out again for Jamestown, arriving safely in May of 1610 — to the astonishment of their fellow colonists who were certain they had perished. Gonzalo's extended description of the utopian 'commonwealth' he would establish 'Had I plantation of this isle' (II.i.143, 139) comes virtually verbatim from Montaigne's essay 'Of the Cannibals', widely available in England from 1603 on in John Florio's translation. The name Caliban is an anagram of 'cannibals', the term, not yet associated with the eating of human flesh, that Montaigne used for the natives of the New World. Set on and near a Mediterranean island endowed, strangely, with New World qualities, *The Tempest* stands apart as the Shakespearean play that most directly registers, responds to, and thus helps to determine the impact of the project of trans-Atlantic colonisation on which England embarked in the final decades of Elizabeth's reign. During the first decade of James's, which saw the establishment of the Virginia Company in 1606 and the founding of Jamestown in 1607, it pursued that project with renewed vigour.

Caliban challenges Prospero's right to rule the island, basing his claim on inheritance and prior possession. 'This island's mine,' he insists during his first appearance in the play, 'by Sycorax my mother, / Which thou tak'st from me' (I.ii.333–4). 'I am all the subjects that you have,' he tells Prospero, 'Which first was mine own King' (I.ii.343–4). Soon after, Caliban willingly accepts the drunken Stephano as his new master and king and, subsequently chastened by that experience, he tells Prospero as the play closes, 'I'll be wise hereafter, / And seek for grace' (V.i.294–5). Caliban's early words challenging Prospero have acquired a distinctive resonance during the post-Second World War era, which has seen the breakup of the vast empires that Britain, France and other European countries had acquired in Asia, Africa, and the Caribbean. So compelling is that resonance – so expressive of the displaced and oppressed – that it is not uncommon these days for directors and commentators to regard *The Tempest* as an examination of colonialism.

The presence of Caliban also contributes to the strangeness of *The Tempest* in another way – by virtue of his being a character for whom there is no Shakespearean precedent. Moments before audiences first see him, Prospero calls him 'Thou earth' (I.ii.316) and he is, in many respects, the antithesis of Ariel, whom the First Folio describes as an 'airy spirit' in the 'Names of the Actors' provided at the end of the play. Caliban's presence poses a challenge – beyond that found in any other Shakespearean play – to the capacity, of audiences and characters alike, to distinguish between two categories central to all cultures: the human and the non-human. Taking advantage of the process of performance, *The Tempest* poses that challenge in specifically theatrical terms by setting what audiences and characters see on first encountering Caliban against what they hear.

Of the Europeans who think themselves shipwrecked, the first to encounter Caliban is Trinculo, who sees him before hearing him make any sounds. What he sees is so 'strange' that he takes him to be something other than human. 'What have we here?' he asks, eyeing, sniffing, and perhaps even nudging the creature lying silent before him, 'a man or a fish? dead or alive?' (II.ii.24–5). 'A fish,' he concludes, 'A strange fish' (II.ii.25, 27–8). When Trinculo, seeking shelter against the storm that is 'come again', creeps under the creature's 'gaberdine' (II.ii.38–9), the human and what he regards as the inhuman merge, and when Stephano, the second shipwrecked European to encounter Caliban, enters moments later, he sees a four-legged creature. Like Stephano, he takes it to be something non-human, a 'monster of the isle' (II.ii.66). When that 'monster' utters sounds that he recognises as his own language, Stephano finds himself confronting a paradox. 'Where the devil,' he asks, 'should he learn our language?' (II.ii.67–8). For the Elizabethan–Jacobean era, the capacity to speak was the most direct manifestation of the rationality that sets humankind apart from and above the lower orders of creation, among them the fish. The words coming from Caliban's mouth force Stephano and Trinculo to face the presence of some element of the human within the non-human, in the monstrous and fish-like.

In contrast to Trinculo and Stephano, who see Caliban before they hear him speak, audiences hear Caliban speak before they see him. His first appearance in the play, is orchestrated so that audiences find themselves called upon to face the non-human in a being they initially take to be human. When Prospero calls, 'What, ho! slave! Caliban! / Thou earth, thou! speak', audiences hear a voice answer from '*within*', from offstage or even understage: 'There's wood enough within' (I.ii.315–16). Hearing that voice speaking 'our language', they assume the humanity of the unseen speaker. Prospero then orders Caliban to enter: 'Come forth, I say! . . . Come, thou tortoise! when?' (I.ii.317–18). At that point, a stage direction calls for the entrance of a figure that looks '*like a water-nymph*' (I.ii.318) and proves to be Ariel, not Caliban. The timing of Ariel's entrance not only delays the audience's first sight of Caliban but also provides a contrast with what they behold when they do see him.

The play further delays the audience's first sight of Caliban by having Prospero confer with Ariel: 'Hark in thine ear' (I.ii.320). For readers, the conference lasts no longer than it takes to read 'Hark in thine ear' and move on to Ariel's obedient reply, 'My lord, it shall be done' (I.ii.320). In performance, however, the conference need not be virtually instantaneous, and the longer it lasts, the longer audiences must wait to see the recalcitrant Caliban, whose entrance Prospero, after Ariel's exit, again commands: 'Thou poisonous slave, got by the devil himself / Upon thy wicked dam, come forth!' (I.ii.321–2). This time Caliban obeys, and audiences at last see him. What they see is a character whom the First Folio, in the 'Names of the Actors', describes as 'a salvage [savage] and deformed slave'.

Earlier, the sound of an unseen Caliban speaking 'our language' had prompted them to assume that he is human. Now, his entrance into their field of vision, delayed so as to increase its impact, challenges them to reconcile their sense of what is human with their sight of a figure so non-human in appearance – so 'deformed' – that Trinculo and Stephano, seeing it, take it to be a fish or, to use the term by which they repeatedly address Caliban throughout the play, a 'monster'. Caliban is the Other, the embodiment of that awareness of difference against which, and thus in inescapable relationship to which, one knows one's own identity as an individual and as a member of various social and cultural groupings. To the extent that Caliban's presence prompts audiences to re-conceive and re-work their sense of what is human and extend it to include facets of Caliban, if not Caliban himself, it also prompts them to reconsider their sense of themselves. In so doing, they enter into a complex affiliation with Caliban – involving simultaneous recognition of likeness and difference – akin to that voiced by Prospero, who near the end of *The Tempest* says of Caliban: 'this thing of darkness I / Acknowledge mine' (V.i.275–6). Prospero may be stating that Caliban is his slave or a member of his party rather than Alonso's, but his words also attest to and accept the existence of a bond between them that includes some element of responsibility on his part for what and even who 'this thing of darkness' is. His word for Caliban is 'thing', a term that does not emphasise whatever human qualities Caliban possesses. Prospero explicitly grants freedom to Ariel – '[T]hen to the elements / Be free, and fare thou well' (V.i.317–18) – but Caliban's fate, after he obediently and without delay departs to 'trim' Prospero's cell 'handsomely' (V.i.293), is left disturbingly vague. It is not clear from the playtext whether Caliban goes to Milan with Prospero or remains on the island. Beerbohm Tree's 1904 production responded to that vagueness by showing Caliban, after Prospero's epilogue, alone and gazing mournfully out to sea after the departing ship, towards which he stretches out his arms. In Jonathan Miller's 1988 production at the Old Vic, on the other hand, Caliban found himself facing, after Prospero's withdrawal from the island, not loneliness but the prospect of a new subordination, this time to Ariel, who, having fitted together the parts of the magical staff Prospero had broken, began using it to establish dominance over all who remained on the island.

The wealth flowing into England from the colonies in the New world accelerated the extremely complex process of social change already under way as part of England's movement into the early modern era. On first encountering Caliban, both Trinculo and Stephano see an opportunity to earn riches out of keeping with their social places in the world beyond the island. Calculating Caliban's value as a 'monster' that speaks 'our language', Stephano says, 'If I can recover [cure] him, and keep him tame, and get to Naples with him, he's a present for any emperor that ever trod on neat's-leather' (II.ii.69–72). He does not, however, anticipate making a present of Caliban should he get him back to Naples. Instead, responsive to the financial opportunities of the emerging marketplace economy, he foresees making a profit by selling him, declaring that no price will be too high: 'I will not take too much for him; he shall pay for him that hath him and that soundly' (II.ii.78–80).

Moments before, Trinculo, gazing on Caliban for the first time, had also envisaged the wealth that would be his 'Were I in England now, as once I was, and had but this fish painted, not a holiday-fool there but would give a piece of silver' (II.ii.28–30). 'There,' he adds, thinking about the fortune he could make, 'would this monster make a man; any strange beast there makes a man' (II.ii.30–1).[2] Stephano's vision of charging admission to see Caliban glances at, and almost parodies, what occurred each time the King's Men performed *The Tempest* at Blackfriars or the Globe: audiences paid to see one of those Men 'make' a 'strange beast' named Caliban by playing him. By (dis)playing Caliban on two of Jacobean London's commercial stages, the King's Men appropriated the practice of bringing natives back to England, thereby tapping into the wealth flowing from the New World and diverting some of it into their own pockets.

Still another way in which *The Tempest* is 'strange' is that it departs from Shakespeare's standard compositional practices. In composing the vast majority of his plays across the full span of his career, he typically worked from, with, and on one, occasionally two, major sources, sometimes preserving, sometimes altering, sometimes even – as in *King Lear* and *The Winter's Tale* – inverting what he found there. In fashioning *The Tempest* for performance by the King's Men, however, Shakespeare abandoned that practice. It is his only Jacobean play – and one of but three[3] among the thirty-seven generally attributed to him – for which no major source has been identified.

For *The Tempest*, Shakespeare, instead of working extensively with one or two sources, combined a farrago of writings, some contemporary, some classical. Elements from accounts of what happened in the New World to those aboard *The Sea-Adventure* co-exist with echoes of Virgil's *Aeneid*, most prominently the discussion of Dido (II.i.73–97). The combination associates the voyage from Tunis to Italy that Alonso and his court are making when the opening storm (seemingly) destroys their ship, with both a specific voyage to the New World in the recent past and the voyage that Aeneas, abandoning Dido in Carthage, undertook at some point in the far-distant epic past. That voyage led to the founding of Rome, with whose first emperor, Caesar Augustus, James was often compared in order to distinguish his style of rule from Elizabeth's.[4] The founding of Rome in turn led to the founding of Britain by Brutus, Aeneas's grandson, and James saw, in the sovereignty he exercised over England, Wales, and Scotland, an opportunity to re-establish Britain's primeval unity. Gonzalo's 'commonwealth' speech (II.i.139–64) comes from Montaigne's 'Of the Cannibals', and, in a borrowing from Ovid's *Metamorphoses* that blurs the distinction between Prospero and Sycorax, 'white' and 'black' magic, Shakespeare lifts from the sorceress Medea's incantation of the powers she commands much of the long speech (V.i.33–57) in which Prospero describes the scope of his 'so potent Art'.

The change in Shakespeare's compositional practices is related to *The Tempest*'s associations with the New World. One impact of the discovery and colonisation of the New World was a change in the conception and construction of authority in European cultures.[5] In the Middle Ages, authority flowed from the ability of thinkers and writers to make events meaningful by placing them in a context provided by the books that formed the basis for the systems of knowledge by which people of that epoch made sense of their world: the Bible in theology and the writings of Ptolemy in astronomy, Constantine in medicine, Boethius in arithmetic, Cicero in rhetoric, Aristole in dialectic, and the ancient poets in grammar. What could not be explained in terms sanctioned by those authoritative books was not acknowledged as having any reality. The engagement with the New World shattered that conception and construction of authority by bringing Europeans into contact with utterly new systems of realities – peoples, languages, artifacts, laws, customs, plants, animals – of which those books made no mention and which in some cases could not even be named, let alone comprehended, using the terms they provided. To speak about what lay in the New World required making up new words or borrowing words from the natives – required, that is to say, changing what Ferdinand, encountering Miranda for the first time, proprietarily calls 'my language' (I.ii.431) and what Stephano, encountering Caliban for the first time, calls 'our language' (II.ii.68). To English, the language of *The Tempest*, the New World contributed such words as *canoe, hurricane,* and *skunk,* and Caliban's list of the delicacies he will provide for Trinculo and Stephano includes 'young scamels' (II.ii.172), a word whose precise meaning remains unknown to this day.

The gap between what was found in the New World on the one hand and in the authoritative books of the Old World on the other spurred the development of a novel and competing conception of authority based not on the capacity to apply traditional cultural precedents but on the capacity to represent what was new, different, other, 'strange', by assembling, fabricating – from whatever diverse elements are at hand – a framework within which the events presented take on cultural coherence and meaning. The mixture of writings, contemporary as well as classical, upon which *The Tempest* draws is an example of such fabrication, and by endowing a Mediterranean island with New World qualities and placing on it a creature such as Caliban, the King's Men and their playwright claimed for themselves and for the recently emergent institution that was commercial theatre the authority to represent that which was radically new.

* * *

The Tempest is also 'strange' because, at least partly in response to the challenge such representation poses, it arises from and incorporates the equivalent of 'a sea-change' in the handling of dramatic place and time typical of the other plays Shakespeare provided for the Lord Chamberlain's–King's Men over the course of an association that, at the time *The Tempest* was most likely written – late 1610 or early 1611 – had lasted more than sixteen years. In 1595, the year after Shakespeare helped to found the Lord Chamberlain's Men and became that company's attached playwright, Sir Philip Sidney's *Defence of Poesy*, written in the early 1580s, was posthumously published. It includes a forceful critique of contemporary plays for 'being faulty both in place and time, the two necessary companions of all corporal actions':

> For where the stage should always represent but one place, and the uttermost time presupposed in it should be, both by Aristotle's precept and common reason, but one day, there is both many days and many places inartificially [i.e., unartfully] imagined. (1965, p. 134)

By Sidney's standards, every play but one that Shakespeare provided for the Lord Chamberlain's–King's Men from 1594 on is glaringly 'faulty'. The single exception is *The Tempest*. With all action situated on an island and its adjacent waters, it comes close to observing unity of place, and it conforms to the unity of time by concentrating events within a single day, the hours between sometime after two in the afternoon and six in the evening specified in the following exchange:

PROSPERO: What is the time o'th'day?
ARIEL: Past the mid season.

PROSPERO: At least two glasses. The time 'twixt six and now
  Must by us both be spent most preciously.

(I.ii.239–41)

The Tempest comes closer than any other Shakespearean play to observing the strictest form of unity of time, in which the span of time covered during the play corresponds exactly to the length of time needed to perform it.

That 'sea-change' in the treatment of dramatic time and place is all the more 'strange' if one considers the three plays that, like *The Tempest*, are associated with the closing phase of Shakespeare's career and are included with it in the grouping known variously as his 'last' plays, 'late' plays, 'romances', and 'tragicomedies'.[6] None of them shows any concern with conforming to Sidney's dictum that 'the stage should always represent but one place'. Quite the opposite. They disregard it, sometimes flamboyantly. *Pericles* takes place in half a dozen cities along the coast of the eastern Mediterranean Sea; *Cymbeline* places scenes in Italy and various parts of Britain, including Wales; *The Winter's Tale* opens in Sicily, shifts to a succession of sites in Bohemia, and for the final act returns to Sicily.

Sidney also scorns plays that, failing to confine themselves to the events of a single day, are 'liberal' with time:

For ordinary it is that two young princes fall in love; after many traverses she is got with child, delivered of a fair boy; he is lost, groweth a man, falleth in love, and is ready to get another child, and all this in two hours' space. (1965, p. 134)

Pericles is 'liberal' in almost exactly that way. Pericles meets Thasia early in the second act, and at the start of the third she dies giving birth to their daughter Marina, who, before the play ends, has grown into a young woman of wondrous beauty and virtue. *The Winter's Tale* is also 'liberal' with time. Perdita, with whom her mother is pregnant at the start of the play, appears onstage as an infant in Act III, and by the beginning of Act IV, she is sixteen years of age and ready for marriage.

In subjecting to 'a sea-change' a dramaturgical practice that had shaped his work for some sixteen years, Shakespeare may have been acting upon the willingness to take 'extraordinary risks' that David Daniell says is common in the 'last works' of 'a very great artist'

(1986, p. 119). In addition, there may have been an imitative, perhaps even competitive factor: the desire to match, if not surpass, the example of Ben Jonson's dazzling use of the unities of time and place in *The Alchemist*, which the King's Men performed in 1610. The handling of place and time in *The Tempest* may also be evidence of the lengths to which Shakespeare was willing to go – and capable of going – to help the King's Men cope with the problems – discussed in Chapter 1 – that from 1609 on performing at both the Globe and Blackfriars posed. Such factors are not mutually exclusive, and they interact with pressures arising from the concern, unique to *The Tempest*, with the New World. The compositional technique of the play involves weaving together elements from a potpourri of diverse sources rather than – in accord with the traditional conception of authority – applying or adapting one or two sources. As if in compensation for cutting loose from the kind of authority provided by the use of specific sources, Shakespeare, for the only time during his long association with the Lord Chamberlain's–King's Men, shapes a play that conforms to the unity of time and comes close to observing the unity of place. By thus breaking with his own long-established practice, Shakespeare in effect endows *The Tempest* with the authority of Sidney and Aristotle.

The attention to the unities of place and time that makes *The Tempest* 'strange' in the sense of different from every other play Shakespeare wrote during his association with the Lord Chamberlain's–King's Men is the basis for still another kind of strangeness: its similarity to *The Comedy of Errors*, most likely written in 1590, well before the formation of that acting company in 1594. *The Comedy of Errors* is the only other Shakespearean play that is not by Sidney's criteria 'faulty both in place and time'. The similar treatment of dramatic time and place in *The Tempest* and *The Comedy of Errors* establishes a strange symmetry between what has long been regarded as the final play Shakespeare wrote singlehandedly and what is almost certainly his first comedy and possibly even his first play of any kind. 'In the New World,' Stephen Orgel observes, 'Europe could see its own past, itself in embryo' (1987, p. 35). In writing, towards the end of his career, the play of his that most directly engages the Old World's experience of the New, Shakespeare returned, as the symmetry of *The Tempest* and *The Comedy of Errors* shows, to the embryonic phase of his career, delving into that area of his professional past before 1594 that corresponds to what Prospero, summoning Miranda at age fourteen to tell him of her earliest memories, calls 'the dark backward and abysm of time' (I.ii.50).

Fashioned by a process that, at least in part, involves Shakespeare's reaching far back into his professional memory, *The Tempest* is a play that, as Douglas L. Peterson (1973) has emphasised, insists upon the vital importance of remembering. As it repeatedly requires characters to look into their own pasts, the play links remembering with self-knowledge and with the capacity to act effectively in time by making past actions bear upon present conduct. Prospero's revelation to Miranda, during their first appearance onstage, that the storm and shipwreck are illusions generated by his art changes her sense of what has just passed. Through that revelation, the play brings its audiences to revise their sense of their own immediate theatrical past. They reassess not only the 'direful spectacle' they have just witnessed but also the spectatorly convention, based upon past theatrical experiences, in accordance with which they had construed what they saw and heard in the opening scene as actual events within the dramatic fiction. Prospero goes on to ask Miranda – 'ignorant of what thou art' – if she can 'remember / A time before we came unto this cell' (I.ii.38–9). As he proceeds to tell her 'what' she is, she also learns who she is and who her father is. In effect, Prospero uses his power to remember in order to change – and in changing, to shape – her sense of her own past and thus of her own identity. Across the centuries since they came into being on the stages of early modern London's commercial theatres, *The Tempest* and other Shakespearean plays have come to serve a similar function. In ways that have only recently begun to receive attention, they are now – and have long been – factors in the process of cultural formation, always under way, by which 'this people or that, this period or that, makes sense of itself, to itself' (Geertz, 1980, p. 167). The 'sense' thus collectively made varies from era to era, people to people, but it is in relationship to the specific 'sense' prevailing at a given historical moment that individuals who share that 'sense' develop and preserve a sense of their distinctive personal identities, a consciousness of who (uniquely) each of them is.

Prospero's ability to tell Miranda about their past rests upon his power to remember, and he associates his brother Antonio's act of usurpation with a failure to remember. Interrupting himself three times, twice breaking off in mid-sentence, to ask if Miranda is listening,[7] Prospero tells of giving Antonio 'The manage of my state', thus irresponsibly relinquishing his ducal duties in order to devote himself to 'secret studies' (I.ii.70, 77). He also tells of how, in the process of 'executing th'outward face of royalty, / With all prerogative', Antonio 'Made such a sinner of his memory . . . he did believe / He was indeed the duke' (I.ii.104–5, 101–3). Acting as Prospero's substitute, Antonio in effect forgets his identity. Prospero goes on to describe the usurping ambition that grows from Antonio's violation of his own memory: 'To have no screen between this part he played / And him he play'd it for, he needs will be / Absolute Milan' (I.ii.107–9). Explicitly theatrical, Prospero's terminology directs attention to how, in performance – but not when read – *The Tempest* itself rests upon and arises from memory, from the ability of actors playing dramatic parts to remember not only the words but also the gestures and movements they have rehearsed.

Later in the same scene, when first Ariel and then Caliban object to the work he calls upon them to perform, Prospero responds by imposing his memory of past events upon theirs. Reminded by Ariel of the freedom he has promised to give him, Prospero insists, over Ariel's repeated objections, that Ariel has failed to remember 'From what a torment I did free thee' and proceeds to 'recount what thou hast been, / Which thou forget'st' (I.ii.251, 262–3). When Caliban objects to the confinement imposed upon him – 'here you sty me / In this hard rock, whiles you do keep from me / The rest o'th'island' (I.ii.344–6) – Prospero reminds him of his attempt to rape Miranda.

Prospero uses one of the most spectacular demonstrations of his art – and one of the strangest moments in *The Tempest* – to spur the memories of those responsible for his usurpation: Alonso, Antonio, and Sebastian. To '*Solemn and strage music*', as '*Prosper[o] on the top*' looks on, '*several strange Shapes*' bring in a banquet and invite the three men and those with them to eat (III.iii.17). When they approach the food, however, Ariel, attired 'like a Harpy', enters, '*claps his wings upon the table; and, with a quaint device, the banquet vanishes*' (III.iii.52). Ariel then defines for the 'three men of sin' the relationship between their present situation as they understand it – marooned on 'this island, / Where no man doth inhabit' – and their past evil, which makes them ' 'mongst men . . . most unfit to live' (III.iii.53, 56–8). 'But remember,' he tells them,

> For that's my business to you, – that you three
> From Milan did supplant good Prospero:
> Expos'd unto the sea, which hath requit it,
> Him and his innocent child: for which foul deed

The powers, delaying, not forgetting, have
Incens'd the seas and shores, yea, all the creatures,
Against your peace.

$$\text{(III.iii.68–75)}$$

The next scene includes another spectacular demonstration of the power of Prospero's art that also involves remembering: the entertainment he provides to celebrate the betrothal of Miranda and Ferdinand.[8] It offers the couple a vision of a world in which, with neither 'Venus or her son' Cupid present, the imperatives of sexual desire – 'th'fire in' th'blood' (IV.i.53) – are held in check, to be exercised only within the marital bond. That vision is a reminder to Ferdinand and Miranda of his pledge not to 'break her virgin-knot before / All sanctimonious ceremonies may / With full and holy rite be minister'd' (IV.i.15–17). It is also a foretaste of the blessings that will come if the betrothed couple are 'true' to that pledge instead of indulging in the unrestrained lust that would have peopled the island with Caliban's rape-engendered offspring or Stephano's 'brave brood' (III.ii.103). The entertainment provides a glimpse of a world in which there is no winter – '*Spring come to you at the farthest / In the very end of harvest*' (IV.i.114–15) – and no death.

Prospero calls the entertainment an enactment of 'My present fancies' (IV.i.122), and it takes the form of a Jacobean court masque like those at which the King's Men, as Gentlemen of the Chamber and thus formally members of the royal household, were present and in some of which they may have performed (Orgel, 1987, p. 43). Both the Globe and Blackfriars were commercial theatres, open to anyone, regardless of social rank, who paid the price of admission. In choosing to present Prospero's entertainment as a masque rather than a play-within-a-play, Shakespeare and the King's Men offered all who paid to see *The Tempest* played a representation of, an encounter with, an exclusively royal form of entertainment. Before the masque begins, Prospero instructs Ferdinand and Miranda, its onstage audience, how to behave: 'No tongue! all eyes! be silent' (IV.i.59).[9] Those instructions also function as directions to the play's first audiences on how to conduct themselves while hearing and watching a form of theatricalised entertainment that was 'strange' to the overwhelming majority of them – part of a royal world as far beyond the horizon fixed by their places in Jacobean society as the New World was beyond the western horizon.

The betrothal entertainment occasions the only moment when
Prospero's concentration upon his 'project' falters, and that lapse
takes the form of a failure to remember. As Nymphs and Reapers
summoned by Iris join '*in a graceful dance*' to '*celebrate / A contract of
true love*', '*Prospero starts suddenly and speaks*':

> I had forgot that foul conspiracy
> Of the beast Caliban and his confederates
> Against my life: the minute of their plot
> Is almost come.
>   (IV.i.138, 132–3, 138, 139–42)

Interrupting the dance, itself an instance of human actions performed
in harmony with time, he cuts short the entertainment, abruptly
ordering the spirits performing it to depart – 'Well done! avoid! /
no more' – and '*to a strange, hollow, and confused noise, they heavily vanish*'
(IV.i.142–3, 138). Prospero's forgetfulness is a consequence of his
absorption with the entertainment, and that absorption with what he
himself calls 'some vanity of mine Art' (IV.i.41) briefly repeats the
more extended fascination with 'secret studies' that, twelve years before,
made him vulnerable to another, and more successful, set of usurpers.

Disturbed and angry – at his own lapse as well as the perfidy of
the approaching assassins – Prospero voices, in lines frequently taken
as expressing Shakespeare's personal feelings, a despairing, keenly
felt sense of the transience and insubstantiality of human structures
and human life itself. Like the 'vision' provided for Ferdinand and
Miranda that has abruptly ended, 'The cloud-capp'd towers, the
gorgeous palaces, / The solemn temples', even 'the great globe itself'
and 'all which it inherit, shall dissolve' (IV.i.152–4) leaving nothing
behind. 'We are,' Prospero goes on to tell the betrothed couple, 'such
stuff / As dreams are made on; and our little life / Is rounded with
a sleep' (IV.i.156–8). His despair is intense, but it is only briefly
disabling. After apologising for 'my weakness' and 'my infirmity'
(IV.i.159, 160), he sends Ferdinand and Miranda away and, summoning Ariel, prepares to deal with Caliban and his confederates,
whom he easily defeats, at least in part because of another lapse of
memory. Drawn to the '*glistering apparel*' (IV.i.193) hanging on a line,
Stephano and Trinculo, disregarding Caliban's instructions on how
to deal with Prospero, fail to 'Remember / First to possess his books
. . . Burn but his books' (III.ii.89–90, 93).

Prospero's passage from despair to action demonstrates how, although he is not immune to the temptations that made him vulnerable twelve years before, he is capable now – as he was not then – of the self-conquest required of a ruler. Another such moment occurs when, with all his enemies now at his mercy, he sets 'my nobler reason 'gainst my fury' (V.i.26). Choosing 'the rarer action', which lies 'In virtue [rather] than in vengeance', he decides to forgive rather than take full revenge on Alonso, Antonio, and Sebastian, with whose 'high wrongs I am struck to th'quick' (V.i.27, 28, 25). '[T]hey being penitent,' he tells Ariel, 'The sole drift of my purpose doth extend / Not a frown further' (V.i.28–30). Prospero goes on to renounce not only vengeance but also, in what can be regarded as still another act of self-conquest, 'the rough magic' that in Milan made him vulnerable to his enemies and that now on the island gives him nearly total power over them. 'I'll break my staff,' he declares, 'Bury it certain fadoms in the earth, / And deeper than did ever plummet sound /I'll drown my book' (V.i.54–7).

In fact, however, the playtext never specifies the moment when Prospero executes his pledge to 'break my staff' and 'drown my book' (V.i.54, 57), thereby leaving those who perform the play free to determine when Prospero carries out his pledge. Perhaps while Prospero is waiting for Ariel to return with his ducal attire. Perhaps as Prospero says, 'so, so, so' (V.i.96), after, with Ariel's help, he is newly attired as Duke of Milan. Perhaps at the conclusion of the Epilogue, when Prospero calls upon audiences to set him free. Perhaps not at all.

The playtext also leaves open the issue of whether all who have wronged Prospero 'to th'quick' do in fact come to feel 'penitent' and thus leaves undetermined the related issues of the success of his project and the full efficacy of his art. His political success is beyond doubt. He regains his dukedom, and he succeeds, via the impending marriage of Ferdinand and Miranda, in reconciling the longstanding enmity between Naples and Milan that prompted Alonso to assist Antonio in overthrowing him. That marriage is part of Prospero's design, but it is also one to which the other parties freely assent. Prospero brings Ferdinand and Miranda into one another's presence, but the love they feel for one another comes from their hearts, not his art. He does not, for example, apply to their eyes a love juice like that employed in *A Midsummer Night's Dream*. Alonso, still convinced that Ferdinand is dead, responds to Prospero's revelation that

'I / Have lost my daughter' by spontaneously wishing for the marriage: 'O heavens that they were living both in Naples, / The King
and Queen there' (V.i.147–8, 149–50). There is also no doubt that
Alonso feels the penitence that Prospero says completes his 'purpose'.
Seeing Prospero for the first time in the play, he declares, un-
prompted, 'Thy dukedom I resign, and do entreat / Thou pardon
me my wrongs' (V.i.118–19).

The response of Antonio – Alonso's co-conspirator as well as Prospero's brother – is sharply different, however. He says nothing at all
when Prospero tells him:

> For you, most wicked sir, whom to call brother
> Would even infect my mouth, I do forgive
> Thy rankest fault, – all of them; and require
> My dukedom of thee, which perforce, I know,
> Thou must restore.
>
>   (V.i.130–4)

For readers the silence that follows those words lasts no longer than
it takes for their eyes to move to the next speech, but in performance
Antonio's wordlessness begins a silence that can be lengthy or short,
depending on how long the actor playing Alonso waits before ending
it by calling on Prospero to 'Give us particulars of thy preservation'
(V.i.135). Having Alonso be the one who speaks sets Antonio's
silence against the voice of the man whose support made it possible
for him to usurp Prospero's dukedom. Antonio never assents in
words to relinquishing the dukedom, never acknowledges verbally
any 'fault', even the 'rankest', and – in contrast to Alonso – never
asks Prospero or anyone else to 'pardon me my wrongs'.

In fact, Antonio speaks but once during the final scene, when he
says of Caliban, newly entered with Stephano and Trinculo, 'one of
them / Is a plain fish, and, no doubt, marketable' (V.i.265–6).[10] Those
words help to bring into focus another contrast – between Antonio's
silence when Prospero forgives him and Caliban's use of language
during the play's final moments. During Caliban's first appearance,
Miranda asserts that when he could 'but gabble like / A thing most
brutish', she 'Took pains to make thee speak' and 'endow'd thy
purposes / With words that made them known' (I.ii.356–60). Caliban
replies, 'You taught me language; and my profit on't / Is, I know how
to curse' (I.ii.365–6). During his final moments onstage, however,

Caliban, who like Antonio has instigated a conspiracy to unseat Prospero, uses that language to express purposes unlike any he has uttered before. Ordered to trim Prospero's cell, he pledges, 'Ay, that I will; and I'll be wise hereafter, / And seek for grace' (V.i.294–5). His words convey a willingness to obey, a desire to reform, and a sense of penitence that contradict Prospero's characterisation of him as 'A devil, a born devil, on whose nature / Nurture can never stick' and as 'this thing of darkness' (IV.i.188–9; V.i.275). Caliban's final pledge also accentuates the fact that, even when he does speak, Antonio never uses the language at his command to express such sentiments.

Most productions over recent decades have taken Antonio's silence as evidence of his failure or refusal to feel 'penitent'. In John Barton's 1970 production for the Royal Shakespeare Company, for example, Antonio responded to Prospero's words requiring 'my dukedom of thee' by giving him the badge of office, bowing, and then walking away in silence. His wordless actions conveyed grudging acceptance of what, given Prospero's demonstrated powers, was unavoidable, but there was no sign of any penitence or of any resolve to do good in the future. In Clifford Williams's 1978 production, also for the Royal Shakespeare Company, Antonio broke away from Prospero without returning any badge of office or offering even so much as a perfunctory bow, and for the remainder of the play he kept himself apart from those participating in the developing reconciliation between Naples and Milan. Both productions conveyed the sense that Antonio's malevolence has been checked by Prospero's superior powers but not extirpated, defeated but not destroyed or redeemed. He remains, dangerously, what Prospero, shortly before forgiving him, declares him to be: the 'brother mine' who has 'Expell'd remorse and nature' (V.i.75–6).

During 1988 three major English acting companies staged productions of *The Tempest* that, for all their many differences, concurred in presenting Antonios who were resolutely impenitent. In Nicholas Hytner's production for the Royal Shakespeare Company, Prospero struggled to bring himself to kiss Antonio, who, holding himself motionless, was unmoved by and unresponsive to that gesture of fraternal reconciliation. Even after Prospero required 'My dukedom of thee', the Antonio of Peter Hall's production for the National Theatre continued wearing the ducal coronet, and he kept his back to both the audience and to the others onstage. In Jonathan Miller's

Old Vic production, Alonso removed a ring from his finger and gave it to Prospero as he told him, 'thy dukedom I resign'. That 'thy' conveyed his abandonment of Antonio, and when Antonio stared in dismayed surprise at him, the king who had been his partner in the conspiracy to unseat Prospero and make Milan subject to Naples turned away. After Prospero expressed forgiveness and required 'My dukedom' from him, Antonio hesitated perceptibly, assessing the realignment of power that had just occurred, then, kneeling, kissed the ring his brother now wore. Rising to his feet following that gesture of submission to his brother's authority and Alonso's, Antonio again looked at his erstwhile partner, who avoided his gaze. As the stage cleared following the Epilogue, Prospero and Antonio were the last to leave, and before passing from view, the two brothers exchanged a long, wary stare.

Those presentations of Antonio's silence are consistent with analysis offered in three editions currently widely used in studying, teaching, and performing *The Tempest*. In his vastly influential Arden edition, first published in 1954 and reprinted as recently as 1988, Frank Kermode calls Antonio 'one of Prospero's failures' because 'as far as can be deduced from the closing passages, in which Antonio is silent, he will not choose the good' (1954, p. lxii). Antonio, Kermode insists, is 'another thing of darkness' that 'Prospero must acknowledge' (1954, p. lxii). In his 1987 New Oxford single-volume edition of *The Tempest*, Stephen Orgel comments, 'It is important to observe that Antonio does not repent here – he is, indeed, not *allowed* to repent' (1987, p. 53). In his most recent edition of *The Complete Works of Shakespeare*, David Bevington concurs, stating, 'Antonio never repents' (1992, p. 1528).

'A world without Antonio,' Kermode observes, 'is a world without freedom; Prospero's shipwreck cannot restore him if he desires not to be restored, to life' (1954, p. lxii). Freedom is a major concern in *The Tempest*. Both Ariel and Caliban call for it during their first appearance. Caliban, drunkenly and mistakenly, exults in it after accepting Stephano as his new master: 'Freedom, high day! high-day, freedom! freedom, high-day, freedom!' (II.ii.186–7). In the last song of this most musical of Shakespearean plays, Ariel, helping Prospero to don his ducal attire, sings in anticipation of it: '*Merrily, merrily shall I live now / Under the blossom that hangs on the bough*' (V.i.93–4). Prospero grants it to him as the play nears its conclusion: 'then to the elements / Be free, and fare thou well' (V.i.317–18). 'Free' is also the final word spoken in the play, and it is Prospero who speaks it. At the end of the Epilogue, speaking as a magician who has renounced his magic and as an actor whose part is ending, Prospero, who no longer exercises the extraordinary control over what audiences see and hear that sets him, strangely, apart from every other Shakespearean character, asks those who have watched the play to grant him freedom: '*As you from crimes would pardon'd be, / Let your indulgence set me free*' (V.i.19–20).

Antonio's freedom flows from his silence. Prospero can 'require' him to return the ducal power he usurped, but he cannot compel him to be sincerely and everlastingly 'penitent'. Antonio's freedom goes beyond that which Kermode, rightly, attributes to him. His situation, as *The Tempest* draws to an end, is not one in which he 'never repents' or is 'not *allowed* to repent'. More accurately, it is one in which the Shakespearean playtext never allows him to *say* that he repents. He is given no words to speak equivalent to Alonso's asking pardon or Caliban's pledging to reform. It is, however, equally true – and equally significant – that Antonio is also not allowed to *say* that he does not repent.[11] He is given no words to speak revealing what he feels and does, nor is any other character. In *The Winter's Tale*, Hermione, newly returned to life, says nothing at all to her husband Leontes, whose groundless jealousy had caused her 'death' sixteen years earlier. Comments by the amazed onlookers make clear, however, that her silence is not a sign of any resentment or ill-will towards Leontes. 'She embraces him,' says one; 'She hangs about his neck,' says another (V.iii.111, 112). In *The Tempest*, by contrast, no one watching as Prospero forgives his brother and reclaims the dukedom offers any equivalent comment clarifying what Antonio does or feels. In the absence of words – Antonio's or anyone else's – indicating what his silence signifies, it is possible that he does not feel penitent. Most recent productions enact that possibility, and editors such as Kermode, Orgel, and Bevington present it as a certainty. In fact, however, Antonio's silence is also fully compatible with another, directly antithetical possibility: he feels penitence so intense that, in contrast to Alonso and Caliban, he has no words to express it.

Robin Phillips's 1976 production at the Stratford (Ontario) Festival enacted that possibility. Antonio sank speechlessly to his knees on hearing Prospero's words to him, and Prospero, in a gesture confirming the forgiveness he voiced, took his kneeling brother's hands in his. In that production, the silent Antonio was a profoundly penitent man. No longer making 'a sinner of his own memory', he was part

of an extraordinary process, summarised by Gonzalo, that brings
good from evil and from disorientation self-discovery:

> Was Milan thrust from Milan, that his issue
> Should become Kings of Naples? O, rejoice
> Beyond a common joy! and set it down
> With gold on lasting pillars: in one voyage
> Did Claribel her husband find at Tunis,
> And Ferdinand, her brother, found a wife
> Where he himself was lost; Prospero his dukedom
> In a poor isle, and all of us ourselves
> When no man was his own.
>
> (V.i.205–13)

In Phillips's production, the 'all of us' who have found 'ourselves'
included Antonio, penitent beyond words.

Such inclusion, however, is contrary to what is becoming an
editorial-critical consensus that takes Antonio's silence as evidence of
resolute, enduring impenitence that sets him apart from 'all of us'.
That consensus is another, highly typical instance of how any era,
responding to and seeking confirmation of its own vision(s) of the
human condition, tends to focus and thus to narrow the possibilities
presented by a Shakespearean playtext. The currently developing
consensus reflects a deep, prevailing scepticism about, on the one
hand, the capacity of individuals to change and, on the other, the
efficacy of authority, particularly governmental authority, in dealing
with evil. The irony, in this instance, is that, under the guise of
preserving Antonio's freedom, the emerging editorial-critical consensus in fact restricts it, transforming the freedom to be impenitent
that his silence allows into a mandate that he must not feel 'penitent'.
In so doing, that consensus denies the freedom to be penitent that
likewise flows from his silence.

The freedom thus compromised is not Antonio's alone. It is also
the freedom of the actors who play him and of those who direct them.
In the absence of words specifying what Antonio feels and does when
Prospero forgives him and requires the return of the dukedom,
responsibility for determining what he feels and does passes to them.
More than that, the freedom being compromised is that which the
play itself possesses. *The Tempest* is a play that – edited and performed
at and for a given moment in history – presents Antonio's mal-

evolence as beyond the scope of Prospero's art, as checked but not transformed by 'rough magic' capable of dimming the noon-time sun and waking the dead. It is also, however, a play that – performed and edited at and for a different moment of history – allows that 'rough magic' to awaken in Antonio a capacity for remorse and for goodness so long dormant that its revival leaves him wordless.

Epilogue

During both the Elizabethan and the Jacobean phases of his career, Shakespeare participated in creating what are widely considered to be the greatest plays in the English language and, many would say, the greatest that humanity possesses. Their claim to greatness rests in very considerable measure upon a universality that has manifested itself in a variety of ways. A production of *Coriolanus* that opened in Paris on 9 December 1933 triggered riots that contributed to a change in the government of France. Germans such as Goethe and Schlegel played indispensable roles in establishing the excellence of Shakespeare's works, and the Nazi government that came to power in Germany during the 1930s included Shakespeare's plays among the works that it designated as properly German. The journal *Hamlet Studies* is published in New Delhi, India. Grigori Kozintsev has filmed Russian versions of *King Lear* and *Hamlet*, and among the films of the great Japanese director Akira Kurosawa are two – *Throne of Blood* and *Ran* – based upon *Macbeth* and *King Lear* respectively. The 1986 meeting of the International Shakespeare Association took place not in Stratford-upon-Avon or even London, not in Washington, D. C., or Toronto, but in the western sector of a Berlin that was then still divided by the Wall and the Cold War. The site of the ISA's 1991 meeting was Tokyo.

The greatness and universality with which Shakespeare's plays have been invested should not, however, blind us to the fact that in his own time and place – his own historical and cultural moment(s) – Shakespeare was an actor and professional playwright penning plays for performance by an acting company in the profits of which he shared. He was part of an enterprise that was at least as much commercial as 'artistic'. The company's quasi-feudal relationship to its patron – the Lord Chamberlain until Elizabeth's death and then King James himself – gave them the right to perform, but they earned their livelihood by how they fared in the marketplace, by what they took in at the box office. The fate of John Fletcher's tragicomedy *The Faithful Shepherdess* provides a glimpse of Shakespeare's attentiveness to box-office considerations as well as aesthetic concerns. Fletcher's play was a commercial failure when performed in 1608, and in an address 'To the Reader' in the published version, Fletcher, who later succeeded Shakespeare as the King's Men's attached playwright, explains why. It did not give audiences what they wanted and expected, in particular features associated with traditional folk festivals. 'Missing Whitsunales, cream, wassil and morris-dances', Fletcher comments, audiences 'began to be angry.' In composing *The Winter's Tale* within three years of the failure of *The Faithful Shepherdess*, Shakespeare made sure its audiences have no such reasons 'to be angry'. It gives them a sustained taste of folk ritual through the sheep-shearing festival (IV.iv) – among the longest and most complex scenes in all of Shakespeare – which includes dancing, ballads, and a catch.

The esteem in which, since the late eighteenth century, various eras down to the present have held Shakespeare and his plays is one measure of his success. Another measure – and one more true to his actual situation – is the money he earned. During the years he worked with the Lord Chamberlain's–King's Men, Shakespeare, the son of a small businessman (probably a glover) who went broke, became wealthy enough to buy the second most imposing residence in his native Stratford-upon-Avon and to retire there at or before the age of fifty. The presence of Shakespeare's figure on the back of the £20 notes currently in circulation in Britain testifies to his involvement, even now, in commercial processes. His plays made money for him and for his acting company when Elizabeth I and James I ruled, and today, when Elizabeth II sits on the British throne and her son and heir, Charles, Prince of Wales, bears the same name as James's son and successor, those plays continue to do so for many others. 'Others' includes not only those who perform them in theatres and for film and television, but also shopowners, restauranteurs, guides, tour operators, and hotel proprietors in places like Stratford-upon-Avon and Stratford, Ontario, as well as the publishing companies that market editions of his plays and books about them. 'Others' also includes those who write such books, including this one.

Notes

Introduction

1. Quoted in Bentley, 1971, pp. 52–3.

2. They were called 'sharers', Bentley explains, 'because their remuneration was not a weekly wage, as in the case of the hired men, or valuable training as in the case of the [boy] apprentices, but a share in the receipts of each performance' (1984, p. 25).

3. Quoted in Elam, 1980, p. 7.

4. A book in folio format is made up of sheets of paper folded once to produce two leaves and four pages. A book in quarto consists of sheets folded twice to produce four leaves and eight pages. The plays included in the First Folio were assembled by John Heminge and Henry Condell, who, like Shakespeare, were founding members of the Lord Chamberlain's–King's Men.

5. In fact, any number of Shakespearean characters powerfully articulate it, most notably Ulysses in his speech on 'degree' in *Troilus and Cressida* (I.iii.75–137).

1. Shakespeare's Jacobean Plays

1. Their adult rivals, the Lord Admiral's Men and the Lord Worcester's Men, became the Prince's Men and the Queen's Men respectively, and the two companies of boy players competing with them were renamed Children of the King's Revels and Children of the Queen's Revels. That act completed the process, under way since 1572, by which the crown asserted authority over players, playing, and theatres.

2. The last contemporary reference to Shakespeare as an actor is to his performance in Ben Jonson's *Sejanus* in 1603. Thus, it is

possible that in succeeding years his acting responsibilities were reduced, if not eliminated.

3. Like the Globe, Blackfriars was a commercial theatre, open to all who paid the admission price. It was a 'private' theatre because, in contrast to a 'public' theatre such as the Globe, it was located in what was technically a private house.

4. History proved unkind. James's first son, Henry, died in 1612, and James was succeeded in 1625 by his second son, Charles, who was publicly beheaded in 1649, and the issue of royal succession became the paramount issue of the last half of the seventeenth century.

5. Ironically, James himself became king of England in a way that made him something of a woman's man. His primary claim to the English throne was through his mother – Mary, Queen of Scots – and he became king of England because with her dying words another woman, Elizabeth I, chose him to be. By endowing Elizabeth with a greatness it withholds from him, history has fixed James with the status of a woman's man in still another way. It regards him as *her* successor far more often than it looks on her as *his* predecessor.

6. The remainder of this paragraph draws extensively on Jonathan Goldberg's *James I and the Politics of Literature*, 1983, pp. 110–18.

7. The technical description of blank verse is unrhymed iambic pentameter.

8. *1 Henry VI*, *2 Henry VI*, *Richard II*, and *King John*.

2. *Measure for Measure*: 'A Little Brief Authority'

1. I am indebted to Craig A. Bernthal and Steven Mullaney for their accounts of these events.

2. Of his twenty-five Elizabethan plays, the Folio classifies five as tragedies, nine as histories, and eleven as comedies. The Folio lists *The Tempest* and *The Winter's Tale* as comedies, and if one accepts that classification, *Measure* is the last comedy Shakespeare wrote for six years or more. That interval is far longer than any separating his eleven Elizabethan comedies, which were written at the rate of approximately one per year between roughly 1590–91 and 1602. If, on the other hand, one regards the *The Tempest* and *The Winter's Tale* as generically distinct from comedies – as 'romances' or 'tragicomedies' – then *Measure* is not only very probably Shakespeare's first Jacobean play but also his final comedy of any kind.

3. The play opens with still another substitution involving heads. As the Duke's appointed deputy, Angelo takes his place as the head of Vienna.

4. One can, given Bertram's conduct until this point, question the credibility of that declaration, but the point is that he makes it.

5. That the Duke proposes to Isabella is a surprising, if not troubling, development, since he assures Friar Thomas that he is immune to the power of love: 'Believe not that the dribbling dart of love / Can pierce a complete bosom' (I.iii.2–3). Arguably, the Duke's bosom is not as complete as he thinks it is, and his self-knowledge is less than that Escalus attributes to him when he characterises the Duke as 'One that, above all other strifes, contended especially to know himself' (III.ii.226–7)

6. See Leonard Tennenhouse's discussion of comedies of this kind in *Power on Display: The Politics of Shakespeare's Genres*, 1986, pp. 154–9.

3. *Othello*: 'A Pageant to Keep Us in False Gaze'

1. These lines contain one of many significant differences between the two versions of *Othello* that have survived from Shakespeare's era: the Quarto of 1622 and the Folio of 1623. In the Quarto, the Duke tells Brabantio that he will read the law 'after its own sense', but in the Folio he says, 'after your own sense'.

2. The Turkish threat to dominate the Mediterranean was decisively turned back in 1571 in a massive sea battle off the port of Lepanto involving close to six hundred warships. The Turkish threat to Cyprus in *Othello* is one of the background events leading up to that battle about which James I had written a poem, *Lepanto*, published in 1591 and again on his accession to the throne of England in 1603.

3. Othello and Desdemona leave for Cyprus within hours of their appearance before the Senate on the night of their elopement. Travelling on separate ships, each arrives on Cyprus after Cassio, who has sailed on a third ship. The brawl that disgraces Cassio breaks out that night, and Cassio's appeal for Desdemona's assistance occurs the next day. Act III, Scene iii begins with the conclusion of that appeal, yet as that scene ends, Othello, certain of Desdemona's infidelity, exits determined to find 'some swift means of death' (III.iii.484) for her.

4. 'Virtue' here has the now generally lost meaning of 'power', 'capacity', 'ability', – as in the 'virtue' of sight – as well as the still current meaning of a habit of doing what is morally right and good.

5. Most editions of *Othello* widely used today, including M. R. Ridley's Arden edition, offer a text for the closing moments of III.iii that conflates Quarto and Folio, including both the explicit stage directions, calling for first Othello and then Iago to kneel, found only in the former, and dialogue – principally the simile involving the Pontic Sea – found only in the latter. Thus, the scene as it is most often played, taught, and studied today is different from both Quarto and Folio versions. Pointed brackets indicate Folio-only passages.

6. The corresponding passage in Quarto is

> *Oth.* Never:
>   In the due reverence of a sacred vow,
>   I here engage my words.
> *Iag.* Do not rise yet . . .

7. These words are not in the Quarto.

8. In the Quarto and most modern editions. The Folio's stage direction does not specify that Othello carries a light.

9. Folio has 'My heart's subdued / Even to the very quality of my lord'.

10. In *The Masks of 'Othello'*, an exhaustive study of the play's stage history, Marvin Rosenberg (1961) makes no mention of a production in which Emilia is laid by her mistress's side, and I do not remember seeing any.

11. Folio has 'base Iudean'.

12. See the Introduction for a discussion of how the stage direction for this moment typically provided by modern editors differs from what Quarto and Folio provide.

4. *King Lear*: 'O! See, See'

1. What characters say they hear during this scene is also problematic. Edgar, responding to Gloucester's claim that 'the ground is even', asks, 'do you hear the sea?' (IV.vi.4). When Gloucester says, 'No, truly', Edgar explains, 'Why, then your other senses grow imperfect / By your eyes' anguish' (IV.vi.4–6). Later, however, while describing what he sees from the cliff top, he contradicts that explanation: 'The murmuring surge . . . Cannot be heard so high' (IV.vi.20–2). That complicates what audiences hear – the 'sound effects' of the scene. Are they hearing any sounds of the sea when Edgar asks, 'do you hear the sea?' If not, the effect is to make their

hearing as deficient as Gloucester's. If they do hear such sounds then, what do they hear when Edgar says he stands at the edge of a cliff so high that no sound of the sea below is audible?

2. Three recent exceptions deserve mention. Two are the work of Michael Warren: *The Complete 'King Lear', 1608–1623* (1989a) and *The Parallel 'King Lear', 1608–1623* (1989b). The New Oxford edition of *The Complete Works* (1986) of Shakespeare, edited by Stanley Wells and Gary Taylor, includes both Quarto and Folio versions of *Lear*.

3. Audiences these days typically see an entrance different in important respects from both Quarto and Folio. Goneril and Albany as well as Regan and Cornwall enter paired as husband and wife, not grouped by rank and sex as the Quarto specifies. Lear enters last, not first – a shift that reflects change over the centuries in how rank or importance manifests itself in order of entry. Sometimes Lear is alone, sometimes he moves arm-in-arm with Cordelia. If Cordelia does not enter with Lear, hers is usually the entrance that directly precedes his. In some productions, she comes on alone, in others paired with the Fool, even though neither Quarto nor Folio Lear specifically mentions him in the opening scene.

4. The speech heading '*Cor.*' is ambiguous. Most editors take it to mean Cornwall, thereby making the moment one in which Lear's two sons-in-law, the immediate beneficiaries of his decision to disinherit Cordelia, intervene. However, '*Cor.*' is also the speech heading the Folio gives for many of Cordelia's speeches in this scene, including all on the page on which this dialogue appears. If '*Cor.*' is Cordelia, audiences see the most faithful of Lear's three daughters and the more faithful of his sons-in-law join to protect Kent. Cornwall's silence and inaction are, under such circumstances, a signal to audiences of differences between Lear's two sons-in-law that will become more apparent as the play proceeds.

5. 'To love my father all' is present only in the Quarto.

6. Quarto *Lear* further accentuates the collapse of judicial processes by including in the scene immediately before Gloucester's ordeal an episode not present in the Folio. Lear, mad, takes a joint stool for Goneril and Regan and puts the two 'she foxes' (III.vi.22) on trial in the hovel where he and his pitiful trio of attendants have sought shelter from the storm. Those whom he calls to sit in judgement – the Fool, Edgar as Poor Tom, and Kent as Caius – are a far cry from the Duke and senators of Venice who in *Othello* hear another father, Brabantio, declare himself the victim of injustice.

7. In historical accounts as ancient as Geoffrey of Monmouth's *History of the British Kings* (1136) and as recent as Raphael Holinshed's *Chronicles of England* (1587), in Book II of Edmund Spenser's epic poem *The Faerie Queene* (1590), and in *The True Chronicle History of King Leir*, an anonymous play acted as early as 1594 and published in 1605.

8. Quarto *Lear*, which claims to be a record of that performance, assigns the play's final lines to Albany. 'Albany' is another name for Scotland, and James himself, who was present at that performance, was himself a Scotsman.

5. *Macbeth*: 'Double, Double'

1. In contrast to the King Duncan in Holinshed's *Chronicles* — the major source for *Macbeth* — who has killed to become king.

2. All of III.v and IV.i.39–43 and 125–32. There is evidence that joint authorship was far from unusual in Shakespeare's era. For example, the Lord Admiral's Men, the chief rivals of Shakespeare's acting company, played at the Rose Theatre, owned by Philip Henslowe. His account book, known today as *Henslowe's Diary*, includes entries recording payments to playwrights. They show — surprisingly by our practices — that a majority of the plays purchased for performance by the Lord Admiral's Men between 1591 and 1604 were collaborative works, written by two or more playwrights.

3. The boy actors apprenticed to the Lord Chamberlain's/King's Men are given much the same kind of assistance in a number of other plays — among them *Twelfth Night*, *As You Like It*, *All's Well That Ends Well*, and *Cymbeline* — in which young women disguise themselves as boys for extended periods.

4. Her reference to her father also functions ideologically by invoking the analogy between father and king, family and state that King James himself made explicit in *The Trew Law of Free Monarchies*: 'By the Law of Nature the King becomes a natural Father to all his Lieges at his Coronation' (McIlwain, 1918, p. 55).

5. Especially for audiences who, in contrast to the play's original audiences, are not members of a culture that routinely displays the heads of traitors as a warning to others.

6. *Coriolanus*: 'Author of Himself'

1. That, in turn, lays the basis for the effectiveness of the epithet 'boy' that Aufidius uses during the play's last moments. Taunting

Coriolanus as 'thou boy of tears' (V.vi.100), Aufidius goads him into
pride-filled rage that provokes him into reminding the Volsci surrounding him of his feats of battle against them within the walls of
Corioli: 'Alone I did it' (V.vi.116).

2. Volumnia's is not the only silence besides Coriolanus's. Virgilia,
young Martius, and Valeria also say nothing, leaving open the
question of how each of them responds.

3. In asserting absolute and divinely ordained authority, James
claimed god-like status of the kind attributed to Coriolanus. For
example, James opens his *Basilikon Doron* – a book on the theory and
practice of kingship widely distributed in London in the spring of 1603
after James succeeded Elizabeth – with a sonnet that justifies the god-
like behaviour of kings: 'God gives not Kings the stile of *Gods* in vaine, /
For on his Throne his Scepter doe they swey' (McIlwain, 1918, p. 3).

4. Plutarch sets Coriolanus's death in Antium, but the play
appears to shift it to Corioli. Note Aufidius's refusal to address Coriolanus by 'thy stol'n name / Coriolanus, in Corioles' (V.vi.89–90).
That refusal has far less dramatic weight if the scene is set in Antium,
which is where many editors locate it, primarily on the basis of the
First Conspirator's reference to how Aufidius received 'no welcomes
home' when he returned to his 'native town' (V.vi.50–1). It seems to
me, however, that the point of the reference is to contrast the
welcome Aufidius did not receive from the city of his birth with the
acclaim the stage direction '*Drums and trumpets sound, with great shouts
of the people*' signals Coriolanus is receiving from a city he once
conquered, in the process shedding the blood of many related to
those who now acclaim him.

7. *The Winter's Tale*: 'Awake Your Faith'

1. See Note 3 of Chapter 1 for an explanation of the term 'private
theatre'.

2. Chapter 1 discusses these differences.

3. See Chapter 1 for a discussion of why such a grouping is
problematic.

4. Audiences never see the King of France whose death is
announced in the final scene of *Love's Labours Lost*, nor Ragozine, the
pirate whose death due to fever enables the Duke in *Measure for
Measure* to obtain the head needed to convince Angelo that Claudio
has been executed.

5. In *Mucedorus*, for example, a play so persistently popular that by 1668 it had been published in seventeen editions, a prince disguised as a shepherd rescues a princess who enters and exits pursued by a bear; in *The Winter's Tale*, Antigonus exits pursued by a bear, and a shepherd saves the infant princess he has abandoned.

6. See Chapter 1 for a fuller discussion of this point.

7. That offer has additional impact if in performance the actor playing Antigonus also plays Camillo. With such doubling, Camillo becomes during the play's final moments a *theatrical* reincarnation of Antigonus, since both characters inhabit the body of the actor playing the roles.

8. In the 1978 Phillips–Moss production at Stratford (Ontario), no betrothal occurred. Paulina exited immediately after declaring her intention to mourn for Antigonus – before Leontes could speak of marriage.

8. *The Tempest*: 'Something Rich and Strange'

1. The tendency to identify Prospero with Shakespeare reached somewhat bizarre fulfilment in Peter Greenaway's 1991 film *Prospero's Books*, which rests on the premise that Prospero himself wrote the play that history knows as *The Tempest*.

2. Trinculo's words also participate in the play's concern with the relationship between the human and non-human. They can mean, as Terence Hawkes (1985) has noted, that in England the 'any strange beast' is taken to be, passes for, a human being.

3. The other two are *A Midsummer Night's Dream* and *The Merry Wives of Windsor*.

4. See Chapter 1 for a fuller discussion of this point.

5. This paragraph draws upon Donald E. Pease's (1990) essay 'Author'.

6. Chapter 1 discusses why this grouping is problematic.

7. These interruptions arise less from any inattentiveness on the part of Miranda than from the force of the feelings that the act of narrating, and therefore remembering, the past stirs in Prospero.

8. *The Tempest* was performed during the festivities before the marriage of James's daughter Elizabeth to the Elector Palatine on 14 February 1613. The first performance on record was at court on 1 November 1611.

9. The behaviour of onstage audiences during the plays-within-the-play in *A Midsummer Night's Dream* and *Hamlet* suggests that far from being silent during performances, audiences of that time tended to be talkative.

10. Like Stephano and Trinculo, Antonio first responds to Caliban in terms of the commercial possibilities he offers.

11. For example, he is given no words like those assigned to him in W. H. Auden's 1945 poem 'The Sea and the Mirror':

> Your all is partial, Prospero;
>   My will is all my own;
> Your need to love shall never know
> Me: I am I, Antonio,
>   By choice myself alone.

Bibliography

Adelman, Janet (1978) ' "Anger's My Meat": Feeding, Dependency, and Aggression in *Coriolanus*', in *Shakespeare: Pattern of Excelling Nature*, ed. David Bevington and Jay L. Halio (Newark: University of Delaware Press; London: Associated University Presses) pp. 108–204.

Barton, Anne (1974) *'Measure for Measure'*, in *The Riverside Shakespeare*, ed. G. Blakemore Evans *et al.* (Boston and London: Houghton Mifflin) pp. 545–9.

Bassnett, Susan E. (1993) *Shakespeare: The Elizabethan Plays* (Basingstoke: Macmillan; New York: St Martin's Press).

Bentley, Gerald Eades (1971) *The Profession of Dramatist in Shakespeare's Time 1590–1642* (Princeton: Princeton University Press).

Bentley, Gerald Eades (1984) *The Profession of Player in Shakespeare's Time 1590–1642* (Princeton: Princeton University Press).

Bernthal, Craig A. (1992) 'Staging Justice: James I and the Trial Scenes of *Measure for Measure*', *SEL: Studies in English Literature 1500–1900*, 32, pp. 247–69.

Berry, Ralph (1981) *Changing Styles in Shakespeare* (London, Boston, Sydney: George Allen & Unwin).

Bevington, David (1992) *The Complete Works of Shakespeare*, 4th edn. (New York: Harper Collins).

Bliss, Lee (1990) 'Pastiche, Burlesque, Tragicomedy', in Braunmuller and Hattaway, pp. 237–61.

Bond, Ronald B. (1987) *Certain Sermons or Homilies (1547) and A Homily against Disobedience and Wilful Rebellion* (Toronto, Baffalo, N.Y., and London: University of Toronto Press).

Booth, Stephen (1983) *'King Lear', 'Macbeth', Indefinition, and Tragedy* (New Haven and London: Yale University Press).

Bradley, A. C. (1904) *Shakespearean Tragedy* (New York: Fawcett; reprinted 1965).

Braunmuller, A. R. and Hattaway, Michael (1990) *The Cambridge Companion to English Renaissance Drama* (Cambridge and New York: Cambridge University Press).

Brockbank, Philip (ed.) (1976) *Coriolanus*, Arden edn (London and New York: Methuen; reprinted 1987).

Brown, John Russell (ed.) (1982) *Focus on 'Macbeth'* (London and Boston: Routledge & Kegan Paul).

Calderwood, James L. (1987) 'Speech and Self in *Othello*', *Shakespeare Quarterly*, 38, pp. 293–303.

Charney, Maurice (1988) 'Introduction', in *'Bad' Shakespeare: Revaluations of the Shakespeare Canon*, ed. Maurice Charney (Rutherford, Madison, Teaneck: Fairleigh Dickinson University Press; London and Toronto: Associated University Presses) pp. 9–18.

Coleridge, Samuel Taylor (1930) *Coleridge's Shakespearean Criticism*, ed. Thomas Middleton Raysor, Vol. I (Cambridge, Mass: Harvard University Press).

Daniell, David (1980) *'Coriolanus' in Europe* (London: Athlone).

Daniell, David (1986) 'Shakespeare and the Traditions of Comedy', in *The Cambridge Companion to Shakespeare Studies*, ed. Stanley Wells (Cambridge, New York, Melbourne: Cambridge University Press; reprinted 1987) pp. 101–41.

Elam, Keir (1980) *The Semiotics of Theatre and Drama* (London and New York: Methuen).

Erickson, Peter (1982) 'Patriarchal Structures in *The Winter's Tale*', *PMLA*, 97, pp. 819–29.

Felperin, Howard (1977) *Shakespearean Representation: Mimesis and Modernity in Elizabethan Tragedy* (Princeton, N. J.: Princeton University Press).

Foakes, R. A. (1990) 'Playhouses and Players', in Braunmuller and Hattaway, pp. 1–52.

Geertz, Clifford (1980) 'Blurred Genres: The Refiguration of Social Thought', *The American Scholar*, 49, pp. 165–79.

Gibbons, Brian (1990) 'Romance and the Heroic Play', in Braunmuller and Hattaway, pp. 207–36.

Goldberg, Jonathan (1983) *James I and the Politics of Literature: Jonson, Shakespeare, Donne, and Their Contemporaries* (Baltimore and London: The Johns Hopkins University Press).

Goldman, Michael (1985) *Acting and Action in Shakespearean Tragedy* (Princeton, New Jersey: Princeton University Press).

Greenblatt, Stephen (1988) *Shakespearean Negotiations: The Circulation of Social Energy in Renaissance England* (Berkeley, Calif.: University of California Press).

Hapgood, Robert (1988) *Shakespeare the Theatre-Poet* (Oxford: Clarendon Press).

Harbage, Alfred (ed.) (1969) *William Shakespeare: The Complete Works*, The Pelican Text Revised (New York: Viking; reprinted 1977).

Hardison, O. B., Jr. (1983) 'Speaking the Speech', *Shakespeare Quarterly*, 34, pp. 133–46.

Hawkes, Terence (1985) 'Swisser-Swatter: Making a Man of English Letters', in *Alternative Shakespeares*, ed. John Drakakis (London and New York: Methuen) pp. 26–46.

Hodgdon, Barbara (1990) *The End Crowns All* (Princeton, N. J.: Princeton University Press).

Kermode, Frank (1954) *The Tempest*, Arden edition (London and New York: Routledge; reprinted 1988).

Kernan, Alvin B. (1970) '*Othello*: An Introduction', in *Modern Shakespearean Criticism*, ed. Alvin B. Kernan (New York: Harcourt, Brace, & World) pp. 351–60.

Lever, J. W. (1965) *Measure for Measure*, Arden edition (London and New York: Methuen; reprinted 1987).

Marcus, Leah S. (1988) *Puzzling Shakespeare: Local Reading and Its Discontents* (Berkeley, Calif., and London: University of California Press).

McGuire, Philip C. (1985) *Speechless Dialect: Shakespeare's Open Silences* (Berkeley, Calif., and London: University of California Press).

McGuire, Philip C., and David A. Samuelson (1979) *Shakespeare: The Theatrical Dimension* (New York: AMS Press).

McIlwain, Charles Howard (ed.) (1918) *The Political Works of James I* (Cambridge, Mass.: Harvard University Press).

Montrose, Louis Adrian (1980) 'The Purpose of Playing: Reflections on a Shakespearean Anthropology', *Helios*, n. s. 7, pp. 51–74.

Muir, Kenneth (ed.) (1972a) *King Lear*, Arden edition (London and New York: Methuen; reprinted 1987).

Muir, Kenneth (ed.) (1972b) *Macbeth*, Arden edition (London and New York: Methuen; reprinted 1986).

Mullaney, Steven (1988) *The Place of the Stage: License, Play, and Power in Renaissance England* (Chicago and London: University of Chicago Press).

Newman, Karen (1987) ' "And Wash the Ethiop White": Feminity and the Monstrous in *Othello*', in *Shakespeare Reproduced: The Text in History and Ideology*, ed. Jean E. Howard and Marion F. O'Connor (New York and London: Methuen) pp. 141–62.

Nightingale, Benedict (1988) 'For the Macbeths, Marriage Is Murder', *New York Times* (1 May), section H: pp. 5, 38.

Orgel, Stephen (1975) *The Illusion of Power: Political Theater in the English Renaissance* (Berkeley, Calif., and London: University of California Press).

Orgel, Stephen (1987) *The Tempest*, The Oxford Shakespeare (Oxford and New York: Oxford University Press).

Pafford, J. H. P. (1963) *The Winter's Tale*, Arden edition (London and New York: Methuen; reprinted 1986).

Pease, Donald E. (1990) 'Author', in *Critical Terms for Literary Study*, ed. Frank Lentricchia and Thomas McLaughlin (Chicago and London: University of Chicago Press) pp. 105–17.

Peterson, Douglas L. (1973) *Time, Tide, and Tempest: A Study of Shakespeare's Romances* (San Marino: The Huntington Library).

Ridley, M. R. (1954) *Antony and Cleopatra*, Arden edition (London and New York: Methuen; reprinted 1986).

Ridley, M. R. (1958) *Othello*, Arden edition (London: Methuen; reprinted 1962).

Rosenberg, Marvin (1961) *The Masks of 'Othello'* (Berkeley, Calif.: University of California Press).

Rosenberg, Marvin (1978) *The Masks of 'Macbeth'* (Berkeley, Calif., and London: University of California Press).

Sidney, Philip (1965) *An Apology for Poetry or The Defence of Poesy*, ed. Geoffrey Shepherd (London: Nelson & Sons).

Siemon, James R. (1986) ' "Nay, that's not next": *Othello*, V.ii in Performance, 1760–1900', *Shakespeare Quarterly*, 37, pp. 38–51.

Stallybrass, Peter (1982) '*Macbeth* and Witchcraft' in Brown (1982) pp. 139–209.

Tennenhouse, Leonard (1986) *Power on Display: The Politics of Shakespeare's Genres* (New York and London: Methuen).

Warren, Michael J. (ed.) (1989a) *The Complete 'King Lear', 1608–1623* (Berkeley, Calif., and London: University of California Press).

Warren, Michael J. (ed.) (1989b) *The Parallel 'King Lear', 1608–1623* (Berkeley, Calif., and London: University of California Press).

Warren, Roger (1986) 'Shakespeare In Britain, 1985', *Shakespeare Quarterly*, 37, pp. 114–20.

Wells, Stanley and Gary Taylor (eds) (1986) *William Shakespeare. The Complete Works* (Oxford: Clarendon Press).

Index